1971

TOLSTOY AND CHEKHOV

TOLSTOY AND CHEKHOV

LOGAN SPEIRS

CAMBRIDGE · AT THE UNIVERSITY PRESS

1971

Published by the Syndics of the Cambridge University Press
Bentley House, 200 Euston Road, London N.W.1
American Branch: 32 East 57th Street, New York, N.Y.10022

© Cambridge University Press 1971

Library of Congress Catalogue Card Number: 79–120195

ISBN: 0 521 07950 0

Printed in Great Britain by
C. Tinling & Co. Ltd, London and Prescot

Contents

Contents

To my Mother and Father

1 . Tolstoy and Chekhov

Tolstoy and Chekhov form a pair in Russian literature. Their art is related, although each uses his own for different purposes. They address two nineteenth-century generations. The world they uncover, often using similar methods of presentation, is different for each, and their art makes us understand this difference, this estrangement beneath a surface similarity. Comparisons between them tend to spring naturally to mind, and these ask to be pursued further. The light that the one sheds on the other can help illuminate the qualities of each, and may add precision to readings of their masterpieces. Careful distinctions are required rather than glaring contrasts.

Tolstoy in *What is Art?* stresses the 'modesty' of the highest forms of literary art:

... artists, and public, and critics, have never (except in childhood and earliest youth before having any discussions on art) experienced that simple feeling familiar to the plainest man and even to a child, that sense of infection with another's feeling – compelling us to rejoice in another's gladness, to sorrow at another's grief and to mingle souls with another – which is the very essence of art. And therefore these people not only cannot distinguish true works of art from counterfeits, but continually mistake for real art the worst and most artificial, while they do not even perceive works of real art, because the counterfeits are always more ornate, while true art is modest.[1]

The effortlessness of Tolstoy's ability to infect his readers is one of the miracles of world literature. This quality is unfailingly present in everything he writes up to his abandonment of art. He makes one perceive the things of every-day as though one were looking at them for the first time.

Tolstoy's early work, *Childhood, Boyhood and Youth* comes as something new in literature. It marks the advent of a wholly original talent. With Tolstoy fiction ceases to be story-telling. The last

---

[1] *What is Art?*, Chapter XIV.

All quotations from Tolstoy are from the Maude translations, unless otherwise stated.

element of artificiality drops away from it, the 'made up' quality, the element of allegory or parable. His characters are not illustrations of elements in experience, rather they are faithful reproductions of experience itself. The secret of this is the part that direct reporting plays in his great work. It is a cause of his amazing fertility and ease of creation. There is nothing which he has not seen with his own eyes. His most elaborate creations are constructed out of direct observations of life. In that sense they are not created but re-created.

Chekhov often draws attention to this aspect of his own work.

I tell you honestly, in all conscience, these men were born in my brain, not by accident, not out of sea foam, or preconceived 'intellectual' ideas. They are the result of observing and studying life. They stand in my brain, and I feel that I have not falsified the truth or exaggerated it a jot.[1]

It is Tolstoy's achievement which makes it easy for Chekhov to think of his work in these terms. It is noticeable, though, that many of the characters in Chekhov's early plays and some of the early stories are, in fact, products of 'intellectual' ideas. This is their weakness. In 1888, the year the letter above was written, Chekhov is at a turning point. There are occasions in this year when he does create directly from his own observation of life – in The Steppe and, more importantly, in The Party, both of which are heavily indebted to Tolstoy.

It is of course unwise to be doctrinaire about literary influences. Chekhov himself provides a salutary corrective to this. He dislikes literary map-making.

I don't believe in the physiology of the novel, and the natural course of its development – that is, there may exist such a physiology in nature, but I don't believe with existing methods it can be detected. Boborikin dismisses Gogol absolutely and refuses to recognise him as a forerunner of Turgenev, Goncharov and Tolstoy . . . He puts him apart, outside the current in which the Russian novel has flowed. Well, I don't understand that. If one takes the standpoint of natural development, it's impossible to put not only Gogol, but even a dog barking, outside the current, for all things in nature influence one another, and even the fact that I have just sneezed is not without its influence on surrounding nature.[2]

Every great artist is an original and develops in his own way.

[1] Letter to A. S. Souvorin, December 1888. In A. Chekhov, Letters on the Short Story, the Drama and other Literary Topics, ed. Louis S. Friedland (London, 1965).

[2] Letter to Souvorin, November 1891. In Letters on the Short Story, etc.

Tolstoy draws a sharp line in *What is Art?* between 'universal art' and 'borrowed art'. The word 'influence' used carelessly can suggest direct imitation, and Chekhov imitates nobody. The fact remains that Chekhov and Tolstoy have much in common. They are artists of the same kind, belonging to the same species, the one a profound admirer of the other. This is why it makes sense to consider them together. But the value of doing so lies in the comparison, in the differences between the uses to which they put their art. They have enough in common for such a comparison to be illuminating. The enormous differences are a question of personality and circumstance – both realised that these are difficult to disentangle from one another.

Both Tolstoy and Chekhov share the quality of first-handness. They are determined to prevent the elaborate business of writing from transforming their original perceptions into something else. They are both passionately concerned to tell the truth. They both have a hint of ruthlessness in their determination to see the world with a steady eye.

It is extraordinary how often the detection of lies comes into Tolstoy's work before *War and Peace* – during his period of apprenticeship, as he saw it, before he could embark on major work. His heroes, Nikolenka in *Childhood, Boyhood and Youth* and Olenin in *The Cossacks*, are tormented by their sophistication, which prevents them from recognising themselves as they really are.

The chief motive behind the writing of *Childhood, Boyhood and Youth* is a training in self-awareness – an attempt to find out exactly how far his feelings towards his mother, his first loves and his first friendships were true or false. The hero torments himself already at the age of six, when he is not sure whether what he feels on seeing the corpse of his mother, and during her burial, is really grief or not.

'Every man lies twenty times daily',[1] Tolstoy once said. Tolstoy's artistic conscience and his private conscience were one and the same. His art was a means to grapple with his conscience. This is true of Chekhov too. The ultimate purpose of their art preoccupies them, and they both see it as being a question of accuracy, of showing life as it really is. Real life is more beautiful than a world of artificial illusion. Beauty for them is the reward of clear vision.

Tolstoy saw Chekhov as his greatest younger contemporary:

[1] Henri Troyat, *Tolstoy* (London, 1968), p. 284.

Chekhov is an incomparable artist, an artist of life. And the merit of his creative work is that he is understood and accepted not only by every Russian, but by all humanity.[1]

Both artists have immense ambitions, and this is a quality they share with most nineteenth-century Russian writers. They set out to cover the whole of life. There is so much to be done in their literature that they deal freely and uninhibitedly with universals. The purpose of art is associated in their minds with the purpose of life, and art is seen as the means of furthering an exploration which is the duty of every man. The vast, unmanageable country they belong to, a world in itself, seems to dictate this attitude in them. They cannot narrow themselves to specialisation. Their society is not sufficiently organised for this to be possible. Life is still too simple, too primitive. The simplest issues in life are too immediate to be forgotten. It is easy to see how an artist might turn into a religious fanatic under the burden of a responsibility which no Western writer could be aware of to anything like the same degree.

The key difference between Chekhov and Tolstoy is in the way each deals with the responsibility which weighs upon him. Tolstoy in *What is Art?* states that all great art is religious art, and he goes on to place true art in two categories, a greater and a lesser, 'religious art' and 'universal art'. Religious art deals with the relationship between man and God. Universal art is concerned in the broadest sense with ethics. Both are concerned with telling the 'truth'. Universal art often does this unconsciously, since its creators lack a 'definite point of view' – a fault Tolstoy always attributes to Chekhov. By 'truth' the Tolstoy who writes *What is Art?* has come to mean the knowledge which is instilled into every man by God even if he does not recognise its source. In a preface to improving tales for children (1887) Tolstoy wrote:

> He does not write the truth who describes only what has happened and what this or that man has done, but he who shows what people do that is right – that is, in accord with God's will; and what people do wrong – that is, contrary to God's will.

[1] Quoted by Ernest J. Simmons in *Introduction to Tolstoy's Writings* (Chicago and London, 1968), p. 127.

In 1898 Tolstoy persuaded Marx, the publisher who was bringing out *Resurrection*, to bring out the first complete edition of Chekhov. He told him that Chekhov was more important than Turgenev or Goncharov.

Truth is a path. Christ said, 'I am the way, the truth, and the life' . . .
And in order to show that path one must not describe merely what
happens in the world. The world abides in evil and is full of offence.
If one is to describe the world as it is, one will describe much evil and the
truth will be lacking. In order that there may be truth in what one describes, it is necessary to write not about what is, but about what should be;
to write not the truth of what is, but of the kingdom of God which is
drawing nigh unto us but is not as yet. That is why there are mountains
of books in which we are told what really has happened, yet they are all
false if those who write them do not themselves know what is good and
what is evil, and do not know and do not show the one path which leads
to the kingdom of God.

Telling one sort of truth has failed to satisfy Tolstoy. He has even
learned to hate and fear the truth of his perceptions, and seeks
instead an inner light. The sense of wonder at God's plenty, which is a
real religious feeling, goes as an allegedly spiritual old age sets in.
The bitter knowledge grows in Tolstoy that his own joy has been
transitory. It is a selfish feeling which Tolstoy seeks to hide under a
cloak of righteousness. His late tales are written out of the false
wisdom of old age under the guise of lofty condescension. *Resurrection*
is the story of a young man who acts in the way an envious old man
would wish young men to act. *Hadji Murad* is the exception in Tolstoy's
old age, one of those miraculous moments when old age is calmly
generous. The fear of death has struck at Tolstoy in the prime of life
and is his obsession thereafter, colouring all his thought and distorting his judgement. It is as though he is paying the penalty of
having experienced too much. In his own life and in his re-creation
of it in writing he has lived through more than most men will ever
know at first hand. He now looks back over what he has written and
feels that it was all the wrong thing, that it was all an irretrievable
mistake. Yet a constant element of self-doubt, of discontent about
the quality of his experience has once been of decisive value in
Tolstoy's art.

Tolstoy has gazed upon life with such fanatical, unremitting
intensity that he is suddenly horrified at no longer seeing anything
in it, at a sudden revulsion from it. Chekhov, a less passionate man,
never suffers quite this. He does not suddenly throw everything up in
despair as Tolstoy does. His ambition is never so strong. The limits
have been set for him in literature, since he is of the next generation.
It was for Tolstoy to suffer the agony of discovering what the limits

of his kind of art were, and the sudden suspicion that there were other kinds of art which were perhaps superior to his own. His malevolent, deliberately stupid and bullying affectation of deafness, in his explosion of the 'myth' of Shakespeare, his amused refusal to attend to poetry unless it told a story such as a child or peasant could comprehend are in fact more significant than his definitions of the 'universal' art he asserts that he intends to produce henceforth. He has wished to do everything, and he refuses to admit his lack of qualification in some fields. Chekhov does not feel a need for this. He once wrote to a poet friend:

> Verse is not in my line. I have never written poetry; my mind refuses to memorise poetry, and I can only take hold of it like a *muzhik*, but I cannot state definitely why it pleases me or wearies me . . . Some time ago I tried to get in touch with poets and to set my views before them, but nothing came of it, and I soon gave the matter up, like a man who means well, but who cannot express his ideas in clear and definite form. Now I usually confine myself to writing 'I like this,' or, 'I do not like it.' Your poem I like.
>
> As to the story you are writing, – that is a different matter, and I am ready to pass judgement on it to the extent of twenty sheets of paper; if you send it to me and ask me to give you my opinion I shall read it with pleasure. I shall answer you with some definiteness, and shall feel free.[1]

Chekhov is always decisive and ruthlessly professional when he writes to friends about prose works of theirs. Both Chekhov and Tolstoy have trained themselves in a particular way to the exclusion of other ways. Tolstoy later thinks he might have made a mistake, but it is too late to change himself and he puts a bold face on it.

Both Tolstoy and Chekhov are deliberately the most practical of writers. They exclude everything from their work which cannot be immediately verified by every one of their readers from his own experience. One of Tolstoy's dicta about art is – 'usually it seems to the recipient of a truly artistic impression that he knew the thing before, but had been unable to express it'.[2] Both Tolstoy and Chekhov train themselves to exclude everything that is unusual in order to give priority to the most common concerns of people in the midst of living their lives. They are both wary of the imagination and carefully control the workings of the imagination in themselves. This is caused by their circumstances, by a purpose they both assign

[1] Letter to A. V. Zhirkevich, March 1895. In *Letters on the Short Story, etc.*
[2] *What is Art?*

to their art. They see themselves as living in a land of vague dreamers who must be shown facts. Facts in their country are more important than dreams, deeds are more important than visions. It is evident to both that what Russia needs is hard prose. But in reality both are poets. Tolstoy has more in common with Shakespeare than he realises. The awareness of inexplicable depths within the human consciousness is present in everything he does. There are kinds of communication which can only be made through art — 'The business of art lies just in this: to make that understood and felt which in the form of an argument might be incomprehensible and inaccessible.'[1] Tolstoy communicated more of the mystery of art in his autobiographical story *Schoolboys and Art*, written two years before he began *War and Peace*, than he could do in his deliberate treatise on the subject or in his critical essays. Tolstoy went walking one night with some boys from his school at Yasnaya Polyana:

... They remembered a Caucasian tale I had told them long ago, and I again told them of 'braves', of Cossacks, and of Hadji Murad ...

Everyone who knows anything of Russian peasant children knows that they are not accustomed to, and cannot bear, any caresses, affectionate words, kisses, hand-touchings, and so forth ... I was therefore particularly struck when Fedka, walking beside me, at the most terrible part of the story suddenly touched me lightly with his sleeve, and then clasped two of my fingers in his hand and kept hold of them. As soon as I stopped speaking, Fedka demanded that I should go on, and did this in such a beseeching and agitated voice that it was impossible not to comply with his wish ...

We had passed the wood and were approaching the village from the other end.

'Let's go on,' said all the boys when the lights became visible. 'Let us take another turn!'

We went on in silence, sinking here and there in the snow which was not hardened by much traffic. A white darkness seemed to sway before our eyes, the clouds hung low, as though something had heaped them upon us. There was no end to the whiteness amid which we alone crunched along the snow. The wind sounded through the bare tops of the aspens, but where we were, behind the woods, it was calm ...

... Fedka suddenly stopped.

'How was it, you told us, your Aunt had her throat cut?' he asked. (He had not yet had enough of horrors.) 'Tell us! Tell us!'

[1] *What is Art?*

I again told them that terrible story of the murder of Countess Tolstoy, and they stood silently about me watching my face.

'The fellow got caught!' said Semka.

'He was afraid to go away in the night while she was lying with her throat cut!' said Fedka; 'I should have run away!' and he gathered my two fingers yet more closely in his hand . . .

'Lev Nikolaevich,' said Fedka to me (I thought he was again going to speak about the Countess), 'why does one learn singing? I often think, why, really, does one?'

What made him jump from the terror of the murder to this question, heaven only knows; yet by the tone of his voice, the seriousness with which he demanded an answer, and the attentive silence of the other two, one felt that there was some vital and legitimate connection between this question and our preceding talk. Whether the connection lay in some response to my suggestion that crime might be explained by lack of education (I had spoken of that), or whether he was testing himself – transferring himself into the mind of the murderer and remembering his own favourite occupation (he has a wonderful voice and immense musical talent), or whether the connection lay in the fact that he felt that now was the time for sincere conversation, and all the problems demanding solution rose in his mind – at any rate his question surprised none of us.

'And what is drawing for? And why write well?' said I, not knowing at all how to explain to him what art is for.

'What is drawing for?' repeated he thoughtfully. He was really asking, What is Art for? And I neither dared nor could explain.

Tolstoy will demonstrate rather than explain. The 'explanation' only comes when his art has withered away. *War and Peace*, and *Anna Karenina*, come before.

TOLSTOY

2. Family Happiness: A Prelude

Family Happiness was written by Tolstoy at the age of thirty, about five years before he began War and Peace. It is the most interesting forerunner of the great novels. Like nearly all Tolstoy's work it is founded on personal experience. Tolstoy felt guilty at having decided at the last minute not to marry a girl whose guardian he was. The story is an exploration of what would have happened if they had married, an attempt to find out whether his decision not to marry her has been the right one. It is the story of three years in the life of a newly married couple. The work is harshly moral. The woman learns to feel ashamed of her society life as a result of her husband's disapproval, and even comes to criticise him for not having been strict enough with her. V. P. Botkin, a critic and friend of Tolstoy, told him that Family Happiness was marred by its puritanism. Moral sternness is present in Tolstoy from the very beginning – the opinion that there is a right way to live and a wrong one, and that the right one demands courage. In Family Happiness Tolstoy castigates himself for his own want of courage.

The short novel is a study in human weakness, but at the same time shows the moments of courage and selflessness which human nature is also capable of, moments which can never be experienced if one hesitates to act because of a fear of consequences. This aspect of Family Happiness makes one think of Chekhov. It is the closest the productions of the two writers come to direct similarity. Tolstoy thereafter musters his forces for the vast masterpieces of his middle years, and Family Happiness looks oddly slight as a forerunner of those.

Family Happiness disgusted Tolstoy as soon as it was written. He felt that it lacked force. In fact this is not entirely true. In a way it has too much force. Its delicate structure is occasionally shaken by rumbles of Tolstoyan indignation at human frailty, auguries of the late Tolstoy. His discontent will be appeased during the writing of War and Peace and Anna Karenina, but will burst forth with redoubled vigour thereafter.

At the time of writing Family Happiness Tolstoy was pondering about his duties as an artist. The Sebastopol Sketches upon which his fame largely rested could not be repeated, neither could those vivid accounts of the early stages of a man's life, *Childhood, Boyhood and Youth*, the last of which was published before *Family Happiness*. Tolstoy has prepared certain material out of his experience, but he does not consider that he has used it to the full. He has prepared lay figures which are interesting in themselves and are worth looking at, but he has not clothed them. What he will do next is the question.

On joining the Moscow Society of Lovers of Russian Literature in 1859 (the year *Family Happiness* was published) Tolstoy made his first public speech. He described the sort of major literature which Russia needed – a literature

... reflecting eternal and universally human interests, the most precious, sincere consciousness of the people, a literature accessible to every people and to all times, a literature without which no single people, gifted with strength and richness, has ever developed.[1]

The vast ambition, the quest for universal themes in his art, for the eternal rather than the transient, is there already. The discrepancy between the late and middle Tolstoy is not altogether as great as it seems. The assumption of leadership in all he undertakes, the desire to pursue the highest purposes, will eventually result in an attempt to alter the whole of human life.

Chekhov is more self-effacing by nature than Tolstoy. The height of his ambition will be to earn the knowledge '– that to men who devote themselves to the study of life I am as necessary as a star to an astronomer'[2] – the interpretation of experience being the private activity of every individual and entitled to respect as such. Much of Tolstoy's *Family Happiness* is Chekhov's kind of art.

Family Happiness is narrated by the wife; it is an interesting exercise of the sympathetic imagination – even though Tolstoy has not yet acquired his full understanding of the feminine mind. Sergey Mikhaylych is the only man the heroine knows, since she lives alone in the country with her sister. She is faintly disturbed at his silence about his own life but, childlike, gets used to his intellectual separateness from her. It is plain that the decision to marry is hers. Her childish will exerted on the man makes her almost impossible to oppose. Much can be inferred from the one or two facts which are

[1] As quoted in E. J. Simmons, *Leo Tolstoy* (London, 1949).
[2] Letter to Souvorin, December 1888. In *Letters on the Short Story, etc.*

arranged before us. The story is more complicated than it looks because the account is biased by the girl in her own favour. Consequently, there are many different ways of interpreting the simplest situation in it. Though the flow of the story seems effortless and leisurely, it is in fact very compressed. Tolstoy will continue to use the sparse method of the short story writer in his great novels. This accounts for the extraordinary quantity of experience he is able to pack into them so that in retrospect they seem even larger than they are.

The girl works herself into a religious ecstasy, deciding to purify herself by taking Holy Communion on her name-day, making herself beautiful and yet fragile to the man so that he will not be able to oppose her will. The description of the church service is the fore-runner of Natasha's religious experience in *War and Peace*. It is indeed beautiful, yet it is necessary to come to a decision about its value. Tolstoy does not go in for the poetry of feeling for its own sake. He is no Turgenev. By the end of the story the girl will have been taught that this period of her existence did not merit her wistful regrets at its loss.

Out on the verandah she forces Sergey Mikhaylych to declare himself. Speaking to her as to a child, he postulates likely results of a proposal. One is that she consents to be his wife, but that later 'she saw herself that she had deceived him and that he had deceived her'. Sergey's pessimistic forecast will be partially correct. One can infer that he possesses a more accurate knowledge of her states of mind than she ever does.

The first year or so of the marriage is shown in outline, a period of contentment in Sergey Mikhaylych's old-fashioned country house; then comes restlessness and a desire for the bright lights of Petersburg. The responsibility for the marriage is the man's, and the wife grows to realise this. She grows to resent his distaste for the life she soon finds herself leading. In the end, shocked at almost being seduced by a contemptuous young man, she returns, a mother of two children, to country retirement with her husband. She visits the house of her childhood and thinks over what has happened in the last three years. 'My vague confused dreams had become a reality, and the reality had become an oppressive, difficult, and joyless life. All remained the same – . . . and yet, in everything such a terrible inconceivable change!' She tries to evoke memories in her husband of their romance. She draws him out onto the verandah in the

evening. The women of the house are out for a walk, and it begins to
rain.

'Where are you going?' I asked, trying to keep him; 'it is so pleasant here.'
'We must send them an umbrella and goloshes,' he replied.

More is conveyed in this prosaic remark than in the explanation of
their present relations which the wife forces out of her surprised
husband, who has become used to a peaceful and amiable separateness from her.

The couple manage to piece together a certain understanding in the
conversation which follows. Experience has made the wife more
modest in her demands from life. But after this portrayal of human
resilience in adversity Tolstoy suddenly tries to make out that
adversity is now at an end. His desire to state conclusive answers to
life's problems leads him to round off the story in an unacceptable
way.

. . . a new feeling of love for my children and the father of my children
laid the foundation of a new life and a quite different happiness; and that
life and happiness have lasted to the present time.

A painful ending interestingly close to the kind of experience
Chekhov was to explore[1] is wilfully amended.

Tolstoy must say something large about human life, and *Family
Happiness* is too specialised a case for him to base any broad conclusions upon. He needs more space to move about in. At the
moment the subjects which have offered themselves seem flimsy and
insubstantial to him. He has no faith in them. *Family Happiness*
appears to him the culmination of his literary career. In the year of
its publication (1859) he wrote to A. V. Druzhinin, a friend and
critic:

I have written nothing more since *Family Happiness* and it seems to me that I
never shall write any more . . . Were I haunted by ideas that tormented me,
forced themselves to leap out, and aroused boldness, audacity, and force
in me – that would be different. But at the age of thirty-one to write very
pretty stories agreeable to read – no on my word I am incapable of lifting
a finger to do it![2]

[1] Chekhov can be seen to have received many suggestions from *Family
Happiness* in his own short novel *Three Years*.

[2] As quoted by Aylmer Maude, Introduction to *The Kreutzer Sonata and Other
Tales* (The World's Classics, London, 1924).

Tolstoy requires a grand design. He can see no sense in a fragment of life taken in isolation. Not until the whole has been grasped can the parts be understood. He must find the means to accomplish this. With amazing audacity he will shortly be making the attempt by surveying the generations of men as they succeed one another in the nations of Europe. His cramped energies will be released. Having created a panorama of life for himself, having liberated his powers, he will then in *Anna Karenina* explore the theme of marriage again, this time in all its aspects and from all points of view.

3. Introduction to a Study of *War and Peace*

One's first assessment of the opening chapters of *War and Peace* might chance to be similar to Turgenev's snap judgement on them:

> The thing is positively bad, boring and a failure ... All those little details so cleverly noted ... those psychological remarks which the author digs out of his heroes' armpits and other dark places in the name of verisimilitude ... one feels so strongly the writer's lack of imagination and naïveté![1]

When Turgenev refers to the author's 'lack of imagination' he means that too much comes obviously out of jottings in notebooks and diaries, that the ability to note down details which have struck one personally does not in itself constitute artistic ability.

Tolstoy talked about 'leaving a part of his life in the inkwell'.[2] He gave away his personal motive for becoming a writer in his diary: 'I don't wish to die, but I want and love immortality.'[3] *War and Peace* lives and breathes for ever; in it Tolstoy conquers death. Tolstoy's writings are openly projections of himself. It is this openness which Turgenev is deploring as a breach of professional conduct. Tolstoy is making his own rules. If literature is to extend people's knowledge of what is going on around them and within themselves, then all that Tolstoy can honestly contribute is his own experience. He does not claim extraordinary powers of perception for the artist. He does not see the artist as belonging to a species different from other men, more perceptive than other men. He would have agreed with Turgenev about his 'lack of imagination'. At the age of twenty-two Tolstoy wrote: 'It seems to me that it is really impossible to describe a man, but it is possible to describe the effect he produces on me.'[4] At the time of writing *War and Peace* he had not revised that opinion. A work of art must be a faithful reflection of what the artist sees. Analysis and explanation is a matter

---

[1] As quoted in Troyat, *Tolstoy.*
[2] Ibid. p. 282.
[3] Quoted in Simmons, *Leo Tolstoy,* Chapter XVII.
[4] As quoted in R. F. Christian, *Tolstoy's 'War and Peace'* (London, 1962), p. 32.

of half-truths at one remove from his original, spontaneous perceptions – and half-truths are worse than lies because they are harder to detect than a lie is. Tolstoy is always conscious of this in *War and Peace*.

Shortly before embarking on *War and Peace* Tolstoy wrote of a convention which was making the novel one of the least reliable forms of literature for transmitting experience:

... it's a strange thing that all these descriptions, sometimes dozens of pages long, tell the readers less about the characters than some casually thrown out artistic detail in the course of an action already in progress between people who have not been described at all.[1]

A detail must be placed at the point where it first came to be noticed, and not removed from this context. But Tolstoy did not in any case think the creation of character need necessarily be the first consideration in writing or reading a novel. He defined what he termed 'novelist's poetry' in his diary (September 1865). It lay 'first, in the interest created by juxtaposed events; second, in the portrayal of customs and manners against a background of historical fact; third, in the beauty and vividness of the situations.'[2] He put 'the characters of the people' in fourth place. Life is in constant movement and it is this movement and its rhythm Tolstoy seeks first to capture, the responses of nations, classes and individuals to the progression of events in their time. The beauty and strangeness of the world man inhabits is only visible when he has learnt to contemplate it. This is Tolstoy's starting point. He sees personalities as ephemeral fragments in a vast ever-changing pattern. The pattern, mysterious and profoundly beautiful, is always slightly more important to him than its components. If this were not so his novels would fall apart.

Tolstoy's characters, their thoughts and feelings, are subordinate to the pattern he contemplates. Even his own intellectual findings are subordinate to it. The demands of his reason may cause him great trouble, but he is not a reasonable man by nature. The struggle, the war that *War and Peace* is about, is that between two fundamental attitudes which may be adopted to the world – that of the Westernised Prince Andrew, a product of Petersburg, and that of Pierre, Count Bezukhov, a product of Russia's ancient oriental capital,

[1] Ibid. p. 138.
[2] Troyat, *Tolstoy*.

Moscow. Tolstoy stresses the un-Western character of Moscow. Pierre attempts to conform to the Paris education his father has paid for, and as long as he does so he suffers discomfort, for his deepest nature rejects it. During Borodino, 'the great battle for Moscow', Pierre begins to understand this; and later, although his body falls captive to the French as Moscow itself has, Pierre realises that his spirit is free of the French and all they stand for. This causes the weird, disembodied laughter the retreating French hear one night from their alien prisoner.

> Suddenly he burst out into a fit of his broad, good-natured laughter, so loud that men from various sides turned with surprise to see what this strange and evidently solitary laughter could mean.
> 'Ha-ha-ha!' laughed Pierre. And he said aloud to himself: 'The soldier did not let me pass. They took me and shut me up. They hold me captive. What, me? Me? My immortal soul? Ha-ha-ha! Ha-ha-ha!' and he laughed till the tears started to his eyes.
> A man got up and came to see what this queer big fellow was laughing at all by himself.

This full-bodied, released laughter of Pierre is the physical manifestation of a new pleasure in the whole of himself. Like Karataev, his peasant companion, he now perceives his place in the universe. It is very different from Prince Andrew's wistful glimpse of the immensities his narrow training has locked him out of, the sky above the battlefield of Austerlitz, a battle fought on foreign soil and for mistaken purposes. It is very different from the poignant, deathbed transformation of Prince Andrew's father. Prince Bolkonski, nicknamed 'the King of Prussia' by society, has been one of the engineers of the new Westernised Russia in the previous century. He behaves naturally only at the last moment in a scene which is far more touching than the death of his son. The death of Prince Bolkonski is placed before the Battle of Borodino.

Tolstoy sees 'the interest created by juxtaposed events' as the first requisite in the art of the novelist. He sees his novels as significant arrangements. The material arranges itself in the mind of the artist as he works. While completing *Anna Karenina*, Tolstoy wrote to a friend:

> ... every thought expressed separately in words loses its meaning and is terribly impoverished when taken by itself out of the connection in which it occurs ... But now that nine-tenths of everything printed is

criticism, art criticism needs people who can show the folly of looking for thoughts in a work of art, and can continually guide readers in that endless labyrinth of connections which is the essence of art.[1]

Tolstoy never adheres to this unreservedly, though. One side of him hates and fears mysteries, as Prince Andrew does. There is a part of Tolstoy that fears the impersonality and passivity of Pierre – the part that craves for personal immortality. This gave Tolstoy his conscious reason for wanting to become a writer in the first place. Pierre could never have written *War and Peace*, but Prince Andrew might have attempted it to protect himself from death. On one level, *War and Peace* is about Tolstoy's struggle to understand himself, about the modern individual's struggle to break his connection with others, to be unique. It is Tolstoy's attempt to combat death, the extinction of his personality.

Tolstoy's neatly arranged conclusions about life in *War and Peace* are in marked contrast to the irregular flux which registers the thought and speech of his characters. The latter shows how people really think. V. V. Starov once wrote in a letter to Tolstoy:

... nearly all authors write monologues which are absolutely correct, consistent, streamlined, polished, ultra-logical ... But is this the way we really think? Of course not. I have only met one exception up to now – Count Leo Tolstoy. He is the only person who in his novels and dramas gives us real monologues with all their irregularity, fortuitousness, incompleteness and jerkiness.[2]

Tolstoy sets down these confused gropings in the way they occur. He depicts the struggle to achieve understanding before death comes, which goes on in each individual endlessly through the generations of men. The individual life is felt to be cheap, lost within a vast scheme which unfolds from generation to generation. This is a Russian feeling. The wastage is unthinkable, colossal. (One of the incidents at the moment Russia reaches victory is the death of Petya Rostov before he has even begun to live.) But Tolstoy, the Westernised aristocrat, must achieve a personal identity. He is tempted to use the opportunity his position gives him to stand apart from the huge flux of Russian humanity and erect a monument to himself. But at the same time he is filled with guilt at his own

[1] Letter to N. N. Strakhov, April 1876. In Christian, *Tolstoy's 'War and Peace'*.
[2] As quoted in Christian, *Tolstoy's 'War and Peace'*.

selfishness. *War and Peace* is both his monument and his expiation for being ambitious for one. It is a monument he dedicated to his nation.

The passage in the novel to which Tolstoy devoted most time and trouble was not the final epilogue, nor yet the Battle of Borodino for all his arduous researches into the tactics used there. It was the story of Natasha's relations with Anatole Kuragin. He referred to it as 'the most difficult passage and the keynote of the whole novel'.[1] Previous to this episode the novel has shown new generations coming to consciousness in a bewildering world. Each individual becomes caught up in the mists of deception, and struggles to find his way like the crowds of soldiers at Austerlitz. It is hard to distinguish between good and evil, between what is valuable and what is worthless. Natasha's tragic mistake over Anatole epitomises this eternal human predicament. Each character in the novel creates the world in his own image, and each reacts in his own way on discovering his mistake. Natasha has lived in an enchanted, child's world, beautifully evoked when the young Rostovs play a dressing-up game the Christmas before Natasha's disaster.

In *War and Peace* Tolstoy attempts to discredit the various illusions men always create for themselves, and to see the world as it really is. Ultimately this is an impossible task, but it is always the aim of great art. The mistake Natasha makes about love, deceived by the conception of it accepted in her society, is echoed by the mistakes whole nations make about the nature of honour, of justice and of bravery. Men crowd together for mutual support and assume that what they are doing is right because so many are doing it. (Sometimes it is. Tolstoy may distrust crowds, but he never simplifies.) Little Captain Tushin acting out his fantasy at the Battle of Schön Grabern, imagining himself a giant hurling cannon balls at the French, is acting in a manner he is convinced is right. Tushin is certain he is on the right side, but in spite of our enthusiastic approval, which Tolstoy shares, we are made aware that, looked at calmly, there is not much to choose between Tushin at this moment and Napoleon as he surveys the battlefield of Austerlitz with the happy expression of a boy in love – or between Napoleon and Pierre as he looks at the beautiful dawn mist over the field of Borodino. Tushin and Pierre

---

[1] Letter to P. I. Bartenev, November 1867. In Christian, *Tolstoy's 'War and Peace'*.

afterwards wake up to the horror of what has occurred. Napoleon's sluggish conscience stirs briefly after Borodino and then sleeps for ever. Both Napoleon and Anatole Kuragin are morally under-developed, and this is what stupidity is, according to Tolstoy.

It is difficult, and I think even impossible, to divide people into the intelligent and the stupid, or the good and the bad; but between the understanding and the non-understanding there is for me such a sharp line, that I cannot help drawing it between all whom I know.[1]

Natasha and Nikolay Rostov may be stupid by conventional stan-dards, but emotionally they are intelligent and capable of growth. *War and Peace* is a training in understanding.

Pierre after his duel with Dolokhov is haunted by the question 'Who is right and who is wrong? No one!' Immediately afterwards in the novel Andrew is confronted with the same question in a more painful form when he returns from the great international duel of Austerlitz. The question in the eyes of his dying wife haunts him. 'I have done no harm to anyone; why must I suffer so? help me!' Both Pierre and Prince Andrew are haunted by guilt at having made the decisions which resulted in these scenes. Men are often both victims and instruments of the organisations they have created – the institutions of society-marriage, government, military command. Man is often caught in a machine that has been created for him by previous generations and which he himself is in the process of creating anew for succeeding generations. Yet there are also institu-tions, creations of the human spirit, which do lend harmony and dignity to human life. The broad Petersburg–Moscow contrast is fundamental to *War and Peace*. The same contrast, the same exploration continues in *Anna Karenina*, Tolstoy's study of the institution of marriage.

It would be too much of a simplification to allow an account of the novel to stop here. In *War and Peace* Tolstoy lives and breathes for ever. It is an amazingly faithful reflection of the emotional and intellectual life of a man – its creator. It is intricate as only a major work of art can be. The more detailed examination which follows is intended as an attempt to discover some of the secrets of its organ-isation. It is an attempt to obey Tolstoy's request to critics – that they should act as guides 'in that endless labyrinth of connections which is the essence of art'. I shall try to keep to only one or two of

[1] Tolstoy's introduction to *Childhood, Boyhood and Youth*.

the many paths through the labyrinth of connections in *War and Peace*, but every detail noted will always suggest connections with many other details within the novel. Not a single detail in it occurs by accident. Each is essential to the pattern which the work assumes. A full commentary on every one of even the few details which follow would take up more space than the novel itself, for *War and Peace* is inexhaustible. Short compressed chapters were Tolstoy's most obvious stylistic idiosyncrasy. His impressionistic method is so successful that he is often accused of packing his scenes with masses of irrelevant details, details which he must have evoked in the imaginations of his critics since they cannot be referring to the three or four observations with which Tolstoy conjures up entire battles, operas and state balls. The precision with which he organises his details is the secret of his art.

4. The Pattern of *War and Peace*

The overall shape of *War and Peace* is majestically simple. The novel divides into two halves. The advance of Napoleon across the Dnieper into Russian territory occurs almost exactly half-way through. In the first half the focus of attention is on the experiences of the Bolkonski family, the Rostov family, and Count Pierre Bezukhov during the picturesque Napoleonic era. In the second half the protagonists are the French army and the inhabitants of an invaded Russia.

Although *War and Peace* is in two sections, it is not two novels. Still less is it a novel and a philosophic-historical treatise. It is an artistic unity. In the course of reading, the questions which arise demand to be pursued further and yet further. The reader, caught up in the events described, gropes for causes, as do the characters whom he accompanies. We hope for solutions to the questions which the subject gives rise to in our minds, and Tolstoy has a mesmerising ability to encourage such hopes. Why? is the first question; Who is responsible? is the question which instinctively follows. 'But who, after all, is doing this?' Pierre will ask in the second half of *War and Peace* as horrified French soldiers execute seven of his fellow prisoners.

War and Peace is a portrait of a nation in the gravest peril. Shakespeare often explored the same subject. With him also, the same thought seems to have occurred as will be found in Tolstoy. 'Leaders' are frequently seen as less effective in public affairs than they assume they are. Great men seldom lead nations in the direction they wish them to go. Nothing ever happens the way men have planned.

War and Peace is presented in fifteen books. These divide into two blocks of eight and seven books respectively. In the first three books the author is seen to be discovering his subject. These first books are visibly a casting about. There are sections in them which are developed out of Tolstoy's reading rather than first-hand experience. When Nikolay Rostov tells soldiers' tales about the Battle of Schön Grabern to his friend Boris, we smile indulgently because we have seen Rostov at the real Battle of Schön Grabern, but a little later

Nikolay will be presented by Tolstoy doing things on the field of Austerlitz which are only done in romances. As one looks back at the beginning, isolated false notes such as this help one to define the quality of truthfulness in the author of *War and Peace* and *Anna Karenina*. They reveal that one has since learned to expect nothing less than the whole truth from him.

THE FIRST HALF OF 'WAR AND PEACE'

The Introduction (Books I, II and III)

It is a measure of the scale of the novel that one can separate off as introductory three books containing about 350 pages which cover in detail an entire war lasting two years, and which end in the Russian defeat at Austerlitz and the supposed death of the man one has so far looked on as the hero of the novel.

In the first of the three introductory books the worlds of Petersburg and Moscow are shown. War will not at first appear to have much to do with the life of either of these cities except that more young men in society become officers. Tolstoy deals with war in Book Two. In Book One it is mentioned in conversation only. First of all the Petersburg–Moscow contrast, so important in the novel, is established – a contrast between two casts of mind, two ways of life.

The soirée at the opening is deceptively the sort of tableau one might expect of a big historical romance. In the first sentence of the novel, the society hostess exclaims patriotically to Prince Vasili, at the exciting prospect of war with the upstart Napoleon:

'Well, Prince, so Genoa and Lucca are now just family estates of the Buonapartes. But I warn you, if you don't tell me that this means war . . . I will have nothing more to do with you.'

Amidst the decorous whirr of society conversation Pierre Bezukhov makes his first social appearance, and worries the hostess by his natural behaviour and his size. He becomes unforgiveably excited, and argues against the opinions of society on contemporary events. Prince Andrew Bolkonski, the friend of Pierre, helps his hostess out in restraining Pierre's enthusiasm. Later the same evening the friends meet at Prince Andrew's.

Prince Andrew is going to war because he has chosen the army as his career. He has done so because he is disgusted with his inactive life. It is the old story; Shakespeare explores it often – war is attractive because it is thought to simplify life. The issues seem more clear-cut than in peace-time. Emotional tangles torment Andrew, and he wants to use the surgeon's knife on them. But it is only later that we really understand and know Andrew and Pierre. The opening of *War and Peace* is a series of experimental sketches which are visibly arranged in sequence. We do not get this impression in *Anna Karenina*, or indeed later in *War and Peace*, although the episodes remain as short, often shorter.

Pierre goes to a midnight party at the Horseguards' barracks. It is held by Prince Vasili's son, Anatole. Anatole and Dolokhov, the man who lives off him, represent a side of high society – the brutality hidden in Prince Vasili's smooth face at the soirée earlier that evening. Dolokhov draining a bottle of rum while he balances precariously outside the high barrack window is one of the tableaux everyone remembers from *War and Peace*. Why do we admire the feat so much? Tolstoy asks by implication. Dolokhov fascinates everyone who sees him. He fascinates and bewilders because he is a scoundrel. He fascinates because bravery is regarded as a virtue, and how can a man so virtuous in one respect be such a villain? This scene whets our appetite for the battles which are sure to come later. Tolstoy will indeed give us gallantry in the field at its most glamorous. Nobody has ever done it better. The scene ends with Pierre in a fit of ferocious enthusiasm waltzing round the room with a tame bear.

The novel now moves to Moscow. The name-day of Countess Rostov and her daughter Natasha in the next chapters balances the Petersburg evening. The children of the house burst into the drawing-room, led by Natasha. It is a picture of innocence and joy in life personified above all by Natasha. Her almost frightening vulnerability is immediately apparent and gives these scenes the charm that is found in fragile things. Count Rostov has allowed his son Nikolay to join the army.

The picture so far is a country in peace-time rousing itself for war. The focus of everyone's attention is the figure of Napoleon whose name comes up in most of the scenes.

There is now an abrupt change of subject. Much of the ending of Book One is taken up with an event which has apparently nothing to do with the emerging pattern. This is the death of the old grandee, Count Bezukhov, and the passing of his vast wealth to Pierre, his bastard son. A complicated campaign is waged about the

B

dying man, but it is Pierre, who understands nothing of what is going on around him, who becomes the millionaire. It is the first episode which is dealt with at length. There are certain to be good reasons when Tolstoy ceases to economise, for everything must take up as little as possible in this most packed of all novels. The apparently muddled and accidental way Pierre becomes a figure in society reminds one of all the unpredictable factors which govern human life. None of the characters struggling so ineffectually in front of Pierre are aware in the heat of the moment that they are all really facilitating the very thing which seems so far off and unimaginable to them. Tolstoy is establishing the standpoint from which greater and greater events will be viewed. This may not be entirely deliberate, and probably is not. It is simply felt that for the future purposes of the novel this passage must carry weight. There is a gravity induced in the writer by his awareness all the while of the great events he must deal with. This gives a quality to the novel which differs completely from that of Tolstoy's other masterpiece, *Anna Karenina*. In *War and Peace* man is felt as less in control of his destiny and therefore, involuntarily, less blame is attached to the actions which he commits. Death is near. Pierre, standing outside the door of the sickroom, is met a little later by Prince Vasili coming out. The Count is dead.

... there was in his voice a sincerity and weakness Pierre had never observed in it before. 'How often we sin, how much we deceive, and all for what? I am near sixty, dear friend ... I too ... All will end in death, all! Death is awful ...' and he burst into tears.

The oppressive theme which dominates the novel has made its appearance.

There is now a transition to the personal affairs of Prince Andrew. Prince Andrew returns to his father's house prior to joining Kutuzov's staff. The old Prince Bolkonski scares and oppresses those he loves most. He wishes to turn his plain, religious daughter into a paragon. With almost hysterical fury he hates her physical clumsiness and her inability to be taught subjects requiring mental discipline.

Andrew is his father's son. Aristocratic pride sends him to war. The old Prince has been a brilliant commander in Suvorov's day. Life has not conformed to his plans and arrangements, and consequently a state of hatred is the old Prince's most characteristic condition. Just as Prince Andrew is finishing his exposition of the military situation to his father, the old man starts humming in his falsetto old voice: 'Malbrook s'en va-t-en guerre. Dieu sait quand reviendra.' Bitter experience lies behind that song.

Pierre and Andrew, the two young men, twin heroes of the novel, have come into their kingdom, the one in Moscow, the other in the world orientated towards Petersburg, the Russian high command where decisions affecting nations are taken, or appear to be taken. Andrew leaves behind the young wife whom he despises for her frivolity. She is shortly to have a child.

The transition in Book Two is to the army campaigning in Austrian territory. With appropriate abruptness the novel moves into what seems a new world. Familiar figures appear, apparently changed by military uniforms. The book opens with a newly arrived infantry regiment drawn up for inspection. The general struts before it, filled with the military pride we are to see so much of. The general is mortified to see a patch of blue discolouring one of the ranks. It is Dolokhov, recently degraded to the ranks, who has not yet been issued with a private's greatcoat. There are many other incidents, all testifying to the impossibility of tidiness in human arrangements.

The inspection is a relative success, and the regiment marches off to a soldiers' song. One of the adjutants rides alongside the singing soldiers, talking to his acquaintance Dolokhov.

'She let the hawk fly upward from her wide right sleeve,' went the song, arousing an involuntary sensation of courage and cheerfulness. Their conversation would probably have been different but for the effect of that song.

'Is it true the Austrians have been beaten?' asked Dolokhov.

'The devil only knows! They say so.'

'I'm glad,' answered Dolokhov briefly and clearly, as the song demanded.

This song, appropriate to the beginning of a campaign, has a peculiar resonance after the old Prince's song earlier on. Individual personality, even Dolokhov's, sinks temporarily beneath the corporate personality of the army with its one or two elementary moods. The regiment selected by Tolstoy will undergo many changes of personnel in the course of the novel. Towards the end, officers from it will be commanded by Prince Andrew, but it will remain always the same, its narrow range of moods bounded by the emotions expressed in the two songs.

The rest of Book Two follows the fortunes of Prince Andrew and

Nikolay Rostov, on the staff and in the field respectively. Prince Andrew suffers the first blow to his idealism on witnessing the average staff officer's behaviour. His Petersburg set have not been miraculously metamorphosed by their uniforms. Perhaps it is because the staff is never in any physical danger. Yet it is very plain that life in the regiments brings no material rewards, and the precise value of the other rewards it brings is problematical. Nikolay Rostov sees the war as the happiest time in his life, while Prince Andrew remains an isolated Hamlet-like figure burdened with the responsibility he feels himself born to of setting the world right. We will see later that in peace-time each will continue to behave in much the same way as in war.

Both men are gaining experience of war. Nikolay has his first taste of action as the army retreats before the rapidly advancing French. There is a series of sketches of the muddle which develops round a bridge-head. The muddle which we have already sensed in human affairs takes its toll of dead soldiers for the first time. From the attitude of regular soldiers it is apparent that there is nothing unusual in the scene. The reader experiences a sense of anticlimax.

But this is merely a rearguard incident. Perhaps a victorious battle brings different rewards. Tolstoy immediately provides what is wanted. As the edifice grows, the details begin to fit better into place. In the next chapter Prince Andrew experiences the rewards of victory. Filled with excitement, he rides with the news of a Russian success to Brünn where the Austrian Emperor is. The disgraced Austrians are in no mood to be congratulated on a Russian victory. Vienna is occupied.

It is soon clear that the Russian army is in danger of annihilation and that only spectacular genius and heroism can save it. Perhaps now the scenes which all inexperienced soldiers look forward to will make their appearance. Tolstoy provides the Battle of Schön Grabern, the climax of this series of sketches of war. Kutuzov is sending General Bagration with a detachment to retard the French. He knows that only a tenth of these men will return. Andrew seizes this opportunity to acquire glory, and joins Bagration. While Prince Andrew leans on a cannon, scribbling plans of action in his notebook, a cannon ball thuds into the ground near by, and the Battle of Schön Grabern has begun. Immediately one asks who is in control. Bagration can do nothing once fighting has begun except maintain morale by his calm bearing. Eventually Bagration's forces manage to retreat.

Meanwhile a gun-battery is left in front of the Russian line. Everybody on both sides assumes somebody is defending it, for it continues firing. It is commanded by a little man called Tushin. Of all the heroic actions witnessed during the battle, none is so moving as the description of Captain Tushin commanding his battery. It is the great Tolstoy making one of his brief appearances in these early books. The little officer communicates his feelings to the men under him. A childish devotion and enthusiasm fills them as Tushin acts out his fantasies surrounded by unimaginable carnage. Prince Andrew delivers the order to withdraw and has his taste of heroism.

Senior officers collect round Bagration, and all reconstruct the battle in their own favour. Bagration at one point sends for the artillery captain to inquire why two of the four guns in his charge have been abandoned. Prince Andrew states his personal opinion firmly:

'. . . we owe to-day's success chiefly to the action of that battery and the heroic endurance of Captain Tushin and his company.'

Bagration is dubious, and indeed Prince Andrew may be giving too much emphasis to Tushin, impressed by his bravery. Bagration delivers the routine thanks and praises to his senior officers on the completion of a battle. He has contributed as much as any general can to the victory. The honour and self-confidence of the army is safe with him. In every organisation it is more practical not to look in too much detail at what goes on. It is whether the organisation as a whole works or not that matters to Bagration. Prince Andrew suffers a bitter reaction – 'It was all so strange, so unlike what he had hoped.'

Book Two can be seen as a reworking of Tolstoy's indictment of war in his Sebastopol sketches. In quality it is similar. It represents a stage in his development, but takes its place in *War and Peace* as a starting point, so that the reader will be able to see the events which follow with an experienced eye. The futile indignation of the reader resulting from his vain hope that justice, as he conceives it, may prevail, that wrongdoers are to be found, will have disappeared by the end of Book Three – by the time Prince Andrew lies wounded on the field of Austerlitz, gazing at the sky. The novel is the story of a war, not a campaign.

Book Three confirms the conclusions we have been guided to in the previous books. The Petersburg world, where decisions are taken, and the world of the Moscow families, are again contrasted both at home and on the battlefield. We are now starting to see something of what it is that produces war. We see it by watching Prince Vasili conducting private campaigns to marry his children to money. Using the weapons of diplomacy, from honeyed words to righteous indignation, he forces his victims into situations where the alternatives are either capitulation or armed resistance. Pierre submits to marriage with the beautiful Helene and is soon to suffer all the miseries of defeat. It is his Austerlitz. Immediately after his victory over Pierre, Vasili directs his forces against the Bolkonskis to appropriate Princess Mary for his son Anatole.

The sinister invasion of Prince Vasili and his son, who accompanies him with only apparent obedience like a big tom-cat, is almost successful. Like Natasha later, Princess Mary does not recognise her danger, for all her delicacy of sentiment. She is on the brink of disaster, has accepted Anatole in principle, when she catches him out making love to her companion, Mademoiselle Bourienne.

At last Mademoiselle Bourienne gave a scream and ran away. Anatole bowed to Princess Mary with a gay smile, as if inviting her to join in a laugh at this strange incident, and then shrugging his shoulders went to the door that led to his own apartments.

Anatole gets himself into the most gaily romantic situations, but like so many happenings in *War and Peace* they lose their glamour on close inspection. It has become clear to the reader that one does not need to join armies to be in danger. Tolstoy, unknown to us, is all the while preparing the ground for the reception of his villain later on in this book. The introduction to the novel will then be complete. Most of the 'wicked' people have by now made their appearance. All have been disconcertingly light-weight, like the devils in Miracle Plays. Napoleon will be no exception.

The Battle of Austerlitz soon follows. At the great parade before Austerlitz Nikolay Rostov suffers an insane rush of love for the Tsar amidst immense crowds of people all experiencing the same thing. Tolstoy seems to share the enthusiasm experienced during the beautiful scene. It is one of the great moments in Nikolay's life.

Prince Andrew, also mysteriously inspired by the proximity of his Emperor, dreams of glory. Not even he can separate himself from the irresistible crowd-impulse which has taken control of every individual.

The battle begins in thick mist. It is while the allies are marching and halting and getting mixed up in the fog that Napoleon makes his first appearance. He is glimpsed standing on a hill looking over the fog, his marshals behind him. On his face is the 'confident, self-complacent happiness that one sees on the face of a boy happily in love'.

Prince Andrew's moment of glory comes very soon now. He snatches up a flag that has fallen, and runs towards the French. After a few ecstatic seconds, he lies wounded. The crowd-frenzy departs from him as though it had never been.

Above him there was now nothing but the sky – the lofty sky, not clear yet still immeasurably lofty, with grey clouds gliding slowly across it.

The rest of the battle is seen through the eyes of Nikolay Rostov. He is given the order to ride eight miles across the lines to deliver a message to Kutuzov. He gets mixed up in crowds of routed soldiers, and finally sees the Tsar standing alone in a field, looking sad.

There is a flagging in the momentum as the battle of Austerlitz unfolds. Tolstoy has given as much space to Schön Grabern as Austerlitz. For the first and last time he falters under his burden of historical data, unsure for a moment where his exploration of war has taken him. It is this that tells one a turning-point is about to be reached. It is only after Austerlitz that the great Tolstoy is in full command. What can possibly come now? asks the reader, looking at the vast bulk of what is to follow.

At the end of this third book Napoleon tours the battlefield. One of the sights that please him is Prince Andrew lying with the standard beside him. Andrew is given the distinction of being tended by Napoleon's personal doctor, Larrey.

'He is a nervous, bilious subject,' said Larrey, 'and will not recover.'

So ends Book Three.

Books IV and V

If one sees the first three books, ending with Austerlitz, as introduction, then the next five books, ending at the moment Napoleon enters Russia, form the first half of the novel proper. Of these five

books the first two (Books IV and V) and the last three (Books VI,
VII, VIII) fall naturally into two units – the first and second
quarters of the novel proper. One can feel the tempo of the novel
increase. Even more experience is packed in. Many incidents are
glimpsed out of the corner of the eye while one witnesses the main
events.

Books Four and Five portray a defeated nation. There are no very
obvious signs of this, but it is felt below the surface. People are
frustrated, aware of their helplessness. This has been brought to
consciousness by the shock of Austerlitz, but it was there before.
In a way, the Russians were defeated before Austerlitz. One remembers the words of Larrey about Prince Andrew – 'he will not
recover'. Andrew's personality was formed long before Austerlitz
and was one of the millions of factors contributing to it. He cannot
change. No character changes in the novel. It is the conditions which
will change and call out hidden qualities in each person. But first
there is a period during which the negative qualities in everyone
have the ascendancy. As in the *Henry IV* plays of Shakespeare, there
is plenty of gaiety and youthful energy, but circumstances make one
more than usually aware of its inevitable transitoriness.

Book Four begins on a note of frantic happiness. A young officer,
Nikolay Rostov, returns home from the wars bringing his idolised
senior officer, Major Vaska Denisov, as his guest. Tolstoy now knows
precisely what he is engaged on. The episodes arise effortlessly in his
mind. The scene has a reality beyond the reader's experience so far.

Rostov was very happy in the love they showed him; but the first
moment of meeting had been so beatific that his present joy seemed
insufficient, and he kept expecting something more, more, and yet more.

The secret lies in a series of such perceptions, each of which strikes
one by its truth.

Happiness is never unmixed except for brief, long remembered
moments. The Rostovs are not characters out of a Russian *Pickwick
Papers*, their good digestions providing a contrast with Andrew's
biliousness. Up to now it was possible to come away with this
impression.

'How strange it is,' said Vera, selecting a moment when all were silent,
'that Sonya and Nikolay now say *you* to one another and meet like strangers.'
Vera's remark was correct as her remarks always were, but like most of
her observations it made every one feel uncomfortable, not only Sonya,

Nikolay, and Natasha, but even the old countess, who – dreading this love affair which might hinder Nikolay from making a brilliant match – blushed like a girl.

If one looks upon an ever-present awareness of the limitations of human happiness as a weakness in Chekhov, then it is a weakness he shares with Tolstoy.

Nikolay's father gets up a dinner in honour of Bagration, hero of the Russian people. Pierre Bezukhov is at the dinner. Dolokhov has a liaison with Pierre's wife and goads Pierre into challenging him. At the duel which follows, Pierre with beginner's luck wounds Dolokhov. Then comes a greater surprise. Dolokhov bursts into tears. It emerges that he lives with his mother and a hunchback sister and is terrified of the shock they will get. This provides a clue to his behaviour and makes him a more disturbing figure. It suggests that his case is incurable ('he will not recover'), that no mercy will ever be shown anyone unfortunate enough to fall into his power.

The impulse to fight, to punish others, meanwhile fills Pierre with horror at himself. The duel has been an instinctive attempt to gain emotional relief. He tries to calm himself by argument. 'Who is right and who is wrong? No one!' Yet the burning sense of an injustice committed against himself, and at the same time of personal indignity in the face of it, leads to a terrible quarrel with his wife. There is violence in the air, in Book Four. Many people feel dishonoured, feel themselves wanting.

Prince Andrew returns during the night of his wife's confinement. His life is filled with coincidences like this. His sudden Hamlet-like appearance from the dead, thin and pale out of the wintry night, amazes Princess Mary, his sister. He enters his wife's bedroom. ' "I love you all and have done no harm to any one; why must I suffer so? help me!" her look seemed to say.' Within minutes she is dead, and Andrew is the father of a son. Everything has passed with breathless rapidity. This is a quality of the novel. There never seems to be enough time.

The rest of Book Four centres round the figures of Natasha and Dolokhov. Dolokhov, even more than Andrew, possesses a special relationship with death in the novel. There is something in him that relates Dolokhov with Andrew. The finer man suffers from the same kind of mind-sickness, the same readiness to hate. Nikolay Rostov is enormously attracted by Dolokhov, as Pierre is by Andrew, thinking him far superior to himself. Dolokhov lets his young friend into his confidence. It is like a caricature of Andrew's proud fastidiousness.

'. . . I don't care a straw about anyone but those I love; but those I love,
I love so that I would give my life for them, and the others I'd throttle if
they stood in my way . . . I have not yet met that divine purity and
devotion I look for in woman. If I found such a one I'd give my life for
her! But those! . . .' and he made a gesture of contempt.

The woman he chooses is Sonya, whom he knows to be in love with
Nikolay. Dolokhov takes the course which will have the most
harmful results. It is his way of asserting his power over events. To
bring about suffering is one form of self-assertion.

Almost immediately, we know that war is to be renewed. The
young men are to leave Moscow again. Sonya rejects Dolokhov. A
delightful ball takes place on the same evening. It is Natasha's and
Sonya's first ball – the first of the major scenes in *War and Peace*,
comparable in their resonance to the great things in *Anna Karenina*.
It has already been as if a veil was removed from before the eyes in
Book Four, and the new clarity has remained until the surprise is
over, but such scenes as this surprise one anew. There is the description of Denisov with clinking spurs whirling Natasha off into
the exciting Polish version of the mazurka.

The picturesque release of energy and the guilty attraction which
later spoils it are placed next to a scene in which Dolokhov assaults
Nikolay. He methodically cheats Nikolay at cards.

One tormenting impression did not leave him [Nikolay]: that those broad-
boned reddish hands with hairy wrists visible from under the shirt-
sleeves, those hands which he loved and hated, held him in their power.

Tolstoy can convey the physical presence of characters in much the
same way as D. H. Lawrence does. As Dolokhov envelops his prey,
Nikolay feels a fascination at being in the power of those hands, an
awareness of being the victim of a sadistic attack. As with all bullying
personalities, we are sharply aware of Dolokhov. Because we are on
our guard we note his slightest movements, as we will later note the
twitching of Napoleon's leg.

Book Five, which is closely associated with Book Four, is mainly
about Pierre and Andrew, who are trying to make sense of the world
after the disasters they have experienced. Pierre broods over the
question: What is life for? An old Freemason is lucky enough to

come upon the influential young man, and offers him the comforts of his order. The Freemasons will turn out badly later on. The discovery will again be made that faith in human organisations cannot survive for long after one has joined one and knows what goes on in it. Pierre becomes a member of the order, and its aims are revealed to him – 'to improve the whole human race'. But it is soon clear that the human race is not improved so easily. A few days later Pierre in a spasm of violence throws out his father-in-law, Prince Vasili Kuragin, who has come on a carefully planned peace-keeping mission. Pierre's natural sense of self-preservation in this scene is more admirable than the desire for power over others, which is present in his ambition to regenerate the human race.

One great question has slowly taken shape out of the smokes of battle and personal intrigue. What is it that determines the path which a nation takes? Is it true to say that a country is directed by its leaders? Are the nations of Europe suffering from defeat because they are badly led?

Prince Andrew is a disappointed leader, convinced for the present that leadership is always impracticable if not worse. He is seen in country retirement. His baby son is sick. Suddenly he hears a noise from the nursery, and the idea comes into his head that the baby is dead.

'All is over,' he thought, and a cold sweat broke out on his forehead. He went to the cot in confusion, sure that he would find it empty and that the nurse had been hiding the dead baby. He drew the curtain aside and for some time his frightened, restless eyes could not find the baby. At last he saw him: the boy had tossed about till he lay across the bed with his head lower than the pillow, and was smacking his lips in his sleep and breathing evenly.

The secret of Tolstoy's distinctive realism is contained in myriad sketches like this. It lies in details such as Prince Andrew's unforeseeable suspicion of the nurse here – Tolstoy's inclusion of those unexpected quirks of thought which occur in even the most rational minds. The apparently trivial little episode transmits a shock of realisation that no one is self-sufficient, that life without an object of devotion is insupportable. Yet it remains plain that Andrew's domestic ties are not enough for him. Andrew's idleness is clearly a strenuous exertion of the will on his part – an attempt to drive out his ambition which he now sees as useless restlessness.

Pierre visits Andrew's grim, efficient estate. Severely, Prince

Andrew recommends a life of non-interference with others. People
are likely to injure their fellows when they seek to help them. Who
has the right to lay down the correct way to live? He sees behind
Pierre's present social activities the self-assertiveness he has learnt
to distrust in himself.

Neither of them can be said to be either right or wrong in his
present opinions. Looked at unsympathetically, Pierre remains
faintly ridiculous to the end – while Andrew is often forbidding and
arid. Andrew's distaste is justified by everything in *War and Peace*, if
one looks through his eyes. His arguments can never be refuted. But
all Andrew is left with is an intensely aristocratic obsession with
personal honour – a determination to dissociate himself and his
from the brutality, stupidity and destructive clumsiness manifest in
the conduct of others. His short life will be a series of arrogant
sorties into the world of action and high command, followed by
equally arrogant periods of fastidious recoil such as the one he is
suffering from now. He will repeatedly search for people as exceptional as himself and will always be disappointed in those he fixes
on. In his period of withdrawal after Austerlitz, the only activity
of his life is one we might have predicted, since we are beginning to
understand him: it is to preserve his father from dishonour. It is
plain that his father's cruelty to his subordinates is a cruelty Andrew
is conscious of in himself. He knows that he has treated his wife
with the same cruelty. Andrew is very aware in himself of the
exasperated impulse to hurt others. In his hatred of irrational
behaviour and his self-tormenting remorse afterwards, Andrew
represents one reaction to life.

Pierre is enormously sorry for his friend. He shyly tries to communicate his new religious feelings to him. Prince Andrew listens
to Pierre's dreams of heaven as they cross a river by ferry.

'Yes, if only it were so!' said Prince Andrew . . . and stepping off the
raft he looked up at the sky to which Pierre had pointed, and for the first
time since Austerlitz saw that high everlasting sky he had seen while
lying on that battlefield.

The mood is dispelled almost instantly, but what remains for
Andrew is the knowledge that he is capable of such a mood, and – if
one dares risk Tolstoyan simplicity – that there is goodness in the
world. Pierre enlivens the whole dreary Bolkonski household by his
niceness. Good men in fiction are seldom so real.

The scene shifts to the army in Prussia. Nikolay, who returns happily to his regiment as a friendly refuge from the ills of civilian life, finds it hideously transformed by sickness and want. Through a series of mischances his friend Denisov breaks military law. Wounded during a reconnaissance, he retires to a military hospital to evade a court martial. Nikolay discovers his friend in the officers' ward morally poisoned, and with a wound that refuses to heal.

The climax of these two books about people tormented by injustice in an unintelligible world comes when Nikolay rides to Tilsit with Denisov's petition to the Tsar for a reprieve. The historic meeting between the Tsar and Napoleon has just taken place. A friendly general presents Denisov's petition. He waylays the Tsar as he leaves his quarters for a review of combined French and Russian troops.

'I cannot do it, General. I cannot, because the law is stronger than I,' and he raised his foot to the stirrup.

The general bowed his head respectfully, and the monarch mounted and rode down the street at a gallop. Beside himself with enthusiasm Rostov ran after him with the crowd.

Nikolay reacts as the crowd does. It is necessary for him to see both himself and Denisov as pawns in a great and benevolent plan.

But the two emperors are in fact ordinary men, immeasurably distant only because they are out of touch with other men. There is really nobody in charge. Nikolay drinks heavily and quarrels with an officer who resents the combined French and Russian review.

So ends, on a note of impotent rage, a sequence (Books IV and V) in which many questions have been raised – questions of justice and of responsibility. In the centre of the stage at the end of Book Five stand Napoleon and Alexander, the 'leaders' of their respective nations.

Books VI, VII and VIII

The next three books (VI, VII and VIII) form the section which takes us to the centre of the novel. The invasion of Russia will occur thereafter. This section has been prepared for by the previous one. It is seen by Tolstoy as the key to the whole novel, though the military scene will not once appear in it. The central figure will be Natasha Rostov. The main events are the great formative ones of Natasha's life in her first years of womanhood. Of these three books, the

middle one (vII) conveys a mood of innocent happiness such as
Prince Andrew has glimpsed during his talk with Pierre. This is
destroyed in the final book (vIII). Natasha's disgrace is intended as
the most disturbing manifestation so far of the destructive impulses
human nature is subject to. It is the climax of this section, as
Austerlitz and then Tilsit were the climaxes of their respective
sections. It is also the climax of the first half of the novel. The
primitive, imperfectly conscious creature Anatole and the mind-torn
Prince Andrew together will be responsible for the near ruin of
Natasha. It seems that neither of them can help themselves.

Two years have passed when Book Six opens. In the spring Prince
Andrew travels on business. An old wintry oak which grimly scorns
the fresh vegetation all around attracts his attention, and he makes
the obvious reflections. Andrew's thoughts here are naïve. Tolstoy
recognises that human responses are occasionally not as complicated
as people imagine.[1]

Andrew's duties entail a visit to Count Rostov. He finds the
family tedious, but his interest is aroused by the adolescent raptures
of Natasha. On the drive home, Prince Andrew finds that the old
oak has become covered with green leaves. Hope has returned. In the
autumn he is in Petersburg, and the whole of the rest of Book Six
takes place there. It seems as though the nation is renewing itself,
and Andrew finds his new mood reflected in many other people. In
War and Peace nations move as huge units, though the surface motives
of individuals are various and seemingly unconnected. One becomes
increasingly aware of this underlying uniformity of movement.

Andrew is determined on a life of action again. He makes precisely
the same mistakes as before. Again he demands too much. Again he
puts his faith in enlightened leadership, again he looks for great
men to attach himself to, and again the cannon ball will thud into
the ground independent of any strategy invented by him. In Russia,
which is now carried away with enthusiasm for Napoleonic
methods, the figure that is worshipped is Speranski the reformer.
Prince Andrew becomes one of Speranski's protegés. After the despair
of the preceding years, a worship of great men, potential saviours
of their nation, is the natural development, and Andrew, one of the
brilliant young men of his time, shares it.

In general the trait of Speranski's mentality which struck Prince Andrew

[1] It is a perception one finds also in Chekhov.

most was his absolute and unshakable belief in the power and authority of reason . . . he had never felt the doubt, 'Is not all I think and believe nonsense?' And it was just this peculiarity of Speranski's mind that particularly attracted Prince Andrew.

Andrew's need to feel himself part of an ordered universe is really the same need which drives Pierre during this period to attempt reforms in Freemasonry. Pierre delivers an eloquent speech advocating certain changes. The meeting he addresses ends in muddle and bad temper.

At that meeting he was struck for the first time by the endless variety of men's minds, which prevents a truth from ever presenting itself identically to two persons. Even those members who seemed to be on his side understood him in their own way, with limitations and alterations he could not agree to.

None but the crudest activity seems possible when many individuals each attempt to put their personal wishes into practice. Free action seems impossible. This torments Andrew and Pierre.

The Rostovs arrive in Petersburg. We are introduced to Natasha again in one of those miraculous Tolstoyan domestic scenes. Natasha visits her mother in bed. The countess intends to put an end to Natasha's courtship by a young social climber, Boris Drubetskoy.

'. . . No, mamma, don't speak to him! What nonsense!' said Natasha in the tone of one being deprived of her property. 'Well, I won't marry, but let him come if he enjoys it and I enjoy it.' Natasha smiled and looked at her mother. 'Not to marry, but just *so*,' she added.
'How *so*, my pet?'
'Just *so*. There's no need for me to marry him. But . . . just *so*.'

The assertiveness combined with vulnerability in the young girl is perfectly done. Her vital self-love and glad sense of naughtiness increase when she returns to her bedroom, feeling very superior to the 'good' Sonya.

This is a prologue to the romantic highlight of a novel which, if one looks at a synopsis only, is the great nineteenth-century romance. The grand Petersburg ball to which Natasha goes takes up three of Tolstoy's very short chapters, and at the end an immense number of things have happened. Again this ability to cram many events into a small space reminds one of Shakespeare. At the ball presided over by the Tsar himself almost all the characters of the novel move in stately dance. It is like a ballet sequence in which the personages express themselves in the dance with a fresh directness. Prince Andrew dances with Natasha. 'Prince Andrew was one of the best dancers of his day, and Natasha danced exquisitely.' Natasha in later life will be lucky in her memories. Like her brother, she is a person to whom joyful things naturally happen. She has a gift for life. Under her brief influence, Prince Andrew acquires it too.

Prince Andrew visits the Rostovs often, and they no longer bore him, though he on his side intimidates the household. When Prince Andrew vanishes to consult his father about remarrying, Natasha although hurt in her feelings is really relieved. The presence of Andrew has been oppressive. Prince Andrew's father demands that he should defer the marriage for a year. In leaving her free and not announcing that they have become engaged, Prince Andrew is really using his father's command to test Natasha. It is a test she will not pass, and Andrew will make no allowances. The standards of perfection the Bolkonskis set for themselves are perverse – always destructive in their consequences.

The following book (VII), the middle one in this group of three, is an idyll immeasurably distant from the tormented Bolkonskis. Time is felt to be short by the reader, who knows what is to befall Russia. Nikolay returns on leave from the army, and he and Natasha cram everything into what both feel to be the last year of their childhood.

It is the end of August, the time for wolf-hunting, and with the summoning of Daniel, the Rostov huntsman, into their country house we are made aware of man's early beginnings. 'To see him in a room was like seeing a horse or a bear on the floor among the furniture and surroundings of human life.' The wolf-hunt celebrates a mood of wild exultation. Nikolay brings honour to his family by heading off an old wolf. It is the most exciting day in the novel – far more so than all the battles, which leave one disgusted by the human carnage, and it is intended to contrast with them.

Nikolay and Natasha end the day at the house of an old relative. Natasha jumps up and dances a peasant dance.

Where, how, and when, had this young countess, educated by an émigrée French governess, imbibed from the Russian air she breathed that spirit ... the movements were inimitable and unteachable Russian ones.

A patriotic fervour is coming out in Tolstoy here, in keeping with the great events which follow. Underlying everything, Tolstoy's absorbed pondering about war is continuing, though nothing is said about it here. The reader is only apparently left alone with his thoughts. Why will all this youthful gaiety be destroyed? Who is to blame?

It soon becomes evident that the Rostov household is no longer a secure one. Financial ruin is very close. The old count has remained a child all his life. He is like his children – too like them. They are what are called exceptional children, but their sort of life cannot be lived in perpetuity. Yet the loss when life has reshaped them will be intense.

One evening Natasha, suffering from a sorrow she cannot really explain, though she attributes it to Andrew's absence, wanders about the house looking for Nikolay who, unlike the rather limited Sonya, is able to share in her perceptions. The quiet talk between Nikolay and Natasha is filled with startling flashes of inspiration which they lack later.

In Book Eight the story of Natasha's betrothal to Andrew is brought to its tragic conclusion. This book also concludes the first half of the novel. Every one of the main characters appears, and every one of them has become a bit older and a bit dull. The scene is Moscow, a city about which everything is known. *War and Peace* has been filled exclusively with disappointments. Natasha will apparently be the final one.

The Rostovs go to the opera – one of the most brilliant sequences in the novel, balancing the sequence containing the ball at which Natasha danced with Prince Andrew.

All Moscow is at the opera, and most of the people we know either intimately or as acquaintances. By this time the reader has the entrée into all Russian society. Not a drawing-room, assembly room or staff officers' meeting can be entered, it seems, without recognising one or two faces. We know so much that we are getting world-weary. Tolstoy never stops creating new acquaintances, though by now the circle of people who are intimately known will not be enlarged. Tolstoy is creating people exactly as they continue to crop up in life. But a sense of overcrowding does not come. Tolstoy's control over all the material he brings forward never slackens.

Before the performance Pierre's wife Helene has rustled into the box next to the Rostovs'. Helene's brother, Anatole Kuragin, appears.

In the interval he conducts an agreeable conversation with Natasha.

When she was not looking at him she felt that he was looking at her shoulders . . . When she turned away she feared he might seize her from behind by her bare arm and kiss her on the neck.

Andrew seems suddenly a figure in the remote past. The other man, by deliberately forcing his physical presence on her, is now far closer to her.

A love letter arrives, composed in fact by Dolokhov, and the 'comedy' is in full swing. All that is missing is an elopement.

There is a tremendous scene at Dolokhov's quarters where he, Anatole and other dare-devils prepare for the abduction, as though it were a hunting expedition, with Natasha as quarry. The plot is foiled, and then follows humiliation and disgrace for Natasha which is so painful one wishes to avert one's eyes.

Pierre, although he understands Natasha, must stand by and watch her suffering. No one is able to help. This appears to have established itself as a law. Natasha struggles in full view of several people all powerless to help. There are the less prominent tragedies of Princess Mary, Pierre and Andrew also in this book, and the same applies to these too.

On hearing of Prince Andrew's arrival Pierre visits the Bolkonskis. He finds Andrew talking politics among his father's friends. Speranski has been dismissed and accused of treachery. Andrew works himself up over the injustice meted out by governments, to escape thinking of the injustice of his personal situation. 'At dinner the talk turned on the war, the approach of which was becoming evident.'

We next survey an international bloodbath. The impulses underlying it are not strange, but very familiar – as familiar as Anatole's wish to add a feather to his cap by making a trophy of Natasha Rostov. But before Tolstoy shifts his ground there is a short scene at the last moment. It describes a success which, for Pierre at least, outweighs the failures that the novel has so far been about. He visits Natasha and impulsively declares his hopeless love for her. When he leaves he looks up at the great comet of 1812. For him, its proclamation of irresistible power is not sinister as it is to others. Pierre has helped Natasha, and everything now seems possible to him. Natasha and Pierre will hold on to life.

It turns out that the bleak society before the invasion still conceals within itself immense latent energy. When every individual reacts at the same moment to the national crisis, this energy will be released. Although, as at all times, the individual defeats and deaths will far outnumber the successes, the successes will outweigh them, as Pierre's success with Natasha outweighs his previous failures.

Tolstoy's choice of a great patriotic war to contrast with the sterile period described in the first half of his novel could easily be seen as a most dangerous one. The answer to that is the attitude Tolstoy attributes to the Russians in this war. It is the same as might be adopted to a great natural disaster. Military successes do not give the nation its inspiration, for there are none. The novel will not celebrate Borodino, but rather a passive rejection by all Russians of the French.

THE SECOND HALF OF 'WAR AND PEACE'

Books IX and X

War and Peace is introduced by three books dealing with the war that ends at Austerlitz. These are followed by ten books (IV–XIII) which make up the bulk of the novel. These ten books fall exactly into two equal blocks (the first of which has been dealt with). After these comes a conclusion consisting of two books (XIV and XV) which describe how war is brought to an end – for that generation at least. Then there are the two epilogues.

The five books (IX–XIII) which now follow are divided into two sections, the first consisting of two books and the second of three, precisely as with the previous five books. The conclusion of the first of these sections (comprising Books Nine and Ten) is to be the Battle of Borodino.

There is now a distinct change in emphasis. The attention is no longer held exclusively by a relatively small number of characters and their concerns. People now move in their masses, in entire nations. A consequence of this is that the author, the organiser of the material, is far more in evidence. Tolstoy drops the role of an impersonal narrator concealed behind his characters. He now uses his private voice and stands in the foreground, selecting and guiding. This is the only honest course. He is now there as a man who is searching for answers, a man who is selecting details to aid this search, and we must be allowed to see what he is up to.

There is a second reason for Tolstoy's abandonment of imper-

sonality. When he dealt for the first time with an immensely confused historical event, the Battle of Austerlitz, the dramatic method of
presentation got in the way of reality. Impossibly much of the battle
had to be seen through the eyes of a few people – in particular,
Nikolay Rostov. Tolstoy himself has never seen battles in the way
Nikolay does, and he hates any distortion of reality in art.

Another reason for Tolstoy's move into the foreground in the
second half of the novel is that he is now faced with the characterisation of historical figures. He must be honest about his personal
attitude to them. This is best illustrated by the way he presents
Napoleon. Tolstoy speaks about Napoleon contemptuously. He
caricatures Napoleon when he personally comments on him – and
he has every right to his own opinion – but when Tolstoy shows
Napoleon in person he is as impressive as a Napoleon would
be.

In the opening chapter of Book Nine Tolstoy outlines his conception of history, which is in harmony with all the experiences we
have been offered so far, and has been arrived at by way of them. The
first sentences are these:

From the close of the year 1811 an intensified arming and concen-
trating of the forces of Western Europe began, and in 1812 these forces –
millions of men reckoning those transporting and feeding the army –
moved from the west eastwards to the Russian frontier, towards which
since 1811 Russian forces had been similarly drawn.

Tolstoy intimates that henceforth each character in the novel is to
be seen from two points of view – 'his individual life' and 'his
elemental swarm-life'. The further away one stands from individuals,
the more clearly one sees how helpless they are in the arrangement
of their affairs. 'We are forced to fall back on fatalism' in history.
The question which immediately arises is whether one must absolve
the individuals in the novel from responsibility for their actions.
The second of Tolstoy's epilogues will therefore be a discussion on
the nature of free will. Tolstoy, throughout *War and Peace*, is concerned with the question of responsibility – the problems of guilt
and retribution.

The province of the historian is to seek out the relations between
past events. If the historian attempts this by analysing the personalities of great historical figures he is bound to be unreliable. Tolstoy
questions the historian's right to indulge in character studies,

because his conjectures can never be verified.[1] The historian would be poaching on the territory of the artist, and diminishing the value of his own activity. Tolstoy's Napoleon in a historical treatise would be a lie, as Tolstoy later feels at liberty to see Thiers' Napoleon to be a lie. But in the novel Tolstoy's Napoleon is no more a lie than Goya's Duke of Wellington or Shakespeare's Henry V.

Tolstoy, in his chapters dealing with the writing of history, is really talking about his art, defining artistic truth by contrasting it with historical 'fact'. It is the attitude of a Napoleon to certain facts in life which interests Tolstoy. Tolstoy's Napoleon is a major creation in the novel and essential to it. He is as important a figure in the second half as Anatole Kuragin is in the first. Morally he is as unformed. He rides over battlefields piled with the dead and remains unperturbed. His being sent to Elba will be like Anatole's being exiled by Pierre to Petersburg. It is irrelevant to think of punishing either of them.

In the introductory chapter to Book Nine, Tolstoy has established his new vantage point. He then goes on to describe the crossing of the Niemen, which begins the invasion of Russia. There is the strange incident of the Polish Uhlans drowning under the eye of their Emperor rather than cross by a ford where he would be out of sight. Books Nine and Ten develop into a series of studies of crowd psychology, the temper of the mass as it manifests itself in each individual Frenchman and Russian respectively. This will be concluded in the account of Borodino.

Sketches illustrating the swashbuckling temper of the French army lead up to the first full-length portrait of Napoleon. Balashev, a Russian general, has been sent with a note of protest from the Tsar. The interview with Napoleon is a terrifying study of a man who holds vast power. Napoleon is unquestionably what is called a great man. He is watched with strained attention as one involuntarily stares at a great man, as though some secret might lie within him, some explanation.

Balashev . . . stood a minute or two waiting. He heard hurried footsteps beyond the door, both halves of it were opened rapidly; all was silent

---

[1] 'Countless are the times I have begun and given up writing the story of 1812 . . . I was afraid that the need to describe important people of 1812 would compel me to be guided by historical documents and not the truth.' Quoted in Christian, Tolstoy's 'War and Peace'.

and then from the study the sound was heard of other steps, firm and resolute – they were those of Napoleon. He had just finished dressing for his ride, and wore a blue uniform opening in front over a white waistcoat, so long that it covered his rotund stomach, white leather breeches tightly fitting the fat thighs of his short legs, and Hessian boots. His short hair had evidently just been brushed, but one lock hung down in the middle of his broad forehead. His plump white neck stood out sharply above the black collar of his uniform, and he smelt of eau-de-cologne.

Already there is an overpowering impression – closeness to a familiar figure only glimpsed from afar or seen in pictures. The closeness is such that Balashev can even smell Napoleon. The fat short legs, the plump white body, the smell of eau-de-cologne are not comic – they are terrifying because of the incongruity of the soft envelope and the immense secret it conceals (or appears to conceal). Napoleon thinks that he is a world conqueror. Balashev thinks he is too. Tolstoy has already told us that, looked at philosophically, he is not, but once placed in close proximity with the man, theory becomes irrelevant. Tolstoy does not diminish one sort of truth to give weight to another.

Napoleon is a great leader, as fully in control of the military situation as any man can be. Napoleon's contempt for his adversaries is backed up by a confident series of assertions which are difficult to fault, even if looked at coolly – which Napoleon makes it impossible for Balashev to do in his presence.

'. . . Barclay is said to be the most capable of them all, but I cannot say so judging by his first movements. And what are they doing, all these courtiers? Pfuel proposes, Armfelt disputes, Bennigsen considers, and Barclay, called on to act, does not know what to decide on, and time passes bringing no result. Bagration alone is a military man. He's stupid, but he has experience, a quick eye, and resolution . . . And what role is your young monarch playing in that monstrous crowd? They compromise him and throw on him the responsibility for all that happens. A sovereign should not be with the army unless he is a general!' said Napoleon, evidently uttering these words as a direct challenge to the Emperor. He knew how Alexander desired to be a military commander.

'The campaign only began a week ago, and you haven't even been able to defend Vilna. You are cut in two and have been driven out of the Polish provinces. Your army is grumbling.'

'On the contrary, your Majesty,' said Balashev, hardly able to remember what had been said to him, and following these verbal fireworks with difficulty, 'the troops are burning with eagerness . . .'

'I know everything!' Napoleon interrupted him. 'I know everything. I know the number of your battalions as exactly as I know my own.'

The Tsar's demand that he should retreat behind the Niemen again, even though the frightened Balashev has toned it down to a humble request, has triggered off this brilliant piece of bullying, which in reality is as involuntary as the bullying temper already sensed in every level of the French army. Napoleon enjoys the impression he is making, and grows fiercer, and this also is the process in the French army as a whole. In the final outburst of the interview:

'. . . if you stir up Prussia against me, I'll wipe it off the map of Europe!' he declared, his face pale and distorted by anger, and he struck one of his small hands energetically with the other. 'Yes, I will throw you back beyond the Dvina and beyond the Dnieper, and will re-erect against you that barrier which it was criminal and blind of Europe to allow to be destroyed.'

the excitement and elation of Napoleon represents a force that cannot be stopped. Its impetus will carry him with ease into the heart of Russia. That evening at dinner Napoleon benevolently questions Balashev about the sights of Moscow, assuming the Russian will be flattered by this interest. It has been a sketch of the psychology of a nation on the attack. We do not see Napoleon or the French again till the Battle of Borodino at the end of Book Ten. For the time being, there is no more to be said.

The rest of Book Nine is a portrait of the threatened nation mustering its energies. The subject is introduced by a glimpse of the Bolkonski family. Prince Andrew, once again in military uniform, talks to his sister:

'Ah, my God! my God! When one thinks who and what — what trash — can cause people misery!' he said with a malignity that alarmed Princess Mary.
She understood that when speaking of 'trash' he referred . . . also to the man who had ruined his own happiness.
'Andrew! One thing I beg, I entreat of you! . . . Don't imagine that sorrow is the work of men. . . . Remember that misfortunes come from God, and men are never to blame,' were the last words he heard from his sister when he took leave of her.

The importance of forgiveness in a world where the individual has no right to pass judgement, is an old concept. Mary with her simple religion and her modesty now becomes important in the scheme.

Yet she has always been there in the background. Some qualities are seen clearly only in adversity.

Perhaps the key to Book Nine has been a passage in Napoleon's dinner-time conversation with Balashev, scarcely noticed at the time.

'How many inhabitants are there in Moscow? How many houses? Is it true that Moscow is called "Holy Moscow"? How many churches are there in Moscow?' he asked.

And receiving the reply that there were more than two hundred churches, he remarked:

'Why such a quantity of churches?'

'The Russians are very devout,' replied Balashev.

'But a large number of monasteries and churches is always a sign of the backwardness of a people,' said Napoleon.

The main scene in Book Nine will take place in one of Moscow's churches.

But meanwhile the story follows Prince Andrew to the army. Andrew still wishes to find someone in control of events. He wishes to discover the 'science of war'. The desire for order still drives him, though his disappointments are endless. Any final conclusion that no man can control events will be drawn much against his will. Tolstoy is enforcing the conclusion which is forming in his own mind by means of the man who least wishes to accept it, whose sense of self-preservation is against his accepting it.

Experience has curtailed Andrew's hopes, but he still sees good leadership as the only answer to chaos. By virtue of his position, he is again able to observe councils of war. He hears a furious squabble among sensible, experienced men all unwilling to rely on any plan but their own. Prince Andrew concludes that the only way in which he can be of use will be as a tiny component of the fighting masses. He accepts the relative unimportance of the individual. This, for him, is a gesture of despair – a mortifying blow to his pride.

Attention is now turned to the active army. Nikolay Rostov returns to his regiment. Patriotism is not now an obvious motive, nor is the thought of glory. These are not obvious, either, among his fellow officers as they go about their business. Instead, there is a desire to remain simple and innocent, which is more moving. The boasting and histrionics of the period before Austerlitz are out of place. Rostov is embarrassed when an officer tells him the story of General Raevski charging the enemy with his two sons at his side. Lies are out of place, and the sentiment this one celebrates is

unnatural. 'Why expose his own children in the battle?' Later, when
Nikolay misses the Battle of Borodino, he has no regrets, for he does
not feel that the army alone is of importance. The experience of the
nation at large will be that of weathering a long storm patiently – a
storm which will certainly end. This is what destroys the French, for
their faith in themselves can be shaken. The novel is turning into an
object lesson in attaining the only peace which interests Tolstoy –
peace of mind.

Now comes a scene which raises the most complicated issues. The
Rostovs, together with other families who are staying on in Moscow
that summer, visit their church and hear for the first time the prayer
for the deliverance of Russia which has just been composed. The
entire prayer is given, prepared for by Natasha's fervent response to
the traditional words of the service, and reinforced by the emotion
that is sensed in the congregation. 'Smite down our enemies and
destroy them swiftly beneath the feet of Thy faithful servants!'
The meaning of the words is ugly, yet this does not seem to matter.
The words themselves are not understood and not criticised. The
rest of Book Nine is filled with a fervour which goes beyond words.
The devotion of the people of Moscow to their country is unthink-
ing, irrational. This is what makes it so fine and generous – but also
disturbing, as Tolstoy gradually makes us aware.

Many in Moscow experience feelings of mad generosity and love
at this moment. There is the wonderful account of the fifteen-year-
old Petya Rostov spending a day crushed in the crowds at the
Kremlin, trying to glimpse the newly arrived Tsar. This is indeed
what an excited crowd feels like. For good or ill, all individuality
has disappeared, and all that is left is the excitement of loving or of
hating. The scene is a more disturbing manifestation of emotions
already witnessed in the church scene.

Book Nine ends with the most disturbing crowd scene so far. The
Moscow noblemen meet in their official uniforms to receive the
Tsar. The crowd in its uniforms and with its collective conception of
aristocratic and national honour is temporarily insane in its lust for
self-sacrifice, and also magnificent to watch. The reader responds
completely. This is what everyone always responds to, whether he
wishes to or not. So ends Book Nine, which has begun a study of
man in the mass, in crowds and nations. The question of responsibility has become one degree harder. When the crowds have
dispersed, the individuals in them are surprised at what they have

done. The things people do are not necessarily what they would wish to do, but what they find themselves doing or having done. It is infinitely harder to judge crowds and nations than to judge individuals.

Tolstoy has brought about his great transition in Book Nine, transforming the people we know into members of a nation fighting for its existence. He has accustomed us to the sort of mass emotion which becomes overwhelmingly strong in such circumstances. The section now moves forward to its climax, the Battle of Borodino.

Book Ten also has an introductory chapter. In this, Tolstoy restates his opinions about inevitability in history more strongly. It is as though these opinions gain force the further the French advance into Russia. The contrast between the experience of the time, when no one understood the causes of his actions, and the hugely simple pattern which has emerged in retrospect, dictates such conclusions. The conviction grows that no single man could have affected what was happening. This being so, what was happening *was* inevitable.

Book Ten takes us up to what Tolstoy sees as the great Russian victory of Borodino. Borodino is the expression of Russia's victory over herself. It is a moral victory – like the victory which comes at the end of Conrad's story of that name, or indeed that which comes at the end of *Hamlet*. The process leading up to Borodino is a slow one. Tolstoy sees the disaster which befalls Russia as inevitable. There is no bitterness against the enemy. There was none in his Sebastopol sketches either – even the last terrible one in which he described the taking of Sebastopol. Tolstoy saw Sebastopol as a moral victory. In *War and Peace* a military victory over Napoleon is impossible. Tolstoy swallows a great deal of what one normally thinks of as national pride when he exposes this in detail.

In Book Nine the crowd emotions, the prayers, and the mass adoration of the Tsar had only a temporary significance for those taking part. The long-term acceptance of suffering and privation only comes after the sacking of Smolensk. The story of the fall of Smolensk is told by Tolstoy in conjunction with the story of the collapse of old Prince Bolkonski, Andrew's father. The Bolkonski estate is on Napoleon's route to Moscow. The old Prince refuses to recognise the existence of the war and is peculiarly active in introducing improvements and planning new buildings. This is his last and ultimately insane stand against the realities of the human situation. His attitude is the reverse of Kutuzov's later. He is a barren old man who breaks before the storm.

The fall of Smolensk serves as the pattern for what happens in every town Napoleon advances on. During Napoleon's bombardment of the town itself a change comes over everybody – a sudden acceptance that all is over with their previous lives, that this town is no longer usable and must be abandoned. Its population leaves in great crowds.

Days later, Prince Andrew's regiment passes the abandoned Bolkonski estate. Andrew shares the anger of other Russians, but with an added disgust and nausea which is his own. He sees his soldiers bathing in a pool stagnant with the summer drought.

All this naked white human flesh, laughing and shrieking, floundered about in that dirty pool like carp stuffed into a watering can, and the suggestion of merriment in that floundering mass rendered it specially pathetic

– pathetic because Andrew can see further than they can, or cannot see far enough. He joins them, momentarily conquering his repulsion, but –

'Flesh, bodies, cannon-fodder!' he thought, and he looked at his own naked body and shuddered.

The tale of disaster and defeat in Book Ten ends on a personal note with a moving story of collapse in the Bolkonski family, followed by renewal from an unexpected quarter. This is placed just before the mass victory of Borodino. Old Prince Bolkonski dies. His way of precipitating his death has been curiously like his son's later. He has mustered his energies for a gesture of defiance against the impersonal machine which is about to crush him. He has donned his uniform and gone out to prepare the defence of his estate. In doing so he has collapsed. It has been the last action in a life which has been all of a piece.

It is now that an unexpected change comes over the saintly Princess Mary. To her own horror, she ceases to be a saint. She goes through a succession of emotional crises.

. . . she watched him, and terrible to say, often watched him not with hope of finding signs of improvement but wishing to find symptoms of the approach of the end.

Then there is the sudden realisation that her father's death might after all deprive her own life of all vividness. Later, when he is dead, there is the instinct that to kiss his corpse is an unnatural action, that death has no right to exact this from her.

In part at least, her saintliness has been the expression of an awareness which relates her to Natasha Rostov. One can now see that her 'saintly' interest in the peasant zealots 'God's folk' has provided an outlet for her love of everything open and spontaneous, which she has been prevented from expressing in her relations with her father and brother. The sudden desire for her father's death has been brought about by his decision to die defending his estate. This act of selfishness has been a betrayal beside which war and disaster are only external things. Mary therefore wants her freedom.

Mary now finds herself up against another situation in which she is as powerless as in her relations with her father – a force as irresistible, but different in kind. This is the obstructiveness of the peasants on Prince Andrew's estate to which the family has transferred. The will of the mass has no connection with what the individuals may be like. In the crowd which Mary comes face to face with, 'all eyes were gazing at her with one and the same expression'. Absorption into the mass is as perilous as, at the opposite pole, the old Prince's absorption with himself. It is hard to decide on a course between losing oneself in the emotions of the mass and separating oneself from it entirely. Tolstoy is forcing the reader to try and find his own solutions to the major problems which wartime poses so urgently, and which must be resolved quickly as they come up.

Mary, temporarily ineffective, defeated first by her father and then by the peasants, is rescued by Nikolay Rostov, an average and even rather boring Russian gentleman. The peasants accept his authority immediately. It is with a feeling of relief that they now obey Nikolay and help Princess Mary to leave.

As Nikolay Rostov restores order on the Bolkonski estate, so the Russian forces accept Kutuzov's leadership. Prince Andrew tries to formulate the impression Kutuzov makes on him.

He understands that there is something stronger and more important than his own will – the inevitable course of events, and he can see them and grasp their significance, and seeing that significance can refrain from meddling and renounce his personal wish directed to something else.

This knowledge has come 'because of his old age and experience of life'. The great quality of Kutuzov is his unoriginality. His is the

ripe 'wisdom' of old age, which impresses the intelligent young for
it is something they cannot have. This is a period for Russia when
the old, established things in her are of vital importance. It is the
immensely old things which defeat Napoleon.

There is now a glimpse of Moscow as she appears during the
brief moments before the catastrophe. It is an ugly picture of an
irritable, nervous city. Pierre leaves Moscow to follow the army,
glad to leave this unattractive semblance of life behind.

. . . the deeper he plunged into that sea of troops the more was he overcome
by restless agitation and a new and joyful feeling he had not experienced
before. It was a feeling akin to what he had felt at the Sloboda Palace
during the Emperor's visit – a sense of the necessity of undertaking something and sacrificing something. He now experienced a glad consciousness
that everything that constitutes men's happiness – the comforts of life,
wealth, even life itself – is rubbish it is pleasant to throw away, compared
with something . . . With what? Pierre could not say, and he did not try to
determine for whom and for what he felt such particular delight in sacrificing everything.

Even the present frightened mood of Moscow is preferable to the
mood the idealistic Pierre finds himself in. His joy is for his own
sake, and his object is himself. War is cutting knots which his own
clumsiness has tied. War seems much cleaner than peace. Tolstoy,
like Shakespeare (Henry V, Troilus and Cressida, Coriolanus), finds this
notion dangerous and absurd.

The exciting unknown towards which Pierre is rushing in company
with so many is the Battle of Borodino. Tolstoy now contemplates
the battle for a few moments, with coldly sceptical, analytic eyes.
All professional historians who do not see with such eyes are, he
has already implied, simply writers of poor epic fiction. It does not
matter whether Tolstoy himself is getting his facts right here. It does
not even matter whether Tolstoy personally believes that his facts
coincide with the truth. He is showing how the great efforts of the
past always appear when the shouting and the clash of arms have
died away, when the decisions of the leaders come to be criticised
by historians. The battle was a series of blunders, and Kutuzov
blundered as much as anyone. This is one sort of truth about any
war. All the rest belongs to the artist and is the truth as we experience
it – life rather than documents.

Pierre, as he approaches the field the day before the battle, sees
many scenes in the morning sunshine. He stares at the serious

expression he sees on every face, especially in the crowd that collects round a holy icon which is being carried through the lines. There is a glimpse of Prince Andrew alone in his quarters, bitterly contemplating the futility of life. Yet, in the company of his fellow officers and the newly arrived Pierre, Andrew knows what he is there for, he understands the purpose of the following day:

... 'Take no prisoners, but kill and be killed!...

War is not courtesy but the most horrible thing in life; and we ought to understand that, and not play at war. We ought to accept this terrible necessity sternly and seriously.'

There is little difference between him as he is here and the soldiers who have refused their regular ration of vodka because 'It's not the day for that!' It is impossible for any man to stand back from a crowd when he is in the midst of it.

The result of the following day will depend primarily on the mood of the opposing armies, and accordingly the scene now shifts to Napoleon, the representative of the French.

The French soldiers went to kill and be killed at the battle of Borodino not because of Napoleon's orders ... The whole army – French, Italian, German, Polish, and Dutch – hungry, ragged, and weary of the campaign, felt at the sight of an army blocking their road to Moscow, that the wine was drawn and must be drunk.

Yet, Tolstoy goes on, 'Napoleon at the battle of Borodino fulfilled his office as representative of authority as well as, and even better than, at other battles.' In conversation with his adjutant, Napoleon defines the art of war: 'It is the art of being stronger than the enemy at a given moment. That's all.' It is plain that he is as capable as we are of seeing all the possible interpretations of this. But he is not the sort of person who holds one's interest for long. The battle is a more important event in the lives of many other people than it is in Napoleon's.

Pierre finds a vantage point at the gun-battery which will become famous for the tens of thousands slaughtered over it. '... just because he happened to be there he thought it one of the least significant parts of the field.' The episode of the battery is the greatest thing in the second half of War and Peace. It remains a burning memory and yet it is one of the shortest episodes in Tolstoy. It seems to last only a few minutes, but everything is there. Pierre has his experience of glory. It is different and finer than anything he had foreseen. Heroism in Tolstoy's art, as in Shakespeare's, is treated as one of the most impressive manifestations of the human spirit. Tolstoy sees it as the moral force to endure terrible bondage sanely, the ability to stand still when necessary rather than to run, even though it be forward. It is the quality which connects Pierre's soldiers to their fellows with such strength. The Russians gain the victory by staying where they are for a whole day, bound to one another unshakably. The whole novel is an attempt to examine such bonds. The battle is the last of Tolstoy's studies of crowds in these two books (IX and X).

Kutuzov is the better general because his troops make him so. At the height of the slaughter he issues his impossible command for an attack on the morrow. It is already expected before he gives it. Great generals are the ones most in touch with the spirit of their armies. Both Kutuzov and Napoleon are.

It is now that the action shifts to Prince Andrew, who receives his death wound. In spite of the bloodshed all around, his destruction shocks one by its perversity. A grenade lands at his feet, and he does not fling himself to the ground like those around him.

'I cannot, I do not wish to die. I love life – I love this grass, this earth, this air . . .' He thought this, and at the same time remembered that people were looking at him.

He receives death because his fear of ridicule is stronger than his instinct to live. He dies because he is an aristocrat, a being apart. It is both magnificent and ugly, like the fates of Shakespeare's aristocrats.

Prince Andrew will be a long time dying. In the hospital tent where he is brought, a man whose leg has been cut off is suddenly revealed as Anatole Kuragin. Prince Andrew experiences the same feeling as we witnessed, long ago, so unexpectedly in Anatole's father, Prince Vasili, after the death of old Count Bezukhov. 'Prince Andrew . . . wept tender loving tears for his fellow men, for himself, and for his own, and their errors.'

Books XI, XII and XIII

The occupation of Moscow is the subject of Books Eleven to Thirteen. The study of personalities drops still further into the background after the experience of Borodino. The emotions which sway nations are not instilled by leaders. 'Every time there have been conquests there have been conquerors', to which human reason replies, says Tolstoy, 'but this does not prove that the conquerors caused the wars'.

Kutuzov must give the order to retreat beyond Moscow. He bravely shoulders the responsibility for the inevitable command. Count Rostopchin, Governor of Moscow, who has postured dwarfishly in the face of events and embarrassed the citizens by demanding heroic feats of last-ditch heroism is not obeyed, because he gave the wrong orders. The citizens of Moscow 'who went away, taking what they could and abandoning their houses and half their belongings, did so from that latent patriotism which expresses itself not by phrases or by giving one's children to save the fatherland, and by similar unnatural exploits, but unobtrusively, simply, organically, and therefore in the way that always produces the most powerful results'. There is a grand simplicity in this identical decision of numberless families.

The Rostovs are also leaving. A convoy of wounded soldiers arrives in the street. Under the silent influence of the wounded men, the Rostov family now produces its act of heroism. They offer their carts and become a mere appendage to the convoy. (A carriage which has attached itself to the cavalcade carries Prince Andrew.) The self-sacrifice of the Rostovs will live in the memory as the Raevski redoubt has done.

It is now, though, that Tolstoy chooses to define the position from which the events following Borodino are to be seen. He makes it clear that everything he has just described with such breathtaking vividness has been relatively unimportant. It was vast numbers of men standing their ground who won Borodino. It is a vast city emptying itself which wins the war. The exceptional actions, heroic or otherwise, are kept firmly in proportion within a vaster scheme.

The occupation of Moscow is now imminent. There is the wonderful description of the great city as a 'dying queenless hive'.

Here and there among the cells containing dead brood and honey an angry buzzing can sometimes be heard. Here and there a couple of bees, by force of habit and custom, clean out the brood cells . . . In another corner two old bees are languidly fighting, or cleaning themselves, or feeding one another, without themselves knowing whether they do it with friendly or hostile intent. In a third place a crowd of bees, crushing one another, attack some victim and fight and smother it.

The essential fact, though, is that the hive has been deserted. The same kind of desultory incidents occur in Moscow. There is a description of a mob murder:

'Hit him with an axe, eh!... Crushed?... Traitor, he sold Christ... Still alive... serve him right!... Use the hatchet!... What — still alive?'

The Shakespearian reservations about crowds, together with a Shakespearian ability to handle crowd scenes, have been present all along. This scene is a perfectly placed comment on the great crowd at Borodino, magnificent as that was — a sudden reminder of a side of Tolstoy which remains always detached and contemplative — a slightly unnerving reminder.

Tolstoy now calmly begins exposing the long-term futility even of acts of heroism. The rout of the French will be impressive precisely because it lacks drama, because it is inevitable. Tolstoy begins to take up his final position. He declares that the burning of Moscow was not done by a heroic peasantry. 'How much must the probability of fire be increased in an abandoned wooden town where foreign troops are quartered!'

The early days of the French occupation are experienced with Pierre. Inspired by the heroism he has witnessed at Borodino, he determines to do something heroic too — to assassinate Napoleon. Yet the first thing that Pierre does is to save the life of a Frenchman. The grateful Frenchman pays a series of complacent compliments on the behaviour of the Russians at Borodino, and Pierre shows his good breeding by responding humanely and sympathetically. This is Pierre as he was meant to be.

Pierre, ashamed of his 'weakness', hurries through the streets of Moscow in search of Napoleon, thinking to settle the fate of Russia single-handed. Instead, he helps two parents who have lost a child. Moments later, making a romantic attempt to save an oriental beauty from assault, he is overpowered by a French patrol and arrested.

The following book (XII), the central one in this group of three, describes a period of status quo between the Russians and the French. Both live alongside one another, each maintaining their own kind of order. Surprisingly, Russia is not seething with grief, heroism and self-sacrifice except verbally, 'with unconscious hypocrisy'. Every person has more immediate things to attend to —

C

and this, collectively, is what is important. Nikolay Rostov acts the
part of a dashing hussar in a provincial society which remains the
same as it has always been, except for the influx of rich Moscow
citizens and the fact that 'the inevitable small talk, instead of turning
on the weather and mutual acquaintances, now turned on Moscow,
the army, and Napoleon'. Nikolay meets Princess Mary again. The
love between them grows. Ordinary life goes on.

Meanwhile, imprisoned by the French, Pierre is a witness to what
would now be called a war crime — the execution of Russians
suspected of arson.

On the faces of all the Russian, and of the French soldiers and officers
without exception, he read the same dismay, horror, and conflict that were
in his own heart. 'But who, after all, is doing this? They are all suffering
as I am. Who then is it? who?'

He can find no one to blame. That is what frightens Pierre more than
anything.

Pierre is transferred to a new group of prisoners and finds himself
next to the peasant Karataev who has an attitude to life Pierre wishes
to understand. Karataev's talk is refreshing and strange. It reflects a
method of dealing with life which no one man could have evolved
for himself.

'And do you feel sad here?' Pierre inquired.
'. . . How is one to help feeling sad? Moscow — she's the mother of cities.
How can one see all this and not feel sad? But "the maggot gnaws the
cabbage, yet dies first"; that's what the old folk used to tell us,' he added
rapidly.
'What? What did you say?' asked Pierre.
'Who? I?' said Karataev. 'I say things happen not as we plan but as God
judges,' he replied, thinking that he was repeating what he had said before.

The connection between the two men cannot last. It is clear that
Karataev is not capable of anything so sophisticated as friendship.
'He loved his dog, his comrades, the French, and Pierre who was his
neighbour, but Pierre felt that in spite of Karataev's affectionate
tenderness for him . . . he would not have grieved for a moment at
parting from him. And Pierre began to feel in the same way towards
Karataev.' Yet Pierre sees Karataev as the personification of everything
kindly and Russian. Tolstoy states that this is only the way Pierre
sees Karataev. The other prisoners find him ordinary. Pierre never
understands him, yet something of what he sees in Karataev is

undoubtedly there. It does not occur to Karataev to pass judgement on anything or anyone, and so he remains happy. His energy is not sapped by thoughts of his own weakness in the face of life's troubles, for these are in God's control. Karataev teaches Pierre gratitude for the pleasures of being alive.

Pierre's friend, Prince Andrew, gives himself up to death in the next chapters. Andrew's death is watched by Mary and Natasha with whom he has been reunited. The moment Prince Andrew loses his hold on life for ever, Tolstoy's interest shifts to the onlookers. Prince Andrew turns away from Natasha for the second time. His pursuit of complete answers to unanswerable questions finally betrays him into breaking the link with her. The moment of no return comes. Natasha sits by his sick-bed. Andrew pursues his own thoughts, taking Natasha as his starting-point.

'Love hinders death. Love is life. All, everything that I understand, I understand only because I love. Everything is, everything exists, only because I love. Everything is united by it alone. Love is God, and to die means that I, a particle of love, shall return to the general and eternal source.' These thoughts seemed to him comforting. But they were only thoughts. Something was lacking in them, they were not clear, they were too one-sidedly personal and brain-spun.

He is shortly contemplating the experience of death with interest. There is something hard and separate about him finally, which alienates even Natasha. It is almost a relief when Prince Andrew dies. His oppressive presence, always near the foreground hitherto, has been removed.

Suddenly the affairs of the Russian nation are seen to have reached their turning-point. The French have inflicted no national humiliation. There is no Russian curiosity about the French, no interest in anything they bring, simply a universal desire for them to go, for the discomforts of the time to be over. It is really this which defeats the French. It is a war which brings them no increase in self-esteem. Napoleon's proclamations and skilful plans for the future are no longer accepted by his army which is depressed and bewildered like himself, not knowing what to do with the empty city. The retreat begins.

In the midst of the disintegrating French army Pierre lives on next to Karataev. Each Frenchman is trapped by the mass of his fellows, so that individual escape is impossible though it is what everyone wants.

The Conclusion
(Books XIV and XV)

The next two books (XIV and XV) form the conclusion of the novel. They deal with the destruction of the French and the marriage of Pierre and Natasha.

Tolstoy shows no sign of flagging energies as he finishes his immense task. There is an account of a typical partisan raid undertaken by groups led by Denisov and Dolokhov. The sixteen-year old Petya Rostov is involved in the raid. In his childish excitement he blinds himself to the knowledge that Dolokhov initiates atrocities. All Petya allows himself to see is the bravery of the heroes he finds himself with. A bullet through the brain finishes him, for his enthusiasm makes him inefficient.

Among the prisoners rescued in the raid is Pierre. Karataev has died a short time before. He has taught Pierre to conquer his despair at understanding nothing. 'To love life is to love God. Harder and more blessed than all else is to love this life in one's sufferings, in innocent sufferings.' Pierre is contemplated by Tolstoy, as Pierre has contemplated Karataev. Pierre's knowledge of his spiritual strength gives him serenity, and this serenity is felt by many Russians – for the time at least. Tolstoy is not complacent. These concluding books depict an interim period, and there are the epilogues yet to come.

Natasha dominates the last book (XV). As always, she displays a gift for living, a vitality which enables her wounds to heal, sometimes with indecorous speed. At first she broods over the last days of Prince Andrew.

'One thing would be terrible,' said he, 'to bind oneself for ever to a suffering man. It would be continual torture.' And he looked searchingly at her. Natasha, as usual, answered before she had time to think what she would say. She said: 'This can't go on – it won't. You will get well – quite well.'

She now saw him from the commencement of that scene and re-lived what she had then felt. She recalled his long sad and severe look at those words, and understood the meaning of the rebuke and despair in that protracted gaze.

'I agreed,' Natasha now said to herself, 'that it would be dreadful if he always continued to suffer. I said it then only because it would have been dreadful for him, but he understood it differently. He thought it would be dreadful for me. He then still wished to live and feared death. And I said it so awkwardly and stupidly! I did not say what I meant. I thought quite differently. Had I said what I thought, I should have said: even if he had to go on dying, to die continually before my eyes, I should have been happy compared with what I am now.'

But her reply at that moment had been the inevitable one for her, although she does not now want to admit it. The defensive reaction came before she was aware, and she had not been responsible for it. The judgement Prince Andrew passed on her as a result was un-realistic as were all the demands he made from life. He wanted more than he had the right to expect. There is nothing noble about Natasha. Once Prince Andrew is dead she can find no consolation, no peace. She lacks this kind of nobility too. She wears herself out with suffering. ' "I love thee! . . . thee! I love, love . . ." she said, con-vulsively pressing her hands and setting her teeth with a desperate effort.' But soon there is another life to fight for; the news comes of Petya's death, and Natasha's 'persevering and patient love seemed completely to surround the countess every moment, not explaining or consoling but recalling her to life'. Then Pierre reappears and captivates Natasha almost from the first moment. He infects her with his happiness at having experienced the brotherhood of man.

The whole second half of *War and Peace* has been about the ability to conquer despair. This ability is always called forth in a nation by great and terrible events, and seldom outlives them although its memory remains even when the events themselves fade. We are left with the knowledge of what people can be like.

The Epilogues

At the beginning of his first epilogue Tolstoy re-states the position from which he has just been looking at the events of history. The individual takes part in events which he cannot control, and which he has not initiated. The only important thing is the attitude he adopts to them.

The first epilogue is mainly a picture of family life among the Rostovs and the Bezukhovs seven years after the war. (The main events of the novel occupied the seven years between 1805 and 1812.) The heroes and heroines have lost their heroic qualities. It is difficult to overcome one's disappointment in them as they now are. Their natures remain the same, but are seen under different circum-stances. The scenes, all domestic ones, are as vivid here as in the body of the book. The energy which fills the characters is still there, especially in Natasha, yet it is Natasha who disappoints one most. She is almost unrecognisable to Denisov when he sees her in the midst of her family. She has become slovenly in appearance and manner. To Denisov's disgust she can talk of nothing but her husband and children, to whom she is obsessively devoted. Pierre seems to thrive on it, though.

Nikolay has married a very different sort of woman – Princess Mary, who keeps a diary in which she notes down every significant action of her children. This is to help her choose the most suitable method of educating them. Nikolay, a bluff, paternalistic landowner who treats his wife clumsily in their domestic quarrels, is yet adored by her. Nikolay is the strongest member of the whole clan. He asks nothing further from life. He is satisfied. Only, he is by turns irritated and wistful at the evidence of mental suffering he detects on occasion in his wife and Pierre – and in the young son of Prince Andrew, whom he cannot like.

Prince Andrew's son is given the last spoken words in *War and Peace*. 'Everyone shall know of me, shall love me, and admire me . . .'[1] Coexistent with this aspiration is his knowledge that, as was the case with his father, it will not be satisfied, and he bursts into tears.

In the second epilogue Tolstoy goes on to establish his conclusions about the experiences he has brought us through. 'What force moves the nations?' he asks. It does not reside in individual 'great men', who have attracted the attention of historians.

So long as histories are written of separate individuals, whether Caesars, Alexanders, Luthers, or Voltaires, and not the histories of *all*, absolutely *all*, those who take part in an event, it is quite impossible to describe the movement of humanity . . .

. . . history shows that the expression of the will of historical personages does not in most cases produce any effect, that is to say, their commands are often not executed, and sometimes the very opposite of what they order occurs.

No man is free. The more minutely we examine life the clearer it becomes that 'free will' is immensely circumscribed. But this is always rejected instinctively. Man perceives 'that his every action depends on his organisation, his character, and the motives acting

---

[1] Constance Garnett. Her translation is more accurate here.

upon him; yet man never submits to the deductions of these experiments and arguments'. It is the deep feeling that he is trapped which causes Nikolinka's tears at the end of *War and Peace*. For the novel has really ended with these tears. The tears of bafflement and frustration over those things man can never possess. It is in the last analysis an immensely sad novel, like *Anna Karenina*.

Tolstoy has been led on further and further by his subject. He has not been able to stop until he has found himself stopped. The pattern is now established in all its symmetry, but it has not miraculously ceased to be baffling. Tolstoy has been driven to grasp all human life, to say everything he can about experience, all experience, and this means both the direct experience of living and the conclusions which have always been drawn from it, which will always be the same. It is these last he rifles through in his second epilogue, rejecting all false comforts. That Tolstoy now finally eliminates all cause for self-congratulation on the part of the heroes and heroines of the novel does not destroy what has gone before. In fact it renders more impressive, because more unfathomable, the powerful drives which have carried them through, and which Tolstoy has shown in the only way they can be shown – dramatically.

The question 'why?' which has led him on through the stages of the novel and is the reason for it, is finally left unanswered – it has been proved that it can never be answered. It is this question which has compelled the absorbed examination of experience which is the novel. Tolstoy constantly feels himself on the brink of a discovery and we follow him, perhaps making discoveries of our own or, like Tolstoy himself, hoping to, and lured on. Pierre, perhaps because of his limitations, has acquired a peace Tolstoy himself cannot reach. He is different from the author, who looks at him enviously. There is as much of Prince Andrew in Tolstoy as of Pierre.

Yet if Tolstoy had not constantly wished to discover order in the world, to give mankind the answer to the great question 'why?' and so achieve immortality, monstrous as the ungrateful reader may find such arrogance and self-assertion, monstrous as Tolstoy himself still knows it to be, he would not have written his two great novels, for he would not have been compelled to write them.

5. Tolstoy's Thinking in *War and Peace*

The task which Tolstoy sets himself in *War and Peace* is nothing less than to discover the meaning of life. He embarks on the quest which will continue for the rest of his career.

In *War and Peace* Tolstoy portrays the life of the generations just previous to his own. This gives him an enormous range of possible vantage points from which to survey life – from a position of close intimacy with people he has created out of his memories, to an extreme of impersonal remoteness. His exploration ends in two epilogues reflecting these extremes, two contrasting resolutions, each of which is acceptable only on its own terms. The antithetical epilogues represent the point to which the unworked immensity upon which Tolstoy started has been resolved by him, a point beyond which he has been convinced he cannot go – for the time being. The stuff of the two epilogues cannot be reconciled.

In the course of the novel Tolstoy presented general conclusions based on incidents which had just occurred in his work, but as he proceeded further he became aware that each conclusion had depended utterly on the occurrence which suggested it. Each generalisation was overthrown by situations where it no longer applied.

The title *War and Peace* immediately calls to mind all the bewildering irreconcilables in human experience and activity. These are contemplated in different ways within the novel, in moods fluctuating between terrified rejection and joyous acceptance of God's plenty. 'What wealth God has! He gives each day something to distinguish it from the rest,'[1] Tolstoy once exclaimed when he had embarked on his great work.

Tolstoy's second epilogue is inspired, among other things, by a conception of life a little like one of Pierre's several conceptions. But there is no reason why it should be a point of rest for Tolstoy any more than the soap-bubble image, which excited Pierre at that particular moment in his life, turned out to be for Pierre.

[1] Aylmer Maude, *The Life of Tolstoy* (The World's Classics, London, 1930), I, 305.

... This globe was alive – a vibrating ball without fixed dimensions. Its whole surface consisted of drops closely pressed together, and all these drops moved and changed places, sometimes several of them merging into one, sometimes one dividing into many. Each drop tried to spread out and occupy as much space as possible, but others, striving to do the same, compressed it, sometimes destroyed it, and sometimes merged with it.

'That is life,' said the old teacher.

'How simple and clear it is,' thought Pierre. 'How is it I did not know it before?'

'God is in the midst, and each drop tries to expand so as to reflect Him to the greatest extent.'[1]

No man can trap all of life within the pages of a book. Tolstoy, caught up in the process of writing, was under the illusion that he could – otherwise the extraordinary achievement would have been impossible. In retrospect, years later, Tolstoy's illusion that he had almost succeeded in saying everything led to his commitment to opinions expressed in the second epilogue of *War and Peace*. It may be true that in this epilogue he has distanced himself from his created world; nevertheless the second epilogue remains an essential part of the novel and should never be read separately from it. Tolstoy's later use of ideas which appear in the second epilogue does no damage to the work which was their first context.

Tolstoy later conveniently forgot that it was the balance and juxtaposition of the second epilogue with the first which gave meaning to both. Out of its context, the second epilogue withers away. It expresses a part of what Pierre once thought he saw, and a good deal of what Prince Andrew saw when he neared his end, but no more than that. Tolstoy in the second epilogue, as he looks back over his creation, is very close to having placed himself at one remove from life by the very success of his creative faculty – the apparent completeness of the world he has created – but this has not happened yet. It only happens when time has passed and Tolstoy views his edifice from a much greater distance. By then, like one of Brueghel's majestic towers of Babel, part organic, part mechanical, it has become remote, has fallen silent and seems to require little

[1] The Maude translation (The World's Classics, edition in three volumes, London, 1933), III, 330.

Page references after quotations which may be difficult to locate will be to this edition.

to perfect it and smooth it off. Fortunately, *Anna Karenina* is written before Tolstoy commits himself to this.

One is always asked first to assess the people who hold the opinions expressed in the novel, not the opinions themselves. Pierre glares bloodthirstily through his spectacles, imagining himself slaughtering those enemies of progress, the opponents of Napoleon, and later imagines himself assassinating Napoleon whom he now sees as Antichrist, but he is always the same Pierre whose smile expresses that 'Opinions are opinions, but you see what a capital, good-natured fellow I am' (I, 27). The Prince Andrew who frowns when his arm is touched at Anna Pavlovna's reception is visibly the same Andrew who, while Natasha sings, ponders 'the terrible contrast between something infinitely great and illimitable within him and that limited and material something that he, and even she, was' (II, 60). And the Napoleon who on St. Helena broods over the millennium he might have brought about is the same Napoleon who terrorises Balashev with 'What a splendid reign the Emperor Alexander's might have been!' – and so on through all the characters selected for scrutiny on various levels. Circumstances appear to force people to arrive at certain conclusions about life, but their personalities are really the decisive factors. No man sees the truth.

Tolstoy's moments of rest in *War and Peace* are increasingly the moments when he claims to have found 'what he sought at his very feet' (III, 386). This has been present at the back of his mind from the beginning of *War and Peace*. It is the reasonable Christianity which Tolstoy will later on in his life proclaim with such incongruous aggressiveness, with such oppressive humility. Princess Mary expresses it early on:

. . . how can we, miserable sinners that we are, know the terrible and holy secrets of Providence while we remain in this flesh which forms an impenetrable veil between us and the Eternal? Let us rather confine ourselves to studying those sublime rules which our divine Saviour has left for our guidance here below. Let us try to conform to them and follow them, and let us be persuaded that the less we let our feeble human minds roam, the better we shall please God, who rejects all knowledge that does not come from Him.

There is always this to bow to in the last resort, but the whole of the novel implies a dissatisfaction with this conception of the meaning of life. Mary says that 'Religion alone can explain to us what without its help man cannot comprehend' (II, 90). This is the issue bald and frightening. Tolstoy distrusts the ideas he has been fed on since infancy. The torments of the ageing Tolstoy will be caused by his capitulation to them. It is only when he cannot go on, when he has exhausted and tormented himself with all the possibilities which have suggested themselves to him that he will attempt to convince himself that he has arrived at the position Pierre reached at the end of *War and Peace*.

> . . . suddenly in his captivity he had learnt, not by words or reasoning but by direct feeling, what his nurse had told him long ago: that God is here and everywhere . . . He felt like a man who, after straining his eyes to see into the far distance, finds what he sought at his very feet.

But Tolstoy's final position in his own life will be very far from Pierre's position. Tolstoy's captivity is more like Prince Andrew's mental captivity, and his discovery of God is never a product of 'direct feeling'. He is like Prince Andrew after Austerlitz.

> '. . . How happy and calm I should be if I could now say: "Lord, have mercy on me!" . . . but to whom should I say that? Either to a Power indefinable, incomprehensible, which I not only cannot address but which I cannot even express in words – the Great All or Nothing –' said he to himself, 'or to that God who has been sewn into this amulet by Mary!' (I, 385)

It is 'the Great All' Tolstoy wants, but he never finds Him. Prince Andrew on his deathbed is convinced he has at last found this 'Great All', but Tolstoy is plainly not satisfied. 'Is it possible that the meaning of life was not disclosed to him before he died?' (III, 396) Pierre will say piously to Natasha, thinking of his own comfortable God of the family hearth. There is sad irony in this. Natasha will allow Pierre to retain his illusion that he and Prince Andrew have found the same thing. She has her memories of the dehumanised presence Prince Andrew became in his last days. Prince Andrew's God, the God of the second epilogue, and Pierre's God, that of the first epilogue, must be *one* – but Tolstoy can never connect the two in his mind, can never feel the two as one.

One day Tolstoy will return cap in hand to the God worshipped by Princess Mary, who is not Prince Andrew's sister for nothing, whose eyes in the midst of her married bliss 'expressed a quiet sadness, as though she felt, through her happiness, that there is another sort of happiness unattainable in this life' (III, 452), and who is secretly at war with her husband's (Nikolay Rostov's) animal personality.

But it is Pierre and Natasha who dominate the end of *War and Peace*, and in their own terms demolish both the conclusions of the second epilogue and the religion of Princess Mary. They are spontaneous, unorderly in their thinking like the peasant Karataev, who stands for the soil from which they have sprung. Pierre is like Karataev in that he also often says 'the exact opposite of what he had said on a previous occasion, yet both would be right' (III, 204). Natasha secretly feared Prince Andrew. She could never write to him because she 'could not conceive the possibility of expressing sincerely in a letter even a thousandth part of what she expressed by voice, smile and glance'. But Tolstoy cannot go on perpetually in the company of Pierres and Natashas. They do not satisfy him. Already in the first epilogue the portrait of Natasha's brother, Nikolay, the slightly brutal masculine representative of the Rostov breed, is an expression of Tolstoy's dissatisfaction.

Tolstoy's relations with the Russian peasant will become like Princess Mary's flirtation with 'God's folk', the peasant pilgrims whose simplicity refreshes her like the scent of flowers. In other words, the real Karataev will exist for Tolstoy only for as long as Pierre and Natasha do. He has no more to do with Tolstoy's post-*Confession* period than they have. One day Princess Mary will win – the sister of Prince Andrew.

War and Peace is never at rest. It is never calm and Olympian. Prince Andrew, in the midst of dreams about achieving his 'Toulon' in the great battle (Austerlitz), thought 'well ... what then? ...' (I, 346). There is always a fresh 'what then?' A question always springs up just when rest seems to have been achieved, and sets all in motion again in a contrary direction. The novel can only end when Tolstoy is satisfied that all his questions have at least been put correctly. The mysteries have acquired a pattern, but have not been solved. This is a great curtailment of the vast and impossible hopes which have driven Tolstoy on through amazing achievements.

The restless, apparently random movement among opinions and emotions at the beginning of the novel gradually falls into a definite oscillation between two poles, and it is this which is eventually frozen in the two epilogues. It is this process which gives the novel its shape. At first there is a violent disorder in the imagery used to describe the thinking of Pierre and Andrew, a confusion in the apparent similarity and merging of their aims as they embark upon their lives and discuss life together. They both appear to be seeking the same things. They both look forward to their 'Toulon'. The hero of both is Napoleon. At first the imagery used to describe the strivings of each is to a large extent mechanical. They see life as a matter of screws and cog-wheels which, in time, they will learn the secrets of and be able to manipulate to their own advantages. But soon human activity comes to be compared in the same breath to a clock and also a bee-hive. Gradually these two conceptions (the rational and the instinctive) become disentangled from one another and are set further and further apart. War is compared at one moment with a game of chess, and at another with a zoological migration. Each concept seems valid until the other shows it to be wildly wrong on its own, very different terms.

It becomes clear that Prince Andrew temperamentally favours mechanical imagery, the great clock, the dial of history. He sees armies and states as mechanisms, clumsy ones with a lot of un-necessary gadgetry which ought to be replaced. These mechanisms are rendered effective by certain 'cog-wheels' within them which drive everything if they are not obstructed. The activity of armies fosters this illusion of Prince Andrew's and dictates his choice of career. The 'cog-wheels' seem easy to find always – Tushin, Timo-khin, Dolokhov, and Andrew himself at the Battle of Schön Grabern; Bagration at Borodino; Dokhturov, Konovnitsyn, Denisov in the pursuit of Napoleon out of Russia. The starting mechanisms, the keys, are Napoleon, Alexander and Kutuzov. It is easy to see war like this. Tolstoy himself often presents it so throughout the novel.

Before Austerlitz, Tolstoy said:

One wheel slowly moved, another was set in motion, and a third, and wheels began to revolve faster and faster, levers and cogwheels to work, chimes to play, figures to pop out, and the hands to advance with regular motion as a result of all that activity.

But, as Tolstoy goes on contemplating the event of Austerlitz, the image he has chosen begins to cover too much.

Just as in a clock the result of the complicated motion of innumerable wheels and pulleys is merely a slow and regular movement of the hands which show the time, so the result of all the complicated human activities of 160,000 Russians and French – all their passions, desires, remorse, humiliations, sufferings, outbursts of pride, fear and enthusiasm – was only the loss of the Battle of Austerlitz, the so-called battle of the three Emperors – that is to say, a slow movement of the hand on the dial of history.

The mechanical conception of human life annihilates life. Prince Andrew, the rationalist and man of action, oscillates violently between the conception of life as a machine or, to put it better, a vast composite game of chess (this becomes his preferred image) played by robots, and moments of elevation into an abstracted condition of mystical, disembodied 'love', an escape from his mind and personality, from himself in fact.

'A happiness lying beyond material forces, outside the material influences that act on man – a happiness of the soul alone . . . love . . . which does not require an object.' (III, 134)

It is a state Tolstoy cannot put much confidence in, but which he is forced into selecting when he thinks along Prince Andrew's lines. It may be the answer to the robot nightmare, but it is only an equal and opposite nightmare.

As the clock, soon felt as a tormented robot whose dial registers degrees of agony, comes to be associated with Prince Andrew, so the beehive comes to be associated with Pierre. The beehive image is used in its final form at the beginning of the first epilogue.

A bee settling on a flower has stung a child. And the child is afraid of bees and declares that bees exist to sting people. A poet admires the bee sucking from the chalice of a flower, and says it exists to suck the fragrance of flowers. A beekeeper, seeing the bee collect pollen from flowers and carry it to the hive, says that it exists to gather honey. Another beekeeper who has studied the life of the hive more closely, says that the bee gathers pollen-dust to feed the young bees and rear a queen, and that it exists to perpetuate its race. A botanist notices that the bee flying with the pollen of a male flower to a pistil fertilises the latter, and sees in this the purpose of the bee's existence. Another, observing the migration of plants, notices that the bee helps in this work, and may say that in this lies the purpose of the bee. But the ultimate purpose of the bee is not exhausted by the first, the second, or any of the processes the human mind can discern. The higher the human intellect rises in the discovery of these purposes, the more obvious it becomes that the ultimate purpose is beyond our comprehension.

This is the way Pierre has begun to look at life. The temperamental difference between him and Prince Andrew accounts for it. Pierre experiences the world as an organism rather than a machine.

Certainly there is a recurring rhythm in life, discernible for instance in Karataev's simple round of activities, but it is like the repetitiveness of bird-song. Pierre gives up arguing himself into the illusion of being trapped in a machine. At the end we find him contemplating what once bewildered him and brought about those moods of 'confusion and hopelessness to which he was apt to succumb'.

This legitimate peculiarity of each individual ... The difference, and sometimes complete contradiction between men's opinions and their lives, and between one man and another, pleased him and evoked from him an amused and gentle smile. (III, 390)

'Well ... what then? ...' is Prince Andrew's nagging question. But there is always Pierre. One does not arrive at him, one simply remembers him. He is outside logic, but then so is *War and Peace* — so is Tolstoy. Pierre, desiring to be told the meaning of life, listens to the arguments of the old Freemason,

'And thou art more foolish and unreasonable than a little child, who playing with the parts of a skilfully made watch dares to say that, as he does not understand its use, he does not believe in the master who made it'

but it is not the argument he listens to, the image of the watch he notices; it is really 'the speaker's tone of conviction and earnestness, or the tremor of the speaker's voice — which sometimes broke — or those brilliant aged eyes'. Pierre's exposition to Prince Andrew of the brotherhood of man as he perceives it, has little to do with the arguments of the Mason. The difference between the two heroes of *War and Peace* expresses the essential contradiction within it, which is within Tolstoy himself, the emotional, irrational constructor of mechanical systems which only work when powered by himself, his personal energy.

Tolstoy uses machine imagery in order to express his reaction to one aspect of life. When he says of Pierre,

It was as if the thread of the chief screw which held his life together were stripped, so that the screw could not get in or out, but went on turning uselessly in the same place (I, 459)

he is not reducing Pierre's situation to infantile terms. The image expresses both Pierre's immediate fear and also the long-term fear in Tolstoy that if Pierre can indeed think of himself as a clumsy machine, then all is lost, Andrew will have won. But the 'screw' idea eventually disappears from Pierre, rejected as something alien to him, and his life is held together all the better for being rid of it.

There is one image from *War and Peace* which epitomises the mind at work in it.

. . . the mainspring of his life . . . which made everything appear *alive*[1] had suddenly been wrenched out. (III, 197)

Tolstoy's thought is the product of his feelings – his sympathies and in particular his fears. His thoughts are determined by the emotion of the moment. No one is interested in the ideas taken separately from the novel *War and Peace*. The mind at work is the novel, alive and in constant movement. Tolstoy is an immensely complicated person, immensely many-sided. His simplicity is a complete illusion, but his rationality is a masquerade.

Tolstoy's apparently most rational arguments are all emotional in origin. The conclusions have already leapt joyously into his mind or have grimly forced themselves upon him apropos of the latest occurrence in the novel. The lucid illustrations which play the major part in Tolstoy's method of arguing are instruments of self-persuasion. The conclusion is there for the moment and the vigorous diagrams press it home, but other diagrams could be used to lend equal vigour to diametrically opposite conclusions. Everything depends on the preceding experience within the novel which has produced the conclusion in the first place.

Tolstoy always attempts to persuade himself that his interpretation of what he has just seen has a rational basis. This persuasion is beguiling, but just when he presumes that his point has been carried, he himself looks elsewhere. At the time he was writing *War and Peace*, Tolstoy wrote down in his notebook, 'Every man lies twenty times daily'.[2] He himself is never entirely convinced by his own arguments. No man can be, because he knows that they are little more than expressions of his desires. I think this was true of Tolstoy even at the end of his life. He attempts to deceive the world, but he never succeeds ultimately in deceiving himself.

The most disturbing image in *War and Peace* is one Tolstoy introduces towards the end of the novel. It is that of God's 'stencil'.

Of an innumerable series of unexecuted commands of Napoleon's, one

[1] My italics.
[2] Troyat, *Tolstoy*, p. 284.

series, for the campaign of 1812, was carried out – not because those orders differed in any way from the other unexecuted orders, but because they coincided with the course of events that led the French army into Russia; just as in stencil work this or that figure comes out, not because the colour was laid on from this side or in that way, but because it was laid on from all sides over the figure cut in the stencil. (III, 512)

Tolstoy goes on, a little later, to reveal the hidden motive behind his choice of this image.

If any single action is due to freewill, then not a single historical law can exist, nor any conception of historical events. (III, 534)

Tolstoy fears to speculate on what might have happened if an event he records had not occurred in the way it did. At every moment in life there are infinite contingencies which are capable of bringing about an infinite number of different results. But to accept this would lead to an astronomic enlargement of Tolstoy's self-imposed task of discovering order in the world and managing the nearly intolerable confusions within his own mind. It is this awareness of vast disorder and a never ceasing need to escape from it, even if this involves great losses, which provides the impulse for his writing. Everything that occurs in the world has been planned in advance – this must be made to stand immovably as Tolstoy's supreme article of faith. He tries to arrive at it by deduction, but never does. Instead, he is forced to argue from it as though it were proven fact. He hates some of the conclusions it results in, but the alternative for him is chaos, perhaps even his own madness.

Tolstoy refuses to admit the possibility of what might have been because that would cast doubt on the reassuring determinism of God's 'stencil'. He enumerates the various Russian disasters which might have occurred as a result of the Russian army's movement south of Moscow after the abandonment of that city. He uses the fact that these disasters did not occur as proof that the leaders of the Russian army were blindly acting out the wish of God for the destruction of the French! The French acted equally blindly – but in such a way that the Russian flank march proved disastrous for them, not for the Russians.

But very shortly afterwards Tolstoy cannot resist going on to say that the destruction of the French would have been inevitable anyway, whatever anybody did. 'That army could not recover any-where. Since the battle of Borodino and the pillage of Moscow it had

borne within itself, as it were, the chemical elements of dissolution'
(III, 278). Here he is making a generalisation which allows a great
deal of play in it, summarising a general situation in which the
French are going to be defeated wherever they move because of the
moral superiority of their opponents. Tolstoy's secret desire is to
see events in this way too, to have it both ways, because he finds
God's stencil galling. He must give up his freedom but, at the same
time, he hopes he can arrange to get some of it back again.

Tolstoy contemplates God's stencil and the Prince Andrew nightmare it leads to with dissatisfaction. He wishes to conceal the inconsistency of his desire to be able simultaneously to see events in
ways which cancel each other out, and as happens so often he brings
in scientific imagery to lend respectability to his irrationality. The
strangest application of 'science' in the novel is this:

Men who want to fight will always put themselves in the most advantageous
position for fighting. The spirit of an army is the factor which multiplied
by the mass gives the resulting force. To define and express the significance
of this unknown factor – the spirit of an army – is a problem for science . . .
by bringing variously selected historic units (battles, campaigns, periods of
war) into such equations, a series of numbers could be obtained in which
certain laws should exist and might be discovered. (III, 289)

Tolstoy wishes to retain intact his conviction that Russians –
'stencil' or no 'stencil' – are superior to all comers, but to give it
respectability by pretending that this has the authority of 'science'
behind it. But at the same time he does not really want this explanation to hold water either. There is something of the false mag-
nanimity of the victor in the flagrant absurdity of the argument here.
He wants a theory of history, but at the same time he does not want
it to work. He is inviting the scientist, whom he really despises, to
capture Russian love and courage in a test tube.

One of the many contributory reasons for Tolstoy's so-called
theory of history is that he despises generals, yet he will often
generously discount his theory while contemplating the activities
of certain generals he admires. Tolstoy's arguments are all emotional.
They express nothing beyond the desires which produced them, like
the facts and figures at the end of the novel which are part of the
surging crescendo of triumph which the expulsion of the French
from Russian soil calls forth.

Tolstoy wishes for some transcendent order to exist in human

affairs corresponding, perhaps, to Prince Andrew's delicate vision as
he lies dying.

'Yes, a new happiness was revealed to me of which man cannot be
deprived,' he thought as he lay in the semi-darkness of the quiet hut gazing
fixedly before him with feverish, wide-open eyes. 'A happiness lying
beyond material forces, outside the material influences that act on man – a
happiness of the soul alone, the happiness of loving. Every man can understand it, but to conceive it and enjoin it was possible only for God. But how
did God enjoin that law? And why was the Son . . .?'

And suddenly the sequence of these thoughts broke off and Prince
Andrew heard (without knowing whether it was delusion or reality) a
soft, whispering voice incessantly and rhythmically repeating 'piti-piti-piti',
and then 'ti-ti', and then again 'piti-piti-piti', and 'ti-ti' once more. At the
same time he felt that above his face, above the very middle of it, some
strange airy structure was being erected out of slender needles or splinters,
to the sound of this whispered music. He felt that he had to balance carefully (though it was difficult), so that this airy structure should not
collapse; but nevertheless it kept collapsing and again slowly rising to the
sound of whispered rhythmic music – 'it stretches, stretches, spreading out
and stretching,' said Prince Andrew to himself. While listening to this
whispering, and feeling the sensation of this drawing out and the construction of this edifice of needles, he also saw by glimpses a red halo round the
candle, and heard the rustle of the cockroaches and the buzzing of the
fly that flopped against his pillow and his face. Each time the fly touched his
face it gave him a burning sensation and yet to his surprise it did not destroy
the structure, though it knocked against the very region of his face where it
was rising.

The fly attracted by his gangrened flesh does not distract him from
his vision. Natasha does, seconds later, when she appears and
summons him back to life. Prince Andrew's return to his vision will
be marked by the return of his physical dissolution. Scarcely the
most reassuring associations, therefore, are connected with this
tender vision. Tolstoy wishes for some transcendent order to exist,
but at the same time he instinctively shudders at the possible
consequences of discovering it.

Tolstoy is not certain of the validity of Prince Andrew's private
vision in any case. He feels that he himself cannot find what he
seeks, however he racks his brains. One way out is to relegate the
universal order he seeks to some abstract scientific level which is
outside his province. The other is to assume that the life of the
individual is ordered on some metaphysical plane where Tolstoy is

again unqualified to pursue it. In other words, he resorts to faith, to a reverent posture. All is in the hands of God. And lurking at the back of this is the thought Prince Andrew had when he looked into the shallow eyes of Napoleon. 'How good it would be to know where to seek for help in this life' (I, 385). This thought lurks behind the false confidence of Tolstoy's statement that all was suddenly revealed on Andrew's deathbed as it will inevitably be to every man. It lurks wherever 'the simple and solemn mystery' of death is 'accomplished' (III, 221).

Pierre, just before the first epilogue, finds himself thinking about Prince Andrew and Karataev 'and involuntarily began to compare those two men, so different and yet so similar in that they had both lived and both died and in the love he felt for both of them' (III, 396). Pierre has found happiness through abandoning all attempts to be reasonable – his 'insanity consisted in not waiting, as he used to do, to discover personal attributes, which he termed "good qualities", in people before loving them' (III, 414). The first epilogue conveys the thoughts a contemplation of Pierre gives rise to. In this epilogue the study of history, however 'scientific', is seen as futile, mere empty word-spinning.

... let us assume that what is called science can harmonise all contradictions and possesses an unchanging standard of good and bad by which to try historic characters and events: let us say that Alexander could have done everything differently, let us say that ... he might have arranged matters according to the programme his present accusers would have given him – of nationality, freedom, equality, and progress (these I think cover the ground). Let us assume that this programme was possible ... What would then have become of the activity of all those who opposed the tendency that then prevailed in the Government – the activity that in the opinion of the historians was good and beneficent? Their activity would not have existed: there would have been no life, there would have been nothing.

If we admit that human life can be ruled by reason, the possibility of life is destroyed.

Yet the *second* epilogue postulates that it is merely the complexity of God's manoeuvrings with us which gives us the illusion of living free lives – of living at all. Tolstoy says there that

If any single action is due to freewill, then not a single historical law can can exist, nor any conception of historical events. (III, 534)

This is the 'dreadful it' which Pierre was sometimes vaguely conscious of. Tolstoy ignores it entirely in the passage quoted from the first epilogue, the earlier passage above, for at that instant he is expressing a dislike of historians just because they are looking for the very laws which in other places Tolstoy says he wants them to find. But Tolstoy can never leave the 'dreadful it' alone for long. He does not want it, and yet he must have it; he needs it. Another name for 'it' is God's 'stencil' which Tolstoy often feels to be death, or death in life which is the same thing – the scientist's definition of death being a mere matter of chemistry. Pierre, when he is unhappy, feels trapped.

... perhaps all these comrades of mine struggled just like me and sought something new, a path in life of their own, and like me were brought by force of circumstances, society, and race – by that elemental force against which man is powerless – to the condition I am in ... Only not to see it, that dreadful it! (II, 167)

But in other circumstances, when embodied by Karataev, for instance, that very same 'it' is felt as benign, and Pierre experiences paradoxically an elated sense of freedom through his acceptance of God's bondage.[1] He learns to welcome living in God's prison-house, which he grows to recognise as the only alternative to the nightmarish cosmic anarchy he has previously been contemplating. Pierre's semi-articulate acceptance of God's bondage becomes ever more placid. He rests in it and ceases to see his separate personal existence as important. This is achieved through modesty and through his possessing a particular kind of temperament. It is the abandonment of the intellect which Tolstoy expressed in his first epilogue – 'If we admit that human life can be ruled by reason, the possibility of life is destroyed.' Looked at from another angle, it is what Swift in his *Digression on Madness*[2] defines as 'the sublime and refined point of felicity, the possession of being well deceived' – the fool's paradise which the Swift-like Prince Andrew refuses to live in.

The oscillation goes on, back and forth. Tolstoy is neither Pierre nor Prince Andrew. He can find no resting-place. In the second epilogue he paces restlessly but hopefully about his prison-house

[1] Though later, refusing to subject the free movement of his mind to any conventional form of discipline, Tolstoy can describe Pierre's state before his marriage with Natasha like this – 'he felt her presence with his whole being, by the loss of his sense of freedom' (III, 409).

[2] *A Tale of a Tub.*

testing out the extent of his freedom of movement within it, having
left Pierre seated quietly on the earth and therefore suffering no
sense of restriction. 'We feel ourselves to be free', Tolstoy says,
although the complete freedom of which man 'is conscious in
himself is impossible, and . . . his every action depends on his
organisation, his character, and the motives acting upon him' (III,
519). The feeling of freedom, though, cannot be illusion because we
feel it, says Tolstoy; which is no argument. It is like saying an
illusion is not illusory as long as we are taken in by it. But he is
determined to hang on to this as though it were an argument, and
so he gropes about in a realm of metaphysics where his common
sense – which he knows is the only thing he can put any real faith
in – can no longer operate.

If the conception of freedom appears to reason a senseless contradiction,
like the possibility of performing two actions at one and the same instant
of time . . . that only proves that consciousness is not subject to reason.
(III, 520)

But this for Tolstoy is only playing with words, is only a temporary
anodyne and can give no lasting comfort. Such phrases are abandoned as soon as spoken. Tolstoy turns from them dissatisfied, but
allowing them to stand as a sort of insurance policy in case he should
not be able to do without them. Meanwhile, he searches for the
means of escape from his prison so that he can assure himself he
can live outside it whenever he wishes to. While writing the
second epilogue, Tolstoy described what it involved to his friend
Fet:

What I have written there was not simply imagined by me, but torn out
of my cringing entrails.[1]

The consciousness of freedom, and the simultaneous knowledge of
the inevitability of all one does, remains an impossible position for
Tolstoy. He must try and prove some categories of activity to be
really free. Common sense insists on satisfaction, and Tolstoy is its
slave, tormented by it. He pleads, childlike, for what he knows he
cannot have.

But even if – imagining a man quite exempt from all influences, examining only his momentary action in the present unevoked by any cause – we

---

[1] Letter, May 1869, quoted in Troyat, Tolstoy, p. 297.

were to admit so infinitely small a remainder of inevitability as equalled zero, we should even then not have arrived at the conception of complete freedom in man, for a being uninfluenced by the external world, standing outside of time, and independent of cause, is no longer a man.

In the same way we can never imagine the action of a man quite devoid of freedom and entirely subject to the law of inevitability . . . for as soon as there is no freedom there is also no man. (III, 530)

And so he goes on in circles, and so *War and Peace* ends. It ends therefore on a note of near despair – Prince Andrew's despair, which only ended for him with his annihilation.

The only way out seems to be the faith of Princess Mary. This is a simple matter compared with the inner life of Prince Andrew or Pierre. Mary's beliefs are not directly experienced in the novel as theirs are.

I believe that man's true welfare lies in fulfilling God's will, and His will is that men should love one another and should consequently do to others as they wish others to do to them – of which it is said in the Gospels that in this is the law and the prophets.[1]

This is how Tolstoy stated his creed later in life. But there always remains the awareness that everything a man undertakes is distorted by life, or translated into other terms, dictated by God's stencil. The only escape from the pain this knowledge brings is the abolition of the human condition, the cessation of the human race which Tolstoy will contemplate in *Resurrection* and in *The Kreutzer Sonata*.

Tolstoy will return to the nightmare of Prince Andrew, the realisation that he, a powerful personality who needs to assert himself in the world, is simply a product of immutable laws of necessity, 'scientific', metaphysical, or divine. All his heroes later on are God's puppets, and Tolstoy seems resigned to this, even to glory in it. (God is better than nothing.) It is the only way to retain some shreds of self-esteem – to pretend that he desires what he cannot avoid anyway. Being an aristocrat, he must save face. It will be rather ugly to watch. Prince Andrew will have won, but Prince Andrew under the guise of Princess Mary.

At the time of writing the second epilogue to *War and Peace*, Tolstoy discovered that part of the subject matter had been treated already in the writings of Schopenhauer. The Prince Andrew

---

[1] From Tolstoy's reply to the Synod's Edict of Excommunication as quoted in Simmons, *Leo Tolstoy*.

nightmare which he was trying to resolve was also, Tolstoy found, the Schopenhauer nightmare. Schopenhauer had spent his life searching for loopholes in the various kinds of determinism which the human mind has discovered throughout the ages. Tolstoy's interpretation of Schopenhauer is expressed in the aphorism he invents in the second epilogue to *War and Peace* —

Reason gives expression to the laws of inevitability. Consciousness gives expression to the essence of freedom. (III, 532)

In other words, we are bound down mentally and physically to the laws of inevitability, but the entity which is bound down there is free because it remains conscious of itself, though it can do nothing with such freedom. In other words, if it were not bound down it would be free, but it would no longer be human and would be in a state inconceivable to the human intelligence. As far as human experience is concerned it would have gone out of existence, would be dead to the world. The only way out of the Prince Andrew nightmare still remains to all intents and purposes annihilation. Schopenhauer's argumentation merely leads him back again to his starting point, as a disillusioned Tolstoy devastatingly states years later in *A Confession* —

however I may turn these replies of philosophy I can never obtain anything like an answer . . . because here, though all the mental work is directed just to my question, there is no answer, but instead of an answer one gets the same question, only in a complex form.
. . . if it is real philosophy all its labour lies merely in trying to put that question clearly.

The reason Tolstoy had been lured on to read all Schopenhauer in the summer of 1869, and experienced 'unceasing ecstasy'[1] over his work, was the power with which Schopenhauer expressed his image of the world. It lured Tolstoy on as the writing of his own book lured him on — in the hope of illumination. But Schopenhauer had nothing to offer besides his pessimism, which Tolstoy was later to dismiss as a form of 'vulgarity'. Nevertheless he was to some degree an artist; he was original in that his philosophy was experienced by him as a form of art, and this was the reason for his appeal to many nineteenth-century writers. He expresses a personal vision of the world and of the laws which operate in it, 'the constant striving

[1] Letter to Fet, August 1869, quoted Maude, *The Life of Tolstoy.*

without aim or rest',[1] the long disease of life only ended by death.

Schopenhauer never calls philosophy the highest art form, but he implies that it is. The chart of the world which it offers is complete and is therefore superior to the 'fleeting images'[2] the other arts offer. Philosophy is the 'complete and accurate repetition or expression of the essence of the world in very general concepts, for only in these is it possible to get a view of that whole essence which will everywhere be adequate and applicable'.[3] The arts 'speak only the naïve and childlike language of perception, not the abstract and serious language of reflection'.[4]

In fact the philosopher and the artist talk at cross-purposes. The philosopher is unassailable within his system. Schopenhauer is interesting to the artist only because he was tormented by being so. But the cries of Schopenhauer the man trapped within his machine are involuntary, and Schopenhauer the philosopher shuts out his knowledge of the difference in intensity between the parts of his work in which he was most involved (and which Tolstoy and others responded to) and the rest. To him every part is as important as every other, all are equally necessary to the system they comprise.

The artist's answer to the philosopher must ultimately be in his own work. The artist will expose himself to certain ridicule by replying to the philosopher on his own ground. The philosopher will simply request the artist to define his terms. A perilous attempt to state a philosophy of the artist is made by D. H. Lawrence in *Psychoanalysis and the Unconscious*. Lawrence purposely refuses to define his terms in the philosopher's way. 'It is useless to try to determine *what is consciousness* or *what is knowledge*. Who cares anyhow, since we know without definitions.' He expresses an emotional rejection of the world the philosopher constructs so painstakingly. The common sense of the artist is different from the reasonableness of the philosopher.

Knowledge is always a matter of whole experience, what St Paul calls knowing in full, and never a matter of mental conception merely . . .

[1] See Tolstoy on Schopenhauer in *A Confession, etc.* (The World's Classics, London, 1940), p. 33.
[2] *The World as Will and Idea*, trans. R. B. Haldane and J. Kemp (London, 1883), III, 177.
[3] Ibid. I, 342.
[4] Ibid. III, 176.

It is necessary for us to know the unconscious, or we cannot live, just as it is necessary for us to know the sun. But we need not explain the unconscious, any more than we need explain the sun . . . We watch it in all its manifestations, its unfolding incarnations. We watch it in its processes and its unaccountable evolutions and these we register.

Tolstoy's discovery of Schopenhauer, the great pessimist philosopher, was a stroke of luck for him as he embarked upon the final stage of his novel. It suggested fresh matter to bind into an ending which he had already conceived for his work. It is the world-picture as Prince Andrew might have stated it to himself had he written a treatise.

The Pierre of the first epilogue might be seen by a sceptic as occupying a fool's paradise. Perhaps the alternative condition might be designated the fool's hell of Schopenhauer which Prince Andrew inhabits. Tolstoy inhabits it too as he writes the second epilogue. In the first epilogue he was inhabiting the other. He inhabits the novel as a whole, for the novel is the expression of himself.

War and Peace as a totality is incomparably more profound than Schopenhauer's meagre world picture. Tolstoy was aware of this. The last words of *War and Peace* provide a wonderful example of the way the great artist and the philosopher will always be at cross purposes.

. . . it is . . . necessary to renounce a freedom that does not exist, and to recognise a dependence of which we are not conscious. (III, 537)

This looks like Schopenhauer, but it is not, because of its place. It is given a wealth of meaning by all the experiences that have gone before. It is of the same kind as that other unoriginal statement which grows into unexpected meaning by virtue of a vast context – the first words of *Anna Karenina*.

War and Peace is a unity, and the thoughts within it have their place in that unity. One can see that Tolstoy knew this if one compares the thinking within *Some Words about 'War and Peace'* to the thinking within the novel itself. The pondering on freedom in *Some Words* arises apropos of the novel, but it could have no context within it. It would destroy its balance. *War and Peace* is no more a 'baggy monster'[1] than *Anna Karenina* is. The selecting process within Tolstoy,

[1] See James's *Preface to 'The Tragic Muse'*.

the arranging and rejecting has gone on steadily throughout. It is his supreme gift, and not many novelists have had it, far fewer than may be imagined. Nobody else has ever been able to write at such length without getting lost. Tolstoy could predict accurately to his publishers how much space he would need, long before he reached the end of his work.

There is lucidity and harmony in this vast edifice built of human contradictoriness. The whole novel with its multiplicity of experience leaves an impression of sanity, of a vast and firm ordering of the disorder within it. Tolstoy at this stage is in harmony with himself. Though it is a breathlessly precarious harmony, it is all any man can dare hope for. The sheer scale and variousness of the human world has captivated him. The achievement of having stated it to himself, having caught it, almost suffices and partially distracts him from the pain of continuing to know his own limitedness. His ambition is soothed, but not finally placated. He has not found the meaning of life. The novel remains tense with the striving to achieve more than he has been able to – this is what gives it its excitement. The novel registers the life of a man with an extraordinary capacity to live and to render his life. Tolstoy's need to feel himself fully alive amounts to passion. *War and Peace* is the expression of this passion.

6. The Structuring of Anna Karenina

Tolstoy states in *What is Art?* that true art is modest, a display of virtuosity is a sign of bad art. The modesty of Tolstoy's own art is what makes it difficult to deal with. To Henry James and Matthew Arnold, *Anna Karenina* was an interesting slice of life – but what is there artistic in the fact that Levin loses his dress shirt before his wedding? asks Arnold. A lack of economy seems the reason why the novel is so long. The subtleties and the patterning of a George Eliot, James or Lawrence novel seem at first sight to be missing. We do not appear to be given the guidance of an author far more intelligent than ourselves, as we do in the brilliant passages of elucidation to be found in the great English novels. In place of metaphors like the following from *Middlemarch*:

Having once embarked on your marital voyage, it is impossible not to be aware that you make no way and that the sea is not within sight – that, in fact, you are exploring an enclosed basin.

we are given such things as:

Now he experienced a feeling akin to that of a man who, while calmly crossing a precipice by a bridge, should suddenly discover that the bridge is broken, and that there is a chasm below.[1]

The Tolstoy vision seems ordinary.

None of the main characters in *Anna Karenina* are extraordinary people. Vronsky, for instance, Tolstoy tells us, is a type 'turned out by machinery'; he is an officer and a gentleman with a code of behaviour which only requires a brief outline. As for Anna herself, the fact that she succumbs to such a man in itself makes her a far simpler person than the heroines of Jane Austen, George Eliot or James. It is clear, too, that the sort of life she might have lived with Vronsky had they met earlier and married would have imposed no strain on her nerves. She is a woman formed to be at home in the great world, as the awestruck Levin discovers when he finally

[1] I shall quote from Constance Garnett's translation of *Anna Karenina* throughout.

meets her. The torture she is subjected to in her life appears to lack the subtlety, let us say, of Isabel Archer's relations with Gilbert Osmond – a subtlety the Anglo-Saxon reader has learnt to expect.

'Do you see, I love . . . equally, I think, but both more than myself – two creatures, Seryozha and Alexey.'

This is Anna's situation – at least she thinks it is.

Levin, the third major figure in the book, is the one who gives the whole its meaning, and he is perhaps the simplest of all. Levin is a country gentleman, awkward in public, with strong family instincts and an obsession with being better than he is. His sole contribution to the world by the end of the novel is a son.

The Tolstoy vision seems ordinary. There is the frequent inclusion of incidents such as Levin's losing his dress shirt. But of course this appearance of easy naïveté is an illusion. A measure of Tolstoy's subtlety is the critic's difficulty in uncovering it. Tolstoy is as much concerned with the strenuous selection of suggestive details in art as James. Often, where he presents us with a scene in which a mass of detail would pay easy dividends, we do not find it – the ball, the horse-race, the opera, for instance. In these he restricts himself rigorously to essentials. He does the same in delineating the thoughts or feelings of his characters. The effect on anyone reading *Anna Karenina* through is a sense of order and easy control, and this instinctive feeling is the correct one.

The massive novel begins with the little sentence 'Happy families are all alike; every unhappy family is unhappy in its own way'. We are shown a family quarrel. A husband has wrecked the happiness of his wife, but the presentation is gay, even charming. Stepan Oblonsky is a delightful hero of farce. When we see his wife our opinions change, but the situation apparently cannot be helped and Stepan remains delightful. Konstantin Levin has come to town to marry Kitty Shtcherbatsky. He has a conversation with his half-brother Sergey on the meaning of life. It is inconclusive, but Levin is certain of one thing in life, of his love for Kitty. Stepan indiscriminately encourages both Levin and Vronsky in their love for Kitty. He is as charming and dangerous as Chaucer's Pandarus. Levin is shattered by Kitty's rejection of him in favour of Vronsky. Anna, significantly enough the sister of Stepan, appears and a man dies a hideous death, crushed by the train that has carried her to Moscow. In a black dress, Anna appears at a romantic ball where Vronsky and she attract one another, and Kitty is left prostrate and horrified. The gaiety and romance of the opening has evaporated. The unsuccessful Levin visits his younger brother in whom he sees a hideous caricature of his own personality, ineffectual, wicked and suffering. The precariousness of human dignity and achievement is brought home to him. He returns to his estate, where it remains clear to him that he must marry. He tries to channel his feelings into good works on behalf of his peasants – benevolence which we see a little later fails for the time being because it is willed, not felt. Anna returns to Petersburg and her family, but Vronsky is on the same train, and amidst a 'blinding dazzle of red fire' and the clanking of iron their love becomes clear to one another. Anna and Vronsky are then seen in what they have hitherto regarded as their homes. The effect at the end of the first book is that of a precarious lull in a situation which cannot remain inconclusive for long. Dominating the centre of the first book there has been the brilliant ball at which the fascination of Anna was seen with the eyes of Kitty, the girl she ousted. Both Levin and Kitty have been swept aside by people apparently more powerful than themselves.

A tightness of construction is immediately evident from this synopsis of the first book. Clearly, this Russian novel does not, so far, belong to James' category of 'baggy monsters'.

As one reads on one discovers that, as with the first, each book has at its heart one dominating scene which affects one's reactions to the other events in it and also remains with one as a memory which echoes through the novel as a whole. The second book is dominated by the horse-race in which Vronsky breaks the back of his thoroughbred mare through clumsy horsemanship. The nightmare of Vronsky's passionate ride carrying him to a goal he cannot reach, and the contempt he feels for himself, bear a relation to the feeling of senseless waste which Levin and Kitty are experiencing.

The third book has as its key the chapter in which Levin mows his fields in the midst of his peasants, and finds peace and satisfaction in this basic activity. The mood breaks down when he tries to force its continuance by organising his peasants into living closer to him. The third book ends with a vision of death. Levin's younger brother Nikolay appears; a night spent with the dying brother seemingly brings proof of the senselessness of all life, of all striving, even of what appears to be success. This is experienced in the lives of Anna, Vronsky and Karenin in this book, too.

Books Four and Five form the pivot of the whole construction and can be taken as a pair. In them, the growing frustrations of the three previous books are apparently resolved by the coming together of the lovers in two unions, sanctified and unsanctified respectively.

The fourth book is lighted up in an illusory way by a sick-bed reconciliation between Anna and her husband; but as she recovers, her former feelings reassert themselves. Although her situation at home is agonising, the decisive step of beginning life on a new basis has not yet been taken. The betrothal of Levin and Kitty really lightens the book. But the calm is abruptly shattered in the very last chapter by the sudden, uncontrollable escape of Anna and Vronsky to Italy.

The beautiful experience of the marriage between Levin and Kitty, which immediately follows, at the start of the fifth book, provides a firm position from which we can watch the painful progression through sterility to death of the Anna–Vronsky liaison. Levin is developing into more of a personality. When he mislays his dress shirt on his wedding day he becomes ridiculous, but does not lose stature. Vronsky, when he became ridiculous, attempted to shoot himself. Vronsky lives self-consciously according to a military formula. He is doomed to be always separate, always mentally a bachelor however close he is to Anna physically. Immediately after the chapters dealing with Levin's marriage comes the description of Vronsky's attempt at creativity during his 'honeymoon' with Anna. Their marriage is a counterfeit marriage, as his pictures are counterfeit pictures. Many of Anna's feminine emotions are not comprehended by Vronsky and, to be fair to him, this is partly because she herself cannot impart them – the clumsiness Vronsky later displays in dealing with Anna's inexplicable outbursts is only partly his fault. Vronsky's attempts at creativity are indications that his 'married' life does not satisfy him. His desire for expression is echoed by that of other characters in this, the fifth, book – by Sergey's literary efforts, and especially by Karenin's religious mania.

The episode which dominates Book Five is the death of Levin's brother, Nikolay, in the presence of Levin and Kitty. Their confrontation with death brings out the difference between the male and female reactions to basic mysteries, and at the same time shows the effectiveness with which Kitty and Levin are able to act in the face of them. Then, almost at the moment of Nikolay's death, Kitty is found to be pregnant. Children gradually become more important as the novel moves on. The book ends with Anna's abortive visit to her son on his birthday and her subsequent flight from Petersburg to Vronsky's country estate.

The following two books are again a pair. In them the story of Anna and Vronsky is brought to a tragic close. Book Six deals with life in the country, while Book Seven is centred largely in town. The contrast highlights the study of urban life which is a major theme in the novel and which steadily grows in importance.

Book Six begins with a picture of Levin's estate in summer. Kitty's sister, Dolly, visits Vronsky and Anna whose way of life she starts by envying and ends by pitying. Levin visits the local elections where he meets Petersburg and Moscow politicians, among them Sergey and Vronsky playing a game Levin does not understand and which bears no relation to the life of the countryside.

In Book Seven, Levin has moved to town for his wife's confinement. As usual, he becomes bewildered in town, but the experience of the birth of a son soon blots all else from his mind. In agony, while waiting for the birth, Levin quite spontaneously calls to God. The religious emotion brought about by the birth is a stage in his gradual return to the traditional ways of his forefathers.

Anna Karenina kills herself in a state of hatred for life.

Book Eight is mainly about Levin and his half-brother Sergey, their desire to give significance to their lives. Kitty finds her husband's despair over his lack of faith absurd. But Levin in fact is desperately close to suicide. One day a chance remark from one of his peasants makes it clear to him that his way of life is a fruitful one. He now realises that his despair has been caused by abstract reasonings which he has always forgotten when a decision affecting his life has had to be taken. His half-brother Sergey is discredited, although at the end of the book Levin is again defeated by him in argument. Sergey's new-found interest in the Pan-Slavic cause, the latest of his enthusiasms, is obviously a substitute for real emotion, real communication with others. Sergey's references are to newspapers and magazine articles, while Levin's are to his own experience.

'Happy families are all alike; every unhappy family is unhappy in its own way.' Possibly there is no such thing as a 'happy family', but there is a basic sameness in human desires and aspirations, no matter how infinitely numerous are the possible circumstances which thwart them. It is this which Tolstoy is concerned with communicating. 'Sometimes people who are together, if not hostile to one another, are at least estranged in mood and feeling, till perhaps a story, a performance, a picture . . . unites them all as by an electric flash . . . Each is glad that another feels what he feels; glad of the communion established not only between him and all present, but also with all now living who will yet share the same impression; and, more than that, he feels the mysterious gladness of a communion which, reaching beyond the grave, unites us with all men of the past who have been moved by the same feelings and with all men of the future who will yet be touched by them.'[1]

Anna Karenina, for all its bulk, can thus be seen to have the clear lines of a Jane Austen novel. The chapters are short and concise on the analogy of scenes in a play; and the bigger units, the books, are as easily held in Tolstoy's mind as the chapters. What amazes one about Tolstoy is the immense clarity of his artistic vision. He does not simplify anything. It is just that all difficulties of expression are miraculously smoothed out. One feels this the moment the novel opens, and perhaps the opening is worth looking at in more detail.

A marriage which has broken down is presented shortly and yet completely. Dolly is faced with a life which has suddenly lost meaning. She is tied to a man who is intelligent, gay, good-natured, but without morals – a man delightful and yet shallow, like Falstaff or Pandarus. A part of his nature is simply missing, yet he is charming and even slightly mysterious in his oddity – we never quite understand Stepan, yet we are told everything about his inner life, not forgetting his intellectual life, for like George Eliot, Tolstoy is concerned with the total structure of his characters' natures. Stepan is the perfect companion until his company palls, and then he is forgotten. His solution when he senses this happening is to move away and engage the attention of someone else. This solution cannot be applied in his relations with his wife, though, and this causes distress to both of them. It should be made clear that Tolstoy is as concerned with Stepan's distress as with his wife's, and as concerned to show that it is genuine in its way and commands sympathy. Tolstoy's sympathy has an unforced spontaneity the quality of which could be brought out by comparing it to George Eliot's rather more self-conscious concern over her erring characters. Here

---

[1] *What is Art?*, Chapter XVI.

D

is a fragment of the domestic row which comes soon after the opening of the novel:

'You are loathsome to me, repulsive!' she shrieked, getting more and more heated. 'Your tears mean nothing! You have never loved me; you have neither heart nor honourable feeling! You are hateful to me, disgusting, a stranger – yes, a complete stranger!' With pain and wrath she uttered the word so terrible to herself – *stranger*.

He looked at her, and the fury expressed in her face alarmed and amazed him. He did not understand how his pity for her exasperated her. She saw in him sympathy for her, but not love. 'No, she hates me. She will not forgive me,' he thought.

'It is awful! awful!' he said.

At that moment in the next room a child began to cry; probably it had fallen down. Darya Alexandrovna listened, and her face suddenly softened.

She seemed, pulling herself together for a few seconds, as though she did not know where she was, and what she was doing, and getting up rapidly, she moved towards the door.

'Well, she loves my child,' he thought, noticing the change of her face at the child's cry, 'my child: how can she hate me?'

'Dolly, one word more,' he said, following her.

'If you come near me, I will call in the servants, the children! They may all know you are a scoundrel! I am going away at once, and you may live here with your mistress!'

And she went out, slamming the door.

Stepan Arkadyevitch sighed, wiped his face, and with a subdued tread walked out of the room. 'Matvey says she will come round; but how? I don't see the least chance of it. Ah, oh, how horrible it is! And how vulgarly she shouted,' he said to himself, remembering her shriek and the words – 'scoundrel' and 'mistress'. 'And very likely the maids were listening! Horribly vulgar! horrible!' Stepan Arkadyevitch stood a few seconds alone, wiped his face, squared his chest, and walked out of the room.

The childishness of the words, the childishness of these two people in their misery, the slight touch of comedy about the whole situation, does not obscure the very real tragedy of the situation and its complexity – at least for Dolly – although it establishes that the tragedy is a minor one compared to what befalls Anna. Tolstoy's scale of importance is unerring. To it is owing the impression of calm which the novel leaves.

The other tragedy in the novel is the marriage of Anna. Anna is Stepan's sister, and it is when one contemplates this fact that the concealed subtlety of Tolstoy's art first dawns on one. Anna appears to be similar to her brother, an aristocrat, gay, intelligent, well-bred, bursting with health and physical well-being, taking an almost animal satisfaction in life.[1] Yet her life becomes a catastrophe – and this is evidently because she possesses in a large degree whatever it is that Stepan lacks in his make-up. It is what makes her different from her brother which destroys her, in other words her conscience and her loyalty. The value of her personality makes her wasted life tragic, a value which is displayed in the respect she shows her husband when she thinks she is dying, and in the scene where, burdened with remorse, she secretly visits her son on his birthday.

The contrast between Anna's case and her brother's, which is one of the reasons for the novel beginning as it does, clarifies a side of Anna's nature which could have been clarified in no other way. The apparently haphazard start to *Anna Karenina* is an example of the way in which Tolstoy continually defines things through contrast. One character is defined by placing him beside another – Stepan beside Anna, Levin beside Vronsky, Kitty beside Anna, Levin beside each of his two brothers, and so on. 'The business of art', says Tolstoy, 'lies just in this: to make that understood and felt which in the form of an argument might be incomprehensible and inaccessible.'[2]

It becomes clearer and clearer that the huge scale of the novel – the innumerable characters and events – is necessary to the attainment of an immense subtlety. Tolstoy seems to have attempted to include every kind of experience possible to people in his society, all the essential furniture of his characters' minds and conversations (he

---

[1] Tolstoy is as aware of the physical life of his characters as Lawrence is. Here is the description of Vronsky riding in his carriage to meet Anna after his terrible mishap at the races –

> all blended into a general, joyous sense of life. This feeling was so strong that he could not help smiling. He dropped his legs, crossed one leg over the other knee, and taking it in his hand, felt the springy muscle of the calf, where it had been grazed the day before by his fall, and leaning back, he drew several deep breaths.
>
> 'I'm happy, very happy!' he said to himself. He had often before had this sense of physical joy in his own body, but he had never felt so fond of himself, of his own body, as at that moment. He enjoyed the slight ache in his strong leg, he enjoyed the muscular sensation of movement in his chest as he breathed.

[2] *What is Art?*, Chapter X.

takes this as far as artistic economy permits: his common sense always tells him where to stop). The incidents range from the early scene in Vronsky's military bachelor establishment to the failure of Sergey's book. All are essential to give us a full picture of the five or six central characters. Yet the organisation is so skilful that every character and every incident also relates in some way to the two chief characters, Levin and Anna. The memory we are left with after *Anna Karenina* is not confused – it is first of all the distinct recollection of these two people, both high-strung, both vulnerable, one of them miraculously managing to clear the many obstacles in his path, one of them broken (the great race in which Vronsky rides his mare to death is an obstacle race).

ANNA

Having got thus far, making general statements, it might be worth looking more closely at the two main characters, since it is on them that the significance of the novel depends – Anna first of all.

Anna's meeting with Vronsky is associated with a death, an impersonal sort of death which seems no one's fault. Vronsky pays out money to smooth over the fact of death for Anna. It is the first time he spends money on her. She is a woman who, for all her spontaneity and honesty, seems doomed to artificiality in her life. Dolly Oblonsky is immediately suspicious of Anna's peace-making mission – 'there was something artificial in the whole framework of their [the Karenins'] family life'. Like her brother, Anna is enormously accomplished socially and immediately wins Dolly over – 'not only remembering the names, but the years, months, characters, illnesses of all the children, and Dolly could not but appreciate that'. She launches her attack on Dolly instantly – 'yes, I know him [Stepan]. I could not look at him without feeling sorry for him. We both know him. He is good-hearted, but he is proud, and now he is so humiliated. What touched me most . . . (and here Anna guessed what would touch Dolly most) . . .' She is intelligent with her advice, and her motives are warm. It is the sort of understanding conversation which really solves nothing in the long run, but appears to be wise at the time. The smugness here of the sophisticated grand lady is in poignant contrast to her later helplessness.

When 'romance' comes Anna's way, her common sense quickly deserts her, and there is no doubt that Vronsky is a romantic figure.

After the meeting at the station he leaves his card at the Oblonsky household.

When Anna was passing the top of the staircase, a servant was running up to announce the visitor, while the visitor himself was standing under a lamp. Anna glancing down at once recognised Vronsky, and a strange feeling of pleasure and at the same time of dread of something stirred in her heart. He was standing still, not taking off his coat, pulling something out of his pocket. At the instant when she was just facing the stairs, he raised his eyes, caught sight of her, and into the expression of his face there passed a shade of embarrassment and dismay. With a slight inclination of her head she passed, hearing behind her Stepan Arkadyevitch's loud voice calling him to come up, and the quiet, soft and composed voice of Vronsky refusing.

The controlled quietness of Vronsky's movements is conveyed – the slight air of authority which is sensed in his personality. Tolstoy, like Dickens, has the rare gift of commanding the visual imagination. The scenes in *Anna Karenina* really are scenes.

It is in the romantic atmosphere of the ball, wonderfully conveyed, that Anna falls in love. She acquires the temporary hardness and ruthlessness of a huntress. She triumphs over Kitty. Anna is much older than Kitty, older than Vronsky too, but she cannot stop herself. When we next see Anna, she is already alone. She can expect no advice or sympathy from anyone, and she instinctively withdraws into herself. Dolly's children sense this and ignore her. Already, she seems nomadic, someone without a home. After Vronsky's avowal on the platform beside the train carrying her back to Petersburg, her life has begun to split into two. She moves more and more in the society which is far removed from that of her husband – the world of Petersburg fashion where she is pursued by Vronsky. During a scene in Princess Betsy's[1] drawing-room, as frothy as something out of *A School for Scandal*, Karenin notices the way people are looking at Anna and Vronsky. The scene which follows is the counterpart of the earlier domestic scene between the Oblonskys.

He saw that the innermost recesses of her soul, that had always hitherto lain open before him, were closed against him. More than that, he saw from her tone that she was not even perturbed at that, but as it were said straight out to him: 'Yes, it's shut up, and so it must be, and will be in future.' Now he experienced a feeling such as a man might have, returning home and finding his own house locked up.

[1] Vronsky's cousin.

The single image (the house locked up) has the boldness of complete simplicity. The scene – like all the scenes in Karenin's house – is full of memories of years of domestic peace, memories which we almost seem to share, and yet the passage is short. As in that earlier picture of Vronsky standing at the foot of the stairs, the clues seem so few that one doesn't quite know where one has got one's strong impression from.

Anna's reaction brings Karenin face to face with a reality he was incapable of imagining by himself. The living reality is often different from the construction we make of it when we are by ourselves. The interview is very different from the one he has been prepared for because Anna is no longer reacting in the way she has taught him to expect. She has evidently been a tactful and faithful wife. Karenin's dependence on a comforting and acquiescing reaction to the little speech he has prepared proves this. A history of the marriage is never necessary. We know all we need to know about everybody in the novel from simply watching them, so that the novel contains more matter even than its bulk might lead one to expect.

When Karenin is face to face with an Anna newly awakened to more attractive possibilities in life, his prepared phrases give way to statements of his real situation – his dependence on her.

'I am your husband, and I love you . . .' For an instant her face fell, and the mocking gleam in her eyes died away . . . 'But I am not speaking of myself, the most important persons in this matter are our son and yourself.'

It is here that a transformation comes over the novel. Tolstoy's energies become concentrated with extraordinary intentness on the situation which is developing. The issues are no longer abstract, in the mind of the writer. The characters are beginning to push against his directing hand, beginning to determine the pattern which is forming.

A chapter half a page long follows – long enough to convey the empty history of the drifting apart of husband and wife. Tolstoy economises daringly where nothing can be added. Anna has become Vronsky's mistress by the time she next appears. But she is incapable of 'that brilliant, graceful, worldly liaison' which Vronsky's mother had expected for her son, and she carries Vronsky along with her. Her tension weighs on him and enslaves him.

The way she excites Vronsky by her sensitivity and fineness of nature is suggested by the feelings awakened in him at this time by his thoroughbred mare. Before the race he briefly visits the mare.

But the nearer he came, the more excited she grew. Only when he stood by her head, she was suddenly quieter, while the muscles quivered under her soft, delicate coat. Vronsky patted her strong neck, straightened over her sharp withers a stray lock of her mane that had fallen on the other side, and moved his face near her dilated nostrils, transparent as a bat's wing. She drew a loud breath and snorted out through her tense nostrils, started, pricked up her sharp ear, and put out her strong black lip towards Vronsky, as though she would nip hold of his sleeve. But remembering the muzzle, she shook it and again began restlessly stamping one after the other her shapely legs.

. . . The mare's excitement had infected Vronsky. He felt that his heart was throbbing, and that he too, like the mare, longed to move, to bite; it was both dreadful and delicious.[1]

As Vronsky rides over to see Anna, he rides through mud. The racecourse across which he must ride later 'will be a perfect swamp'. His situation fills him with a dull sense of loathing. The sense of loathing is intensified when Anna tells him she is pregnant. She is filled with the same loathing. She is cruel and spiteful about her husband — far crueller than Vronsky would dream of being. Yet Anna cannot allow herself to think of leaving him. The loathing and frustration which builds up in Vronsky destroys his calm for the race, a test for which 'not being upset' is essential. The race makes breathless reading. Its climax is a brutal kick in the stomach Vronsky gives the dying mare. He is furious that she has collapsed before his goal has been reached. But her death has been caused by his clumsiness. 'For the first time in his life he knew the bitterest sort of misfortune, misfortune beyond remedy, and caused by his own fault.' The second time is to come at the end — on the railway platform after Anna's suicide.

Death is never very far away in this novel, as in life. Anna's perception of the nearness of Vronsky's death, when watching the race, makes her realise she cannot afford to live any longer without him. She is hysterically cruel to her husband on the way home.

Karenin's reaction to the rift is extraordinary for so intelligent a man — the determination to keep her in his house and show her daily how much in the wrong she has been. He hides his motives

---

[1] This is extraordinarily close to the method of D. H. Lawrence — too close to be entirely accidental.

from himself, ascribing them to Christian forgiveness. Usually, the more intellectual a Tolstoy character is the more rudimentary is his emotional life. Having made his decision about Anna, Karenin attempts to return to his work (we know as much or even more about Karenin's political manoeuvres as about Lydgate's doctoring in Middlemarch). The description of his work is not satire but the thing itself, absurd only if looked at in relation to realities which Karenin does not wish to see.

Anna's horror at Karenin's letter of reconciliation is justified – although one cannot blame him as she does, for he is an object of sympathy too. 'She cried without restraint as children do when they are punished.' Dignity is lost. She cannot understand why her treatment of her husband is such a terrible thing to her. She visits Princess Betsy. Betsy says 'the very same thing, don't you see, may be looked at tragically, and turned into a misery, or it may be looked at simply and even humorously'. But Anna feels that her crime must be great since she suffers so much.

With almost banal inevitability, it has taken a man like Vronsky, with his prefabricated code of conduct and restricted imagination, to run after a woman like Anna. She remains mysterious to him, a sensitive woman whom he looks on with touching solicitude but whom he has not the skill to handle. For all his grandeur, his aristocratic presence, his manliness, Vronsky is frightened of his own shortcomings, and rightly so. The next time we see him, Tolstoy shows him engaged in showing a foreign prince the pleasures which Russia offers the rich and powerful.

He was a very stupid and very self-satisfied and very healthy and very well-washed man, and nothing else. He was a gentleman – that was true, and Vronsky could not deny it. He was equable and not cringing with his superiors, was free and ingratiating in his behaviour with his equals, and was contemptuously indulgent with his inferiors . . .

'Brainless beef! can I be like that?' Vronsky thought.

As a husband for Anna, Vronsky would have been suitable. As her lover, he would require an order of tact and intelligence which is very rare.

Karenin is one of the most important people in the novel, more important than Vronsky, for it is largely because he is Anna's husband that the tragedy comes about. His suffering imposes a burden of guilt on her which she cannot shake off. Anna grows to hate him for it. The extent of this hatred is a measure of the burden she feels. Later her fear of her husband's accusations will be greater even than her love for Seryozha, her son. 'Let her go as she likes' was the suggestion of the groom to Vronsky about the mare Vronsky subsequently killed. Neither Vronsky nor Karenin allow Anna any freedom of movement. Together, they bring her down with the demands they impose on her.

It is Karenin's nature to be self-centred. It is partly the result of his having received little love in his life, but Anna's presence often awakens a touching glow of life in him. Anna is aware of this. There is something childish, a typically Tolstoyan effect, in his remark on learning her infidelity, 'I cannot be made unhappy by the fact that a contemptible woman has committed a crime'. His distress is a measure of his need, and of the extent of his dependence.

Karenin determines not to separate from Anna after her confession.

'. . . She is bound to be unhappy, but I am not to blame, and so I cannot be unhappy.'

His motive is to punish her. Later he forgives her, but whatever the conscious motive is, the underlying reason remains the necessity to keep her with him. This is 'love' as much as Vronsky's feelings for Anna are.

Anna feels contempt for her husband as she sits trapped in his house, waiting for the birth of her child by Vronsky. She tells Vronsky:

'He's not a man, not a human being – he's a doll! No one knows him; but I know him. Oh, if I'd been in his place, I'd long ago have killed, have torn to pieces a wife like me. I wouldn't have said: "Anna, *ma chère*"!'

Her words are also a reflection on Vronsky which he is partially conscious of. 'You're unfair, very unfair, dearest.'

Tolstoy unobtrusively leads us to become more and more interested in Karenin, so that our memory of him by the end of the novel is clearer than that of Vronsky. Anna exclaims in semi-delirium on what she imagines is her death-bed:

'He's so good, he doesn't know himself how good he is . . . No one knows him. I'm the only one, and it was hard for me even.'

She is conjuring up an ideal husband in her mind, yet the bonds which attach her to Karenin are evident in this desire to idealise him. They have been forced together in a society marriage, yet Anna's loyalty makes her relationship with Karenin as strong as that with Vronsky in spite of herself. Karenin's forgiveness is really a joyful response to this demonstration of the admiration and respect Anna has always desired to feel for him.

The capacity for love that there is in Karenin comes as a happy revelation to him. It extends to Anna's baby who is a new person, a new beginning. But, having brought about a new phase in her relationship with Karenin, Anna finds that she must live with the consequences. Karenin

> was even ready to allow these relations [between Anna and Vronsky] to be renewed, so long as the children were not disgraced, and he was not deprived of them nor forced to change his position. Bad as this might be, it was anyway better than a rupture, which would put her in a hopeless and shameful position, and deprive him of everything he cared for.

Karenin has made it morally impossible for Anna to see Vronsky. She sees him as using her own conscience as a weapon against her. Her hatred increases because she realises that he is not behaving maliciously. 'I hate him for his virtues', she tells her brother. The shock of having his love suddenly rejected brings about Karenin's subsequent bitterness. We are never allowed to laugh at him or to despise him, even for his later attitude to Anna. His conversion to Countess Lydia's religion (which turns him into a laughing-stock) will again be Anna's fault, part of the burden of guilt she sees herself as carrying. Her hatred for Karenin will increase accordingly and swell her hatred at the conditions of her life.

After the episode of Levin's marriage, we follow Anna and Vronsky on their 'honeymoon'. The life away from an accustomed setting and routine brings Vronsky face to face with himself. Anna cannot help him, she cannot see him clearly because she is too absorbed in fears of his affection cooling. There is no real connection between them. The result is that Vronsky's life is not renewed by her. His imitation of the conventions in art, when he turns artist, echoes the conventionality of his public behaviour to Anna. She herself does not provide the inspiration for his portrait of her; it comes less from her than from the pictures Vronsky is imitating. The artist Mihailov's understanding of Anna is greater than Vronsky's.

> 'I have been struggling on for ever so long without doing anything,' he [Vronsky] said of his own portrait of her, 'and he just looked and painted it. That's where technique comes in.'

Vronsky's search for happiness in foreign countries and its conclusion has an almost Johnsonian ring of finality in it. The summing-up of the painting episode is conclusive and weighty.

The same experience befell him as Golenishtchev [Vronsky's acquaintance] who felt that he had nothing to say, and continually deceived himself with the theory that his idea was not yet mature, that he was working it out and collecting materials. This exasperated and tortured Golenishtchev, but Vronsky was incapable of deceiving and torturing himself, and even more incapable of exasperation. With his characteristic decision, without explanation or apology, he simply ceased working at painting.

The emptiness of Vronsky is balanced by what becomes of Karenin. Face to face with himself, the crisis over, Karenin turns to Christ and Countess Lydia, exciting a disgust and pity in the reader akin to the disgust Mihailov feels for Vronsky's painting.

Having only Vronsky, and terrified that he might be getting bored with her, Anna attempts to force an entry for them both into 'normal' life, and is maddened still further when Vronsky fails to understand her motives.

'. . . and why is she putting me in such a position?' he said with a gesture of despair.
With that gesture he knocked against the table, on which there was standing the seltzer water and the decanter of brandy, and almost upset it. He tried to catch it, let it slip, and angrily kicked the table over, and rang.

With foreboding, one remembers the horse-race . . . 'He felt at the same time that his respect for her was diminished, while the sense of her beauty was intensified.' He attempts to restore his equanimity through masculine discussion with Yashvin, a military associate, on buying a horse.

Anna's last refuge is in the country, where we glimpse her when Dolly pays a visit from Levin's estate. The contrast with Levin's married life, and even Dolly's own, defines the strangeness of Anna's way of life. A monotonous gaiety is maintained amidst luxury that reminds Dolly of 'the best hotels abroad'. Nowhere in the novel is Anna so pathetic. The fashionable tone of the establishment and of the guests who take advantage of a hospitality nobody else accepts, the elegant French phrases and the foreign furniture create an impression of slightly shamefaced, raffish unconventionality. Vronsky's humanitarian project, the hospital, reminds one of the imagery of sickness in Shakespearean tragedy. There is a touch of lugubrious insanity in the project.

'And won't you have a lying-in ward?' asked Dolly. 'That's so much needed in the country. I have often . . .'

In spite of his usual courtesy, Vronsky interrupted her.

'This is not a lying-in home, but a hospital for the sick, and is intended for all diseases, except infectious complaints,' he said.

To Vronsky, life seems still ahead of him. He wants a son and heir, and he sees the present as a temporary arrangement which will end when a divorce has been negotiated with Karenin. Anna has already had her life. Her present situation is merely an epilogue to it. She prevents herself from having more children by Vronsky, for the idea of any new development in her life fills her exhausted spirit with fear. She wants Vronsky to go on loving her with the same love which provided the motive for her flight with him.

Both Anna and Vronsky had reached an impasse in their lives at the time they met. This accounted for the immediate centring of their energies on one another. Vronsky's military ambitions had received a setback. Anna could not long remain imprisoned within her un-satisfactory marriage. Later, when they had become lovers, we were told of Vronsky's ambition as still being 'perhaps the chief interest' of his life. We glimpsed Vronsky's family background on seeing the tough old lady of fashion, his mother. The love between Anna and Vronsky is a passion intensified by the unnatural circumstances of their lives.

When Karenin attempted to imprison Anna within her family she exclaimed: 'Haven't I striven, striven with all my strength, to find something to give meaning to my life? . . . What do I know? What do I want? What is there I care for?' Anna's love for her child had a flaw which made her eventual abandonment of him as inevitable as her abandonment of Karenin.

She recalled the partly sincere, though greatly exaggerated role of the mother living for her child, which she had taken up of late years.

At first Anna was received into the Petersburg high society the Vronskys frequented. But when Anna at last broke the society code she had to drop out of that circle. A hell of heartless, unspontaneous banality and boredom underlay the sumptuous façade of Princess Betsy's world, contrasting with the Moscow social life of Anna's brother Stepan. Yet it remains the only social world Vronsky knows, and it is the world he seeks to reproduce for Anna when they live together. It is the old story of the things money cannot buy. In a sense, the whole of *Anna Karenina* is an old story. The morals to be extracted are all very old and recognised as very obvious. Tolstoy is not searching for a new morality, but for principles which always apply in human affairs.

Anna becomes a slave to Vronsky, dependent on his continual presence and on his attention being constantly directed towards herself. When she is without him she is in a vacuum. The question 'what for?' is as important to her as it is to Levin. Without an answer she can see nothing ahead but death. Vronsky is frightened by her demands on him. He cannot see why she does not permit him to have a life apart from her. He thinks of their relationship as a marriage, which ought to provide a stable centre to their individual lives. He cannot understand what Anna wants of him; he does not realise that for her this is not a marriage, and he has had no experience of what marriage is. There are no moments of almost wordless understanding between Anna and Vronsky, as there are between Levin and Kitty. There is only the communication possible between mistress and lover, and it is Anna's responsibility that it is so. Dolly, when she visits them both on Vronsky's estate, is almost more sorry for Vronsky than for Anna. She notices the change which has come over him. She has previously disliked him, but now he has become human and touching. He has been awakened by Anna. He wishes for a marriage, and Anna will not supply it. She cannot bring herself to act the part of either a wife or a mother in Vronsky's establishment. She cannot bring herself even to conduct the management of the house, which Vronsky takes upon himself, ignorant of the way such responsibilities are divided in a civilian household.

Inevitably, Vronsky begins to reject what she offers him. It is not what he wants. 'All was charming, but how many times it had charmed him! And the stern, stony expression that she so dreaded settled upon his face.' Quarrels become regular between them. On the surface, there seems a terrible selfishness in Anna. She has given up a great deal for Vronsky, but she gives him nothing. All the generosity seems to come from him. She knows she has become intolerable, but her fear that she has exchanged her life for an illusion is too great. She is attempting to arrest the march of time, to enjoy a perpetual affair. She is fighting to stay alive.

Anna's self-disgust is complete when she eventually realises that it is her own love for Vronsky which is exhausted. This is what drives her to an inevitable suicide. The last thoughts that pass through Anna's mind as she rides in her carriage from place to place after what turns out to be the final quarrel with Vronsky have all the simplicity of such thoughts. The economy of the presentation is staggering. It is a nightmare built up with the few precise lines of a Goya etching. '. . . we all hate each other like those cab drivers who are abusing each other so angrily.'

The train journey which takes Anna to the end of her life, so like the one which settled matters between her and Vronsky at the beginning, provides the suggestion which leads to her death. The nomadic atmosphere of trains, the sensation of a time out of life which they give, a separation from normal reality and from home, exhilarating in some circumstances, depressive in others, the movement which finally leads Anna to no destination – the part this plays in the Vronsky–Anna relationship is one of the deepest memories one carries away from the novel. The state of mind created in Anna by the last train journey precipitates a suicide already inevitable.

The novel of course does not end with Anna's death. Her final summing-up of life is not the correct one. Tolstoy is convinced that there is a right way of life, though the laws which govern such a life do not lend themselves to any rational means of expression. The novel is about this, and Anna is the most important means of expressing it.

LEVIN

Konstantin Levin could easily have been a weakness in the novel. With him, Tolstoy triumphs over what seems to be the greatest obstacle to any novelist – the convincing embodiment of an ideal. By the end, Levin falls into a pattern of life which is immemorial and as satisfactory as human nature allows. He develops and ripens, and shows signs of becoming like Prince Shtcherbatsky, his father-in-law.

Very soon in the novel we are shown Levin listening to a conversation between his urbane half-brother and a professor of philosophy. Levin seems hampered by slow-wittedness, a man without the right environmental training for intellectual fireworks. He has a mind which, childlike, refuses to react to complexities of argument, and therefore they do not distract him from the first great questions of life. His search for the significance of life is presented at times in a manner that reminds one of *Rasselas*.

... It seemed to Levin that just as they were close upon the real point of the matter, they were again retreating, and he made up his mind to put a question to the professor.

'According to that, if my senses are annihilated, if my body is dead, I can have no existence of any sort?' he queried.

The professor, in annoyance, and as it were mental suffering at the interruption, looked round at the strange inquirer, more like a bargeman than a philosopher, and turned his eyes upon Sergey Ivanovitch, as though to ask: 'What's one to say to him?' But Sergey Ivanovitch, who had been talking with far less heat and one-sidedness than the professor, and who had sufficient breadth of mind to answer the professor and at the same time to comprehend the simple and natural point of view from which the question was put, smiled and said:

'That question we have no right to answer as yet.'

'We have not the requisite data,' chimed in the professor, and he went back to his argument.

A massive common sense is indeed an important element in Tolstoy's wisdom. Tolstoy's purpose with Levin emerges in this chapter. It is to show a man flowering naturally – not forced into an early, sterile maturity as in the urban world – so that he is able to arrive at a personal, and therefore satisfying, solution of essential questions, in particular the question 'how to live'.

A nostalgia for the countryside, the great sea out of which urban man has so recently emerged, is a common theme in the English novel – one thinks of such figures as Adam Bede, or Tom Brangwen. Both represent a nostalgia for a vanished past. What, for practical reasons, neither George Eliot nor Lawrence can do is present a conversation such as the one above. Levin's part in the conversation is so successfully done because the debate is not contrived. Levin is persona grata in the society in which he finds himself. Such juxtapositions of people are still possible in Tolstoy's Russia, while they are not in the more standardised and divided societies of the 'developed' European countries. In this way, perhaps, the Russian novelists possessed one enormous advantage over their contemporaries. With no sense of strain, of the engineered situation, the most heterogeneous people can be made to reveal each other, and a cross-fertilisation of ideas and attitudes is possible. People of great diversity lived on terms of intimacy in the small society which was all the Russia that mattered.

Tolstoy constantly defines by contrasting. Levin's developing personality is held in focus in the novel by frequent meetings with his half-brother Sergey, and with that very different figure, Stepan Arkadyevitch, both of whom affectionately rather despise him. Levin, with his blushes and awkwardness, is adolescent even at the age of thirty-two when he first appears. The mould in which his character must take shape is no longer there ready for him, and his struggle to don the spiritual attire which has hung easily and naturally on his forefathers is a hard one. Tolstoy as much as Lawrence is a critic of the effect on men of the modern metropolis, in which a variety of ephemeral experiences have replaced the old fixed patterns of work and recreation and in which the religious and moral beliefs of men have become confused. This has been the effect of a metropolitan education on Levin. He is one of the dwindling minority which returns to the country after it.

. . . his contemporaries by this time, when he was thirty-two, were already one a colonel, and another a professor, another a director of a bank and railways, or president of a board, like Oblonsky. But he (he knew very well how he must appear to others) was a country gentleman, occupied in breeding cattle, shooting game, and building barns; in other words, a fellow of no ability, who had not turned out well, and who was doing just what, according to the ideas of the world, is done by people fit for nothing else.

'What is "Doing well"?', Hardy makes Clym Yeobright ask his mother in The Return of the Native. It is a question which also occupied D. H. Lawrence – The Rainbow owes more to the Levin part of Anna Karenina than to Hardy or George Eliot. Tolstoy is more convincing than the English writers because the way of life he proposes is no theory. It is the life he himself has lived. If ever a writer wrote from experience it was Tolstoy; this is perhaps his greatest strength. It is the reason for his astonishing simplicity – the lack of strain in all his effects.

Levin is presented to us at the crucial moment in his life. The decision to get married is 'a matter of life and death' to him, as he tells Stepan. The significance he attaches to marriage is greater than either his brother or Oblonsky can conceive. Levin and Kitty are pathetic figures in their childlike delicacy of feeling. 'Lord have pity on us!' Kitty cries when she has refused Levin in favour of Vronsky. Her feeling for Levin is the natural one, but is overlaid by a more conscious and deliberate preference for Vronsky. Kitty's difficulty in distinguishing her true and false affections is the result of a lost spontaneity (like Levin's temporary suppression of his religious feelings through the effects of his education).

After Kitty's rejection of Levin, we are given a horrifying vision of the dangers and pitfalls that lie in wait below the polite surface of life. Levin goes slumming to visit his brother, Nikolay, who has destroyed himself through weaknesses of character which are caricatures of Levin's own. The schemes of action, in case of a loveless future, which Levin wishes to embark on are seen in the distorting mirror of his brother's mind. The nightmare that looms in the background is death with nothing accomplished. On his return to his estate the voices of the past say to Levin, 'No, you're not going to get away from us, and you're not going to be different, but you're going to be the same as you've always been; with doubts, everlasting dissatisfaction with yourself, vain efforts to amend, and falls, and everlasting expectation of a happiness which you won't get, and which isn't possible for you.'

We know from Tolstoy's diaries that Levin's inner life is almost purely autobiographical. Tolstoy evidently sees the essentials in himself and his development as those of Everyman. Having arrived at a measure of happiness at the time he writes *Anna Karenina*, he looks back on the path he has trodden as a necessary one for all. Perhaps the major discovery which Levin will finally make is that his married life involves all the pitfalls and absurdities which he had previously thought he could circumvent. The basic pattern of his married happiness will be identical to everyone else's.

Even the story of Levin's struggle to understand his peasants, in order to teach them to work on more rational principles, is part of Tolstoy's own. It is an attempt which is always muddled and abortive because, as Levin himself realises, there is a lack of connection between the products of the intellect and the living complexities of life. His attempts to do good by rule always fail, as Kitty's did at the time of her partnership with the strange girl Varenka.

The vital similarity of attitude which links Kitty and Levin is pointed in the chapter where Levin's half-brother Sergey visits Levin in the country. Sergey professes greater love for the peasants than Levin, and brands him as a reactionary serf owner. 'That's simply your Russian sloth and old serf owner's ways, and I'm convinced that in you it's a temporary error and will pass.' One thinks back to the sloth Kitty's father has been convicted of.

'But time's money, you forget that,' said the colonel.

'Time, indeed, that depends! Why, there's time one would give a month of for sixpence, and time you wouldn't give half an hour of for any money.'

Levin finds these valuable moments in life occasionally. One such experience is the mowing which he takes part in while Sergey is staying with him.

Levin, though, requires urgently to create something which will survive his death. His servants realise quite simply that what he wants is a wife and children, but in the meantime he puts all his energies into creating a book, although for Levin this involves a misdirection of energy. The events leading up to his marriage follow with complete inevitability. Stepan Arkadyevitch is certain of it when he invites Levin and Kitty to his dinner party on Levin's return from abroad. Stepan's marvellous social gifts are seen at their finest here. The dinner party is his greatest achievement, and Tolstoy makes it clear that it is a delightful and valuable one. The conversations, intellectual and otherwise, the diverse people, are held simultaneously in Tolstoy's mind, so that there is almost a three-dimensional sensation of being in the midst of a convivial gathering, looking round and, above all, noting what is happening between Levin and Kitty.

The marriage of Levin and Kitty and their first month together are dovetailed with the disastrous 'married' life of Anna and Vronsky. The story of Levin and Kitty's marriage as it develops, with its frustrations and rages, is at first almost more painful than what is happening to Anna. There is the death of Levin's brother, Nikolay. Levin feels that Kitty will distract and hamper him at this solemn moment. Marriage seems to have brought him no closer to solving the question 'what is the purpose of life?' after all. This is the question Levin stated to Oblonsky before the dinner which led to his marriage.

'I've not given up thinking of death,' said Levin. 'It's true that it's high time I was dead; and that all this is nonsense. It's the truth I'm telling you. I do value my idea and my work awfully; but in reality only consider this: all this world of ours is nothing but a speck of mildew, which has grown

up on a tiny planet. And for us to suppose we can have something great —
ideas, work — it's all dust and ashes.'

'But all that's as old as the hills, my boy!'

Stepan's reply is at first ours. Only Tolstoy would dare to present
this question with such absurd naïveté. Yet the answer to just this is
plainly the purpose of the novel, and the answer is a lot more
delicate than the question. It becomes clear from the great section
on the death of Levin's brother that Levin and Kitty together are
far more effective than either of them were apart. Levin studies the
scene round his brother's death-bed —

Different as those two women were, Agafea Mihalovna and Katya, as his
brother Nikolay had called her, and as Levin particularly liked to call her
now, they were quite alike in this. Both knew, without a shade of doubt,
what sort of thing life was and what was death, and though neither of
them could have answered, and would even not have understood the
questions that presented themselves to Levin, both had no doubt of the
significance of this event, and were precisely alike in their way of looking
at it, which they shared with millions of people. The proof that they knew
for a certainty the nature of death lay in the fact that they knew without
a second of hesitation how to deal with the dying, and were not afraid of
them.

The attitude of the women to death, clumsily phrased here by
Levin yet understood by the reader through having witnessed what
he has, gives Levin a strength, a sense of support which instills a
new authority into all his subsequent activities. We soon become
aware of this, although Levin is perhaps even more vulnerable to the
shrewd thrusts of his half-brother Sergey. This is because Levin's
reactions to people and circumstances are more direct than Sergey's,
who only selects out of experience what is useful for his purposes
and is blind to the rest. Sergey, the modern intellectual, is by the
end a sadder figure, perhaps, even than Anna Karenina — who has at
least lived. One is impelled to phrase judgements like this because
the novel has qualities of life itself. The reader makes personal
decisions over his attitude to the characters. He is made to feel that
such decisions are his own rather than the author's. The sadness
evoked by the thought of Sergey comes largely from memories of
the failure of his love affair with Varenka, and the failure of his book
— the only child he is likely to have. The latter thought is evidently
Tolstoy's, though it seems to be ours. Again it is a thought vulner-

able to the Oblonsky criticism 'but all that's as old as the hills!'
The same criticism can be levelled at everything in *Anna Karenina*.
That, paradoxically, is its greatness.

Levin's efforts to transcend the life he is born to often result in
mistakes causing distress to himself and sometimes to his wife.
He is constantly trying to get further than his abilities allow. Yet it is
this energy, this eagerness to grow and develop, the kind of hope
that Levin puts into his life, which makes him so delightful. His
energies are constantly exploding in all directions. Levin comes
home after a discussion with fellow-landowners on the problems of
running an estate – 'all was blended in a sense of inward turmoil
and anticipation of some solution near at hand'. There is a willingness, even eagerness, on Levin's part to change his whole way of
life from moment to moment. He does not day-dream; he seriously
sets about putting his dreams into practice – like Pierre in *War and
Peace* – and though sometimes the effects are amusing, one's respect
for Levin's courage grows. His ideas have no permanent value in
themselves; they are important because they are Levin's ideas, part
of his experience. 'This idea threw Levin into great excitement. He
did not sleep half the night, thinking over in detail the putting of his
idea into practice.'

We appear to have been given the whole of Levin's experience in
the years shortly before and after marriage. His married life is not an
idealisation any more than his working life is. The house of Levin and
Kitty, like that of Natasha and Pierre, is simply 'home'. It inevitably
looks better from a distance than near at hand, but it would be
terrible to lose. 'At our place . . . all comers may have as much as
they can eat', states Levin's coachman from the top of his battered
carriage as he drives away from Vronsky's palatial but uninviting
establishment.

Levin, seen through the eyes of strangers, is a particularly fine
example of a Russian country gentleman; he makes people feel
patriotic. To himself he often appears mean-spirited and ignoble.
At times he resentfully sees himself as a superfluous male in Kitty's
stuffy household. Kitty is not an idealisation any more than Levin
is. One was becoming a little bored with her just before her
magnificent behaviour during Nikolay's illness. She had never given
any sign of being capable of heroism before. But there is no doubt
that she was heroic here, and Tolstoy is a great admirer of heroism,
of the reservoir of strength that there is in human nature. 'She

showed that alertness, that swiftness of reflection which comes out
in men before a battle, in conflict, in the dangerous and decisive
moments of life.' In some respects she has much in common with
the later Natasha Rostov. In every-day life she can be as irritating
too. Her feminine chatter, 'Aline-Nadine' as the old Prince calls it,
bores her menfolk, and she fritters away Levin's time and energy
before he learns to mark out an area of his life apart from her. She
is not much good as an intellectual companion. This exasperates
Levin at times. But she is an able manager of the household and,
like Dolly, an excellent mother.

Soon Levin discovers more in Kitty than he has hoped for, after
the disappointment of his exorbitant expectations from marriage.
She is fairly intelligent, even though she does not read much, and
she shows in innumerable ways that she is the product of fine
breeding – the daughter of 'an old, noble, cultivated and honourable
family'. Kitty is a member of Levin's own circle of society, with an
undemonstrative pride in her caste, and shares all the ideals and
assumptions which decide Levin's conduct. Her interest in Vronsky
reflected a temporary curiosity about someone from outside the
world she was brought up in. Levin saw it as an insult not only to
himself but to the sort of people he admires.

'You consider Vronsky an aristocrat, but I don't. A man whose father
crawled up from nothing at all by intrigue, and whose mother – God
knows whom she wasn't mixed up with . . . No, excuse me, but I consider
myself aristocratic, and people like me, who can point back in the past
to three or four honourable generations of their family, of the highest
breeding (talent and intellect, of course that's another matter), and have
never curried favour with anyone, never depended on anyone for anything,
like my father and my grandfather. And I know many such.'

Levin and Kitty embody ideals which Tolstoy thinks are in danger
of dwindling away. It is a triumph of art that Tolstoy does not
idealise Levin and Kitty, does not allow his very natural sympathy
with them to run away with him.

There is an important truth in Kitty's reassurance to Levin just
before their marriage – 'She told him that she loved him because she
understood him completely, because she knew what he would like,
and because everything he liked was good. And this seemed to him
perfectly clear.' As usual in Tolstoy, the context supplies apparently
trite statements with a new depth.

Levin suffers suicidal depression during what ought to be the happiest period of his life, a time of intensive activity, following the birth of a son. The allusions to suicide are matter-of-fact and quietly convincing. Levin's despair arises unexpectedly, just when all the practical details of his life have been settled for ever.

To live the same family life as his fathers and forefathers – that is, in the same conditions of culture – and to bring up his children in the same, was incontestably necessary . . . And all this filled up the whole of Levin's life, which had no meaning at all for him, when he began to think.

He feels cut off from his wife because she has not had his formal education. He cannot talk to her father, Prince Shtcherbatsky, because the questioning of religion which is going on is peculiar to the younger generation. Levin finally sets aside his education as he has already set aside the careers it opened up for him.

The physical organisation, its decay, the indestructibility of matter, the law of the conservation of energy, evolution, were the words which usurped the place of his old belief. These words and the ideas associated with them were very well for intellectual purposes. But for life they yielded nothing.

Levin is able to come to his personal solution through living an isolated life surrounded by peasants leading the most elementary lives. He discovers that they are guided in their better moments by the same principles which guide him, by a knowledge of the difference between right and wrong. This knowledge even Sergey, the most highly educated man of Levin's acquaintance, holds in common with them.

Sergey at this time is much taken up with the Pan-Slavic movement. Prince Shtcherbatsky asks him whom he wants the Russians to fight. They are eating honey near Levin's beehives; a bee has got trapped in Sergey's honey. ' "With the Turks," Sergey Ivanovitch answered, smiling serenely, as he extricated the bee, dark with honey and helplessly kicking, and put it with the knife on a stout aspen leaf.' Tolstoy associates the present aggressiveness of Russia with the desire of those who hold power to make their lives significant ones. One remembers the image in *War and Peace* of Moscow as a huge beehive ransacked by Napoleon. Sergey's decision to inflict this on a foreign nation contrasts with his natural instinct to save the life of a mere bee.

Levin resolves with enviable ease the malaise so many of his contemporaries share. He rediscovers God, and there he is left, having achieved in all departments the fullest measure of happiness possible for him. He tells himself in the last sentence of the novel –

... 'there will be still the same wall between the holy of holies of my soul and other people, even my wife; I shall still go on scolding her for my own terror, and being remorseful for it; I shall still be as unable to understand with my reason why I pray, and I shall still go on praying; but my life now, my whole life apart from anything that can happen to me, every minute of it is no more meaningless, as it was before, but it has the positive meaning of goodness, which I have the power to put into it.'

Among the Levins for at least one further generation all is safe.

Levin perhaps ascribes too large a measure of virtue to his peasants. There was, after all, the peasant girl whom Dolly met on her journey to visit Anna.

'I had a girl baby, but God set me free, I buried her last Lent.'

'Well, did you grieve very much for her?' asked Darya Alexandrovna.

'Why grieve? The old man has grandchildren enough as it is. It was only trouble. No working, nor nothing. Only a tie.'[1]

This answer had struck Darya Alexandrovna as revolting in spite of the good-natured and pleasing face of the young woman; but now she could not help recalling these words. In those cynical words there was indeed a grain of truth.

'Yes, altogether,' thought Darya Alexandrovna, looking back over her whole existence during those fifteen years of her married life, 'pregnancy, sickness, mental incapacity, indifference to everything, and most of all – hideousness. Kitty, young and pretty as she is, even Kitty has lost her looks; and I when I'm with child become hideous, I know it ... fearful pains ...' And there rose again before her imagination ... the death of her last little baby ... '... what's it for? What is to come of it all? ... At the very best they'll simply be decent people. That's all I can hope for. And to gain simply that – what agonies, what toil! ... One's whole life ruined! ... they attack Anna ... How is she to blame? She wants to live.'

Levin apparently has never been privileged with this kind of confidence from a peasant. This truth is held in balance with Levin's truth, and both are partial truths within the novel.

'Yes, the one unmistakable, incontestable manifestation of the Divinity – the law of right and wrong, which has come into the world by revelation, and which I feel in myself, and in the recognition of which ... I am made one with other men in one body of believers'.

[1] See Chekhov's *Peasants*.

Levin is given the last word because Tolstoy wishes this could be the last word; but his novel has shown that there is no such thing as a last word about anything. Levin's mood at the end rings true because it is given a context, because it is Levin's, not Tolstoy's.

Levin hated the mental activity which went on in the advanced Moscow circles which his half-brother frequented. He found that a surfeit of intellectual conversation depressed him and induced a state of nervous irritation. He needed to go away to collect his thoughts, and there seemed nowhere to go while he was in town.

Metrov introduced Levin to the chairman[1] with whom he was talking of the political news. Metrov told the chairman what he had already told Levin, and Levin made the same remarks on his news that he had already made that morning, but for the sake of variety he expressed also a new opinion which had only just struck him. After that the conversation turned again on the university question.

This kind of activity is portrayed by Tolstoy in the same spirit as Chekhov will portray it later. Both are frequent satirists of the shallowness of much so-called intellectual life.

Tolstoy has prejudices, though, which Chekhov does not share. An old landowner friend talks of his land to Levin —

'. . . my son, I must tell you, has no taste for it. There's no doubt he'll be a scientific man. So there'll be no one to keep it up. And yet one does it. Here this year I've planted an orchard.'

Tolstoy foresees the situation Chekhov will deal with in *The Cherry Orchard*, but whereas Chekhov is an impartial observer of the necessary transformations societies undergo, Tolstoy cannot but be worried about them. He is perturbed by the rise of new kinds of people who are destroying in themselves and others the ancient connections between man and the land which sustains him. Ryabinin, the land speculator who cheats Stepan Arkadyevitch, is a striking contrast to Chekhov's Lopahin, the sympathetic businessman in *The Cherry Orchard*. Tolstoy's position is Levin's in the social war which is developing.

'Now the peasants about us buy land, and I don't mind that. The gentleman does nothing, while the peasant works and supplants the idle man. That's as it ought to be. And I'm glad for the peasant. But I do mind seeing the

[1] They are at a literary function.

process of impoverishment from a sort of – I don't know what to call it – innocence. Here a Polish speculator bought for half its value a magnificent estate from a young lady who lives in Nice. And there a merchant will get three acres of land, worth ten roubles, as security for the loan of one rouble.'

Of course Levin's ideas are one-sided, and he admits it. His economic theories adapted to a Russia he wishes to preserve are even more one-sided, but the considered opinions of a man like Levin are as much worth having as those of Chekhov's Lopahin. The personal sympathies of Tolstoy and Chekhov are differently orientated, but both are at pains to show that the ideas expressed in their work arise out of the lives and natures of those who hold them. Levin is upset at the sufferings caused to his own class by the social upheavals which are under way. As so often happens, it is the best in the doomed society which aids its downfall, the unpractical virtues which it has been able to afford during its long material ascendancy. In *Anna Karenina* Tolstoy has not yet arrived at the desperate extreme of seeing the refinements of living as dangerous luxuries because brutal materialism takes advantage of them. Tolstoy's hatred and fear of materialism will turn into a religious creed. He lacks moderation, but he would not be Tolstoy if he did not. Neither would Levin be Levin. His ideas cause his Moscow acquaintances to smile at him affectionately. He looks forward to a pastoral utopia. He makes a cult of contributing his physical labour to the farming of his land, but it is easy for him to do what he likes on his own property, and Tolstoy realises this painfully. Levin has a naïve outlook which Chekhov will smile at ironically when he portrays the same kind of aspiration in a very different setting. In *Three Sisters*, the idealistic pair Irina and Toozenbach find that making a cult of practical work merely lands them in a post-office and a brick factory respectively.

As one reads the episode of the provincial elections in *Anna Karenina*:

'It's a decaying institution that goes on running only by the force of inertia. Just look, the very uniforms tell you that it's an assembly of justices of the peace, permanent members of the court, and so on, but not of noblemen'

one can see that the scene is set during the period between the world of *War and Peace* – the time of Tolstoy's father – and that of

Chekhov. The activity described is muddled and contradictory. The talk, some of it intelligent and informative, is at cross purposes. Bad temper and injustice are the results. Nice people are injured by equally nice people. The situation is tense with the excitement of change, and apprehensive bewilderment in face of an unpredictable future. One thinks back to the great council of the nobility presided over by the Tsar in *War and Peace*, and one thinks ahead to the abortive ball at the Ranyevskaia mansion in Act Three of *The Cherry Orchard*.

Levin remembers a visit to the old marshal of nobility who is being ousted at the provincial elections. 'The big house with the old family furniture; the rather dirty, far from stylish, but respectful footmen, unmistakably old house serfs who had stuck to their master; the stout, good-natured wife in a cap with lace and a Turkish shawl, petting her pretty grandchild . . .' The hint of nostalgia is in place, for the situation demands it.

Contrasted with Levin's life at the end of the novel is the excitement and squalor of national politics – the current enthusiasm over Pan-Slavism. Political events provide Tolstoy with an excellent means of concluding the novel. There is the glimpse of volunteers on the railway platform with their varying selfish motives, Vronsky among them, whose sole idea now is an honourable suicide. The novel, which has brought us close to so many individual lives, ends with a panoramic portrayal of a modern nation acting as a unit. The political madness is a product of instability in each separate member of the ruling society. Modern civilisation is ugly, Tolstoy suggests, because man no longer stands in awe of something holy within himself. He has lost the respect for himself which he had when he considered himself as a special creation of God. The mentality of Prince Shtcherbatsky and Kitty will soon be lost for ever. Levin has just managed to revert to it. We, the future generations, are all now like Sergey. That is really the conclusion. The world which has destroyed Anna is Sergey's world.

'Haven't I striven, striven with all my strength, to find something to give meaning to my life? . . . What do I know? What do I want? What is there I care for?'

Chekhov will spend his artistic career facing the truth which Dolly and Anna experience. 'She wants to live.' So indeed does Sergey, and his incapacity to do so is not caused by an ignorance of the difference between right and wrong, as Tolstoy shows in this most alive of all novels. Tolstoy had to finish it as he had begun it, finding himself unable to modify it to suit his own wish to be a moral reformer. Knowledge of *A Confession* is irrelevant to an interpretation of *Anna Karenina*. In the last chapters of *Anna Karenina* one is aware of the artistic conscience staving off the effects of a cruder form of conscience, that of the moral legislator.

Tolstoy later savagely denounced the contents of *Anna Karenina*, which evidently tortured him because he was aware of their truth. He was by then trying to go further than art could take him. By the time he wrote the essay *What is Art?* he thought works of art should bring about a religious revival. He felt guilty about the questions he had failed to answer in his gigantic novels. His obsession with the plight of the vast mass of mankind made it hard for him to write more fiction. His genius, accustomed to see everything on the grand scale, had gigantically overreached itself.

Although in *What is Art?* Tolstoy looks back on *Anna Karenina* as a decadent piece of society art, it is clear that much in the essay nevertheless springs ultimately out of the experience of writing *Anna Karenina*. His basic remarks on art are perfectly relevant to it — 'We cannot fail to observe that art is one of the means of intercourse between man and man . . . by words a man transmits his thoughts to another, by art he transmits his feelings.'[1] But Tolstoy reduces such statements in the essay to blatant absurdities. He goes on to say that great works of art are only great if they are accessible and comprehensible to every single human being regardless of class or creed. This is the occasion for his dismissing among others Aeschylus, Dante, Shakespeare, Michelangelo, Bach and Beethoven, and himself as an artist, which of course does him little damage.

In spite of infuriating eccentricities Tolstoy still manages in *What is Art?* to make all the most important pronouncements on his own art. (This is why I have felt it relevant to refer to it from time to time.) He lays down two major principles. The criterion for presentation 'is not bulkiness, obscurity and complexity of form . . . but on the contrary, brevity, clearness and simplicity of expression'.[2] The business of art is 'to make that understood and felt which in the form of an argument might be incomprehensible and inaccessible'.[3]

[1] *What is Art?*, Chapter v.
[2] Ibid. Chapter xix.   [3] Ibid. Chapter x.

We are told something more important in *Anna Karenina* itself about Tolstoy's attitude to his own creation. The artist Mihailov is showing his painting of Christ before Pilate to prospective patrons –

Low as was his opinion of Golenishtchev's capacity for understanding art, trifling as was the true remark upon the fidelity of the expression of Pilate as an official, and offensive as might have seemed the utterance of so unimportant an observation while nothing was said of more serious points, Mihailov was in an ecstasy of delight at this observation. He had himself thought about Pilate's figure just what Golenishtchev said. The fact that this reflection was but one of millions of reflections, which, as Mihailov knew for certain, would be true, did not diminish for him the significance of Golenishtchev's remark . . . at once the whole of his picture lived before him in all the indescribable complexity of everything living.

7. Tolstoy's Morality in *Anna Karenina* and in *A Confession*

In *Anna Karenina* two moral attitudes are compared. Essentially they are those of Levin and of Stepan Arkadyevitch. One feels indulgent towards Stepan, but respectful towards Levin. Yet sometimes the grace with which Stepan copes with life is more effective in practice, more helpful than Levin's conscientiousness. Stepan is a social being, yet the social world he inhabits and partly creates around him has its value. He has qualities which Levin is sometimes in danger of losing through his single-minded concentration upon the essential foundations of human existence – bread and discipline. Tolstoy holds the attitudes of Stepan and Levin in balance. He certainly does not dismiss Stepan. Stepan's party, where Levin and Kitty are united, is after all at the exact centre of the novel.

The juxtaposition of two men in *War and Peace*, the man of action and the affectionate dreamer, Prince Andrew and Pierre, was a little simpler. This was fitting in a book which dealt with life on the grandest scale – the large classical patterns of human behaviour which are for ever the same. The contrast between Stepan and Levin, fundamental to the exploration of the human conscience undertaken in *Anna Karenina*, is more careful, more intricate.

The conversation near the beginning of the novel between Stepan and Levin at a Moscow restaurant is worth looking at again. Stepan, lolling back, having just impressed the waiter, says:

'. . . you're very much all of a piece. That's your strong point and your failing. You have a character that's all of a piece, and you want the whole of life to be of a piece too – but that's not how it is. You despise public official work because you want the reality to be invariably corresponding all the while with the aim – and that's not how it is. You want a man's work, too, always to have a defined aim, and love and family life always to be undivided – and that's not how it is. All the variety, all the charm, all the beauty of life is made up of light and shadow.'

Stepan is right, and his statements correct a stern single-mindedness in Levin at this point, which life itself will correct later to a certain extent. Stepan is an embodiment of earthly delight. He neither toils nor spins, yet he has his value. He is associated with the spring, the pleasure of things when they have just begun, before they have become difficult. Stepan's visit to Levin in the country a little later will coincide with the return of spring and will temporarily drive away Levin's memories of his discomfiture with Kitty. Stepan's effectiveness is always temporary, he lives in the moment, yet the description of that spring is one of the most haunting things in Tolstoy. One remembers it when one thinks of Stepan. Stepan is creative in his way. He imparts his experience of life to others.

Early on, Tolstoy elaborates the contrast between the way Stepan Arkadyevitch and Levin look at life by introducing another contrast – Levin's half-brother, Sergey. (Stepan will become a relative of Levin's too.) Levin discovers the same thing about Sergey as Kitty discovers about Varenka, and at about the same time. Levin and Kitty share a quality which Sergey lacks. Anna Karenina has it too. She recognises much of herself in Levin when they eventually meet, introduced to one another by Stepan with his characteristic social instinct, during what is to be Anna's last stay in Moscow.

'Energy rests upon love; and come as it will, there's no forcing it. I took to this child – I could not myself say why.'
And she glanced again at Levin. And her smile and her glance – all told him that it was to him only she was addressing her words, valuing his good opinion, and at the same time sure beforehand that they understood each other.
'I quite understand that,' Levin answered.

Anna recognises much of herself in Levin, but she is flirting with him. In her latest hobby she is flirting also with her earlier domestic self. Watching her bring up the little girl of a servant in preference to the unwanted daughter of Vronsky and herself, one is reminded of the painter Mihailov's reaction to Vronsky's venture as an artist. 'It seemed to him like being forced to watch someone making love to a big wax doll.' Anna's gift for life has been thwarted by Vronsky with his slight banality which is not his fault.

Levin, Kitty, Anna and Stepan are all in their separate ways creative people, all capable of adding something of their own to the life around them. But Levin, Kitty and Anna have the faculty Stepan lacks, though not necessarily to his detriment in our eyes, of directing their affections and energies upon some object.

Anna is trapped between two men, through the failure of each to supply her with a purpose in life. The first failure, that of the eight-year-long ordeal with Karenin (it is important to notice the length of that marriage), cannot be made up for by an attractive, millionaire guards officer whose first relationship this is. Vronsky clings uneasily to the necessity of maintaining his dignity as officer and gentleman in all circumstances. The most touching signs of Anna's hold over him are always the moments when his apparently impregnable dignity breaks down (after their first love-making, after the first quarrel, and on the railway platform after her death). They both become helpless and inarticulate about what exactly it is they want from life. They enter the territory Chekhov was to select as his own, the vast limbo of people who have become severed from their roots.

The essential reason for the waste of Anna's life is the artificiality of her existence. In *War and Peace* the target was Petersburg — Petersburg as opposed to Moscow — the centre of fashion and administration as opposed to the capital city and focal point of the nation. In *Anna Karenina* these contrasts are not so decisively marked as in the earlier novel, the aim being exploration rather than discovery. Levin finds Moscow life almost as distasteful as that of Petersburg or that of any other great city, and yet he will find himself respecting one Petersburg fop at least, the husband of one of Kitty's sisters the society beauty Natalie. Whole series of distinctions are made between the many products of the two places, from the Moscow intellectuals of Levin's acquaintance to the 'Seven Wonders of the World', the stars of Princess Betsy's Petersburg smart set. Tolstoy places Stepan in Moscow and means us to see him specifically as a Moscow product in contrast to Karenin who is a Petersburg product.

Karenin, Vronsky and Anna all belong to Petersburg. Anna is a high-society wife. She is looked upon as an expensive woman, a high-priced commodity. One of Vronsky's qualifications for pursuing her is that he can afford her. A contrast is pointed with the Moscow gentleman Stepan who has an easy disregard for money.

In a letter, Karenin reminds Anna of her debt to him:

'P.S. I enclose the money which may be needed for your expenses.' He read the letter through and felt pleased with it and especially that he had remembered to enclose money. He smoothed down the letter with a massive ivory knife.

Karenin's advance of money shortly before the incident of the horse-race drew blood ('nightingales, we know, can't live on fairy tales'); this should do so even more. Karenin's physical cowardice is recalled to him by the ivory paper-knife in his hand. He has been nervously toying with the idea of calling Vronsky out. He glances up at a society portrait of Anna which hangs in his study – 'the unfathomable eyes gazed ironically and insolently at him . . . the black hair and handsome white hand with one finger lifted, covered with rings.'

Three portraits of Anna are mentioned in the novel. Only one of them is the true representation – the artist Mihailov's. Those associated with Karenin and Vronsky are not. Both Karenin and Vronsky force her to be a sterile woman, in a costume of costly black lace, her small capable hands encumbered with rings. A life spent in the most fruitless activity was conjured up in the itinerary her husband mapped out for her the day she returned from her eventful trip to Moscow. The same kind of activity continues when she lives with Vronsky.

Stepan's reaction to the Karenin–Anna–Vronsky problem is delightfully simple. Shortly after Karenin informed him that Anna was unfaithful, he said: 'I don't – and never would – take on myself to judge either side, and I see no reason why our relations should be affected.' Stepan never takes it upon himself to make moral judgements, and this is why it is important that he should be present in so moral a novel. The social virtues frowned on by the puritan are given full recognition as virtues. Stepan runs off at the end of his interview with Karenin to put the finishing touches to his party, leaving us bewildered and delighted – 'putting on his coat as he went, he patted the footman on the head, chuckled, and went out.' The party is a wonderful successs. At the same time it deepens a tragedy which refined bonhomie cannot resolve. It is an arcadian moment which brings together those who are able to enjoy it, but isolates Karenin. It shows Stepan's effectiveness and also defines his limits. Stepan's way is not Tolstoy's, and Tolstoy makes it clear that, in spite of his charm, Stepan's guidance must often be rejected, though this is a great deal more difficult than the rejection of a Falstaff, for Stepan is much more attractive than Falstaff. Stepan does not understand why such suffering is caused by what could equally be the subject of a charming bedroom frolic. This is why he can be of no help to Anna.

On the day of her death, Anna places before herself the cause of her suicidal distress.

'I'm not jealous, but I'm unsatisfied ... If I could be anything but a mistress, passionately caring for nothing but his caresses; but I can't and I don't care to be anything else. And by that desire I rouse aversion in him, and he rouses fury in me, and it cannot be different ... And is there any new feeling I can awaken between Vronsky and me? Is there possible, if not happiness, some sort of ease from misery? No, no!'

Anna's feeling of degradation is understandable. But it is during such passages as these that Tolstoy causes one slight uneasiness – that the equilibrium of the novel becomes slightly precarious. Throughout, it is difficult to lose one's awareness that Anna's suicide has been prepared for from the beginning, that it is a foregone conclusion. The conclusions of all Tolstoy's future works will also be decided in advance. Tolstoy's moral censure lurks at the ready throughout *Anna Karenina*. It is not only directed against Anna's conduct towards her family, but against her succumbing to physical desire as such. This does not affect the living tissue of the novel as it grows, but the fact remains that Tolstoy's own judgement of his heroine is not necessarily our own. We are sometimes irritated with Tolstoy for an arbitrary aside, but never for any breach of faith in his presentation of what is occurring.

Anna Karenina is a novel with a moral.

Levin could not have believed three months before that after ... forming inappropriately friendly relations with a man with whom his wife had once been in love, and a still more inappropriate call upon a woman who could only be called a lost woman ... he could still go quietly to sleep.

But in spite of Levin's surprise at himself, he sympathises with both Vronsky and Anna – as Tolstoy does. There is only a short time to go before the straitness of Tolstoy's chosen pathway to a heaven upon earth will hamper his creativity, but it has not done so yet. Levin is a delicate organism, as Pierre Bezukhov was; Tolstoy himself will soon cease to be such, and so will his characters, but not yet.

When the novel began, Tolstoy inserted several solemn reflections on the vanity of the world. Of Stepan's crime against his wife, he said: 'There was no solution, but that universal solution which life gives to all questions ... he must forget himself in the dream of daily life.' Tolstoy spoke of Stepan's 'habitually dissipated mode of life', and yet immediately the irrepressible Stepan managed to disarm the disapproval of his author. So long as Tolstoy remains capable of succumbing to his affection for Stepan we are safe.

The decisiveness with which Tolstoy saw everything is the special quality of his art. His imagery is a product of this quality of decisiveness – his illustrations in bright colours which state so much, so quickly.

This child's presence called up both in Vronsky and in Anna a feeling akin to the feeling of a sailor who sees by the compass that the direction in which he is swiftly moving is far from the right one, but that to arrest his motion is not in his power . . . that to admit to himself his deviation from the right direction is the same as admitting his certain ruin.

Tolstoy loves bringing things to firm definition. He never has a blurred effect. Yet this illustration, like many others in *Anna Karenina*, registers a gradual fixing and hardening in his dealings with experience. It is a foretaste of his subsequent use of the parable to drive home lessons.

But the orderliness of Tolstoy's vision is nevertheless the fundamental ingredient of his best work. It can be seen most obviously in the arrangement of his characters. People are first introduced in pairs, and then cross-references are carefully introduced until a perfectly lucid pattern is threaded together amid intricacies which remain intricate. The novel does not form a pattern like that which the inexperienced Levin thought he saw in life at the beginning, during his argument with Stepan. Theories are always contradicted by life itself in *Anna Karenina*. Apparently secure positions have to be modified, or temporarily abandoned, and the novel remains alive to the end.

'To my mind, love . . . both the sorts of love, which you remember Plato defines in his Banquet, serve as the test of men. Some men only understand one sort, and some only the other. And those who only know the non-Platonic love have no need to talk of tragedy. In such love there can be no sort of tragedy. "I'm much obliged for the gratification, my humble respects" – that's all the tragedy. And in Platonic love there can be no tragedy, because in that love all is clear and pure, because . . .'

At that instant Levin recollected his own sins and the inner conflict he had lived through. And he added unexpectedly:

'But perhaps you are right. Very likely . . . I don't know, I don't know.'

The novel lives above all in the thoughts and words of the characters. It is a novel filled with conversations.

The central situation in *Anna Karenina* is sometimes seen as having little relevance to modern life, but this is not so. Anna is regarded by many people within the novel itself as being 'old-fashioned' in her views. She is a perennial human type. Injury sustained through having injured others is an eternal human misfortune. In the plays of Chekhov the apparent coldness, the withdrawn defensiveness of even the most attractive characters in their relations with one another is often simply a manifestation of their awareness of this burden of conscience. Strip *Anna Karenina* down to its dialogue, and the words could easily be mistaken for those of a Chekhov play.

Levin seeks answers to questions 'as to the meaning of life and death to himself, which had of late been more and more often in his mind'.

> 'I work, I want to do something, but I had forgotten it must all end; I had forgotten – death' . . . in looking upon life, he had forgotten one little fact – that death will come, and all ends; that nothing was even worth beginning . . . Yes, it was awful, but it was so.

Tolstoy once again poses the fundamental question of life, the one that includes all the others, and it is in Tolstoy's extravagant nature to be determined to solve it at last, to succeed where everyone else has failed. *A Confession* records something of his personal struggles with it. Levin's aspirations are like Tolstoy's, but Levin's solutions are recognised to be satisfactory only for himself. It is an essential duty of the artist who records life to respect the infinite variety of experience. Tolstoy is writing about somebody in many ways like himself, but more successful in his life than himself. Levin is a product of the creative imagination, whereas *A Confession* will be a direct attempt at self-analysis.

A Confession is moving but, paradoxically, it is reticent as no Tolstoy work of art is. One always knows more about artists from their works than from what they say about themselves; more is let through. In *A Confession* Tolstoy only deals with the facts he deems relevant to an account of his religious crisis. One remembers Chekhov's evocative remark about Tolstoy: 'I feel that I know him well, and that I understand every movement of his brows – and yet I love him.'[1] This suggests more about Tolstoy than all the pages of

[1] Letter to L. A. Avilov, March 1899.

A Confession, What I Believe and so on, and it is the way we know Levin. Tolstoy's wife said of Levin 'this is he, he described himself'.[1] Levin contains more of the living Tolstoy than *A Confession* does. It is significant that Lawrence, who hates the didactic Tolstoy, nevertheless uses the Levin–Kitty situation at least as much as the Anna–Vronsky one for *The Rainbow*.[2]

Tolstoy was not able to be quite like Levin, and his knowledge of this may have precipitated the crisis which is recorded in *A Confession*. In the case of Pierre Bezukhov, Tolstoy was out simply to depict a good man and was not intensely disturbed that he himself was not exactly like this. *War and Peace* was written essentially in a mood of hope; not so *Anna Karenina*. The crisis which coincides with it is reflected in it. There is tension behind the laconic account of Levin's mental sufferings near the end of the novel.

Levin, when his doubts are resolved, meditates peacefully as he looks up at the sky above his land. 'I am incontestably right when I see a solid blue dome, and more right than when I strain my eyes to see behind it.' The serenity at the end of the novel is real, even though it does not reflect the whole truth for Tolstoy himself. It forms a harmonious conclusion to Tolstoy's main artistic opus. But Tolstoy is unable to live instinctively like Levin, he must live rationally. He must have consistency and order. He must be able to state to himself exactly why he does things. An easy conscience alone is not acceptable to him. He must have clear proof that he is not deluding himself. When he decides to live as God wishes him to live he is tormented that circumstances prevent him from doing so consistently. He must give his property away, he must endanger himself by defying the authority of the State over him. Levin does not feel the need to do so much, and Tolstoy envies Levin to the same degree that Levin envies old Prince Shtcherbatsky.

'Well, what would you say about Papa?' asked Kitty. 'Is he a poor creature then, as he does nothing for the public good?'

'He? – no! But then one must have the simplicity, the straightforwardness, the goodness of your father: and I haven't got that.'

– Levin has it more than Tolstoy.

The religious troubles of Levin towards the end of *Anna Karenina*

[1] Quoted in Simmons, *Leo Tolstoy*.
[2] See the final chapter of the present book for a study of the relationship of *The Rainbow* with *Anna Karenina*.

are not extraneous to the novel, a disturbance in its natural flow. But the occasional trace of harshness in Tolstoy's attitude to Anna herself is. There is the suggestion that he has decided exactly what the woman's role in life must be, and that Anna's desertion of Karenin and Seryozha is an offence against this. A patriarchal sternness is present every now and then. Tolstoy is tempted into it as a result of his astounding successes at creating the illusion of having seen the world steadily and seen it whole. He is near convincing himself that his vision, which must necessarily be partial like that of all men, is in fact total. There is the dry, ominous note of disapproval and withdrawal. 'It was the voice of conscience telling him that what he was meaning to do was wrong' (Stepan is asking Karenin to divorce Anna). The temptation to take a decision of this sort proves irresistible occasionally. There are moments when Tolstoy deliberately shuts out experiences which have possessed him so completely that his generosity seemed endless.

In turning himself into a prophet after finishing *Anna Karenina*, Tolstoy the artist is really attempting a move to an impossibly large canvas. He desires to turn the world into a Tolstoyan masterpiece. The ambition becomes fanatical, and the signs of this are just discernible in *Anna Karenina*.

'ANNA KARENINA' AND THE ENGLISH NOVEL: A NOTE

In *Anna Karenina* people are brought to definition against one another through conversation and through their reactions to similar situations. They are constantly presented with alternative courses of action. Choices are made which narrow down inexorably for the individual each time he makes one – narrow down to none at all for Anna – choices which are the only possible ones, but all of which entail penalties of some kind.

Tolstoy's theme is always the desire of people to be better than they are, and their failure or only partial success. One is frequently reminded of George Eliot as the English parallel, contemporary with Tolstoy.

Tolstoy was especially struck with *Adam Bede*. He first read it a few years before writing *War and Peace*, and he singles it out for approval in *What is Art?* as an example of 'the highest art' – 'art transmitting the simplest feelings of common life, but such always as are accessible to all men in the whole world'. This is the virtue he primarily valued it for; though it must be admitted that by the time he writes *What is Art?* he is placing equal value on *The Christmas Carol* and *Uncle Tom's Cabin*.

Adam Bede, which deals with the temptation and weakness of a young man and woman, covers a wide area of experience and with great economy. Tolstoy might easily have chosen the same plot himself. There is the same pondering on the retribution wrong action brings with it, on the rules of conduct which always apply and which are basic to the human situation – rules which Tolstoy refers to metaphorically at the beginning of *Anna Karenina*: 'Vengeance is mine and I will repay.' Both Tolstoy and George Eliot are fascinated by the mystery of the human conscience, which they see as a constant factor even in an age of unprecedented material and intellectual upheaval.

Our deeds determine us, as much as we determine our deeds, and until we know what has been or will be the peculiar combination of outward with inward facts, which constitutes a man's critical actions, it will be better not to think ourselves wise about his character. There is a terrible coercion in our deeds . . . Europe adjusts itself to a *fait accompli*, and so does an individual character – until the placid adjustment is disturbed by a convulsive retribution. (*Adam Bede*, chapter XXIX)

George Eliot, as she develops, becomes more and more conscious of all the many contributing factors which go to make up the individual personality. She is faced with a society far more compli-cated than Tolstoy's, with centuries of vivid and multifarious intellectual life behind it, an endlessly various society in which any given individual might easily be the product of influences and traditions far different from those of his neighbours. She cannot hold on to her original simplicity for long as she probes deeper into the difficulties of living in this society. Her researches into her subject over-prepare her for her work as an artist. Her wittiest *aperçus* throw increasingly narrow beams of light upon the world. Bulstrode in *Middlemarch* succumbing to his temptation is a highly specialised case compared to Arthur Donnithorne in the earlier *Adam Bede*.

Middlemarch does not cohere as obviously as *Anna Karenina* does, and in this George Eliot is being true to her world. She could not have said 'Happy families are all alike' with the serene confidence Tolstoy said it, because the suggestive grain of truth in this would be almost impossible to discern through the demonstrable dissimilarities of all her families to one another – except for the pastoral ones, which become products of a Londoner's nostalgia. Few characters in George Eliot can possess Tolstoy's or, for that matter, Shakespeare's, quality of representativeness, of directly perceivable common humanity, of being everyman or everywoman. It is a quality George Eliot loses early, as multiplying experiences press in upon her. The same thing happens to Henry James in treating the polite society of the Western world.

One can see why 'the Russians' produced such a liberating effect on D. H. Lawrence with his determination to give the English novel a fresh start. By 'the Russians' he demonstrably meant Tolstoy in particular.

Tolstoy founds his work upon the great elementary conditions of human life which will always be the same. The place of man in the natural world, the transitions from youth to age, the passing generations, birth, marriage and death, the interconnection between the life of the country and of the town and city – Tolstoy is constantly reminding us of these lest we should lose sight of them amid the minutiae of special moral and social questions which he raises. Everything rests upon the most stable foundation. Tolstoy has a lordly contempt for quibbling. The function of the Levin side of *Anna Karenina* is to form the foundation upon which all else rests. It is not a sub-plot in the ordinary way, for in a sense it is larger than the main structure. It is the inspiration behind Lawrence's *The Rainbow*.

8. Resurrection and Hadji Murad

Tolstoy completed *Resurrection* in 1899, at the age of seventy-one. He had written it on and off over a period of ten years, but frequently abandoned it in the interests of social work. He finally put his energies into the novel in a burst of creative activity during his seventieth year.

Tolstoy, at the time he embarked on *Resurrection*, told himself in his diary, 'We search for mind, powers, goodness, perfection in all these, but perfection is not given to man in anything',[1] but he could never reconcile himself to this. In *Resurrection* Tolstoy's bitterness at the unperfectibility of man overflows, so that there is not a single attractive personality in the book.

The novel is an indictment of the Russian governing class and the horrifying cruelty with which it seeks to preserve itself in a changing world. Prince Nekhludoff's guilt towards Katusha, the servant girl turned prostitute, leads him to recognise the guilt of the privileged classes towards the oppressed millions who maintain them in luxury. Before accompanying Katusha to Siberia, he gives his peasants some of his land. But, as in all competent tracts, the plot has an air of hard-headed realism – a travesty of the realism Tolstoy once possessed. Nekhludoff does not give away all his land, he does not become ostracised by the best society, where he is indulgently regarded as an enthusiastic eccentric, irritating but good. Nor does he have to marry Katusha, who rejects him because she knows he does not love her. One's interest awakens briefly at this, but this kind of reality threatens to destroy the symmetry of the tract and is quickly suppressed. Another man is at hand who loves Katusha 'platonically', and her first duty is to him.

So Nekhludoff, having investigated the darkest corners of his society, is a wiser man at the end, with a first-hand knowledge of judicial and police methods, of the miseries of the poor, and of convicted criminals. He is equipped to act rightly during the rest of his life.

[1] Simmons, *Leo Tolstoy*.

Tolstoy does not say what Nekhludoff will do next, because he does not know. There is despair behind Tolstoy's apparent self-assurance. He has once again turned to art to clarify his experience of life. This time, like a mirror which always tells the truth, it has revealed Tolstoy's opinionated ignorance – as it once revealed his knowledge. One remembers a remark Chekhov made in 1902 –

'Art does not tolerate a lie ... you can deceive men as much as you like and you can deceive even God himself – such cases have been known – but you cannot practise deception in art.'[1]

Tolstoy discovers virtue in what looks very much like eccentricity, and self-interest in what could equally be seen as generosity in face of Nekhludoff's provoking behaviour. Tolstoy interprets what he sees as he wishes to interpret it.

The novel stops abruptly. Tolstoy wrote in his diary after writing Resurrection: 'I want terribly to write ... an epic continuation of Resurrection; the peasant life of Nekhludoff ...' The desire to experience this life for himself, and tell others about it, leads to Tolstoy's final rejection of the world and its sins, leads to his flight from home, and his death on the railway journey – that favourite symbol in his art of escape with no destination.

Resurrection created great excitement when it was first published because of its brave exposure of the Russian judicial system. The plot serves to string together a series of interviews between Nekhludoff and the various beneficiaries and victims of the prevailing order of things. Even Nekhludoff's relations with Katusha consist almost entirely of a series of interviews with her in jail. Where Nekhludoff is not present the characters become sentimentalised, the realistically observed squalor of prison life merely accentuating the weakness of the characterisation. Sentimentality is a sure sign of ignorance. Disgusted with himself and the world he knows, Tolstoy attempts to explore a world he does not know and can never know. He attempts to write for the masses about the masses. In order to appeal to everybody, to be 'universal', art must be based on first-hand knowledge. Tolstoy ceased to write 'universal art' when he sat down deliberately to write it.

He did not realise that a real Katusha would have more in common with an Anna Karenina or a Kitty Levin than with the

---

[1] Chekhov's conversation with the student Tikhonov as quoted in D. Magarshack, Chekhov: A Life (London, 1952).

heroine of *Resurrection*. By contrast, Chekhov's writing about the depressed classes is far superior because he knows enough about them to be able to place himself in their situation. Chekhov discovers versions of the same difficulties, the same unanswerable questions in their lives as in his own.

Resurrection is a novel which never gets under way because it is about a man who separates himself from others through digust at their weakness. Nekhludoff never becomes sufficiently involved with anybody for the novel to begin. He is a helpless witness of human bestiality and degradation, which tortures him.

The first fifth of the novel is taken up by the trial of Katusha. This comes as a surprise because one has never known Tolstoy to be so diffuse. The length of the episode suggests that the overall project for the novel was a large one. Tolstoy casts about in his usual way for the clues which will set a third great masterpiece surging forward on its purposeful way. He does not find them or, rather, he thinks he has found them, but can do nothing with them. The novel is going to be about the struggle between good and evil in man. Tolstoy reviews Nekhludoff's past life:

In Nekhludoff, as in every man, there were two beings: one the spiritual, seeking only that kind of happiness for himself which should tend towards the happiness of all; the other, the animal man, seeking only his own happiness, and ready to sacrifice to it the happiness of the rest of the world.

This belief in the feasibility of separating good from evil is acted on throughout.

The construction of the novel quickly becomes mechanical. Nekhludoff's defeat of 'the animal man' within him proceeds by stages – 'Fear of the disgrace that would befall him . . . This fear was, *during this first period*,[1] stronger than all else.' Nekhludoff plods steadily forward, getting better in obedience to his author's demands. Tolstoy would perhaps like Nekhludoff to be more volatile.

We may say of a man that he is more often kind than cruel, oftener wise than stupid, oftener energetic than apathetic, or the reverse; but it would be false to say of one man that he is kind and wise, of another that he is wicked and foolish. And yet we always classify mankind in this way. And this is untrue. Men are like rivers; the water is the same in each, and alike in all; but every river is narrow here, is more rapid there, here slower, there broader . . .

[1] My italics.

The air of beneficent large-mindedness with which Tolstoy tries occasionally to lighten the novel is perhaps the most dispiriting aspect of it. This is what Tolstoyan reasonableness has changed into.

Chekhov's concise summing-up on *Resurrection* is unquestionably the right one:

To write and write, and then suddenly to pile everything upon a text from the Gospels – this is entirely too theological. To solve everything by a text from the Gospels – it is just as arbitrary as to divide prisoners into five classes.[1]

The last remark is a reference to this passage in *Resurrection* – 'From his personal relations with the prisoners, from notes by some of those in confinement, and by questioning the advocate and the prison priest, Nekhludoff came to the conclusion that the convicts, the so-called criminals, could be divided into five classes.' – 'Why five and not ten?' asks Chekhov. 'I am sick of theorising of all sorts'.[2] *Resurrection*, as Chekhov well knows, is a product of a period of political upheaval and fanaticism. It is of Chekhov's time and deals with a situation into which he himself is attempting to introduce a measure of good sense and restraint. He wishes to prevent people from attaching labels to one another and refusing to understand one another. It is useless to meet fanaticism with fanaticism. The ageing Tolstoy cannot see this, imprisoned as he has become within the collapsing old order which he has grown to hate but which holds him fast. Chekhov is in his generation the more important of the two, and he knows it.

It seems to me that the writer of fiction should not try to solve such questions as those of God, pessimism, etc. His business is but to describe those who have been speaking or thinking about God and pessimism, how, and under what circumstances . . . My business is . . . to be able to distinguish between important and unimportant statements, to be able to illuminate the characters and speak their language.[3]

Ironically, the inspiration behind these statements is derived, among

---

[1] Letter to M. O. Menshikov, January 1900. In *A. Chekhov, Letters on the Short Story, the Drama and Other Literary Topics*, ed. Louis S. Friedland (London, 1965). All quotations from Chekhov's letters are out of this collection, unless otherwise stated.

[2] Letter to A. S. Souvorin, March 1894.

[3] Letter to Souvorin, May 1888.

other things, from the great masterpieces of Russian literature written
by Tolstoy.

Tolstoy wrote the short novel *Hadji Murad* at intervals between 1896
and 1904. He regarded it rather shamefacedly as a private recreation,
apart from his moral teaching. He first had the idea for it during a
period of difficulty in the laborious process of constructing *Resurrection*. The bigger novel cost him enormous pains by comparison,
probably because of the lack of artistic satisfaction to be derived
from it. He produced *Hadji Murad* for reasons other than a sense of
mission.

In his biography of Tolstoy, Ernest Simmons tells how a guest at
Yasnaya Polyana read out parts of *Hadji Murad* one day to others.
Tolstoy wandered in and out, unable to tear himself away. Finally he
tried to stop the reading of such rubbish. 'If it is so, why did you
write it?' someone said. 'But it's not finished yet', replied Tolstoy
rather inconsistently. Even without this hint one could immediately
perceive the devoted care with which Tolstoy worked over the story.
It is sparse, apparently effortless and, miraculously, some of the
vitality of *War and Peace* is back again. In the passages describing the
monstrous Tsar Nicolas I at council and the ferocious last fight of
Hadji Murad it is as though Tolstoy has become young again. At the
end of his life Tolstoy is perhaps remembering what he has thrown
away. Certainly nobody else has ever written quite like this.

Hadji Murad, a dangerous enemy of Russia in the Caucasus,
breaks all the five commandments of Christ's teaching as elucidated
by Tolstoy, and it is as though Tolstoy is taking a fierce delight in
doing so too – has been using this story as a sort of safety valve. It
stands alone among the works of his last thirty years, and one
wishes it did not.

The code of Hadji Murad is a warrior code, and his conscience is
very different from a Christian conscience. His virtues are according
to his code, and he suffers remorse according to it too. His ideas have
formed him into what he is. The moral questions this gives rise to
seem irrelevant when one is face to face with Hadji Murad himself.
Tolstoy admires his personal magnificence. He is admired precisely
because of his un-Christian separateness. His religion is personal
pride – his strength and his honour as the warrior God has made. It
is impossible to judge Murad by any other code than his own.

Within this story, Tolstoy is of Hadji Murad's party and delights to be so in imagination. The story is really an object lesson in the impossibility of judging others. Hadji Murad abandons his family for the sake of getting Russian help to conduct a blood feud in which his honour is at stake. Oddly enough, the young Tolstoy who sought adventure in the Caucasus found it easier to judge Hadji Murad than the old one does. Tolstoy wrote in 1851, after having seen Hadji Murad – 'he was the leading dare-devil and "brave" of all Circassia, but has been led to commit a mean action'. The old Tolstoy, who has become inured to judging everyone, dividing the good from the bad, stops short when he recalls Hadji Murad. He sees the possibility of being wrong.

The story was suggested to Tolstoy by an experience he noted in his diary.

Yesterday I walked along a fallow, re-ploughed field of black earth. As far as the eye could reach, there was nothing but black earth – not one green blade of grass; and there on the edge of the dusty grey road grew a bush of burdock.

The plant is badly broken but still alive. 'It reminded me of Hadji Murad. I want to write. Life asserts itself to the very end, and here in the midst of this whole field it has somehow asserted itself.'[1] At the beginning of Hadji Murad the narrator of the story recounts a similar experience. Another memory is added also. It is spring, and a Tartar thistle is seen among a vast profusion of meadow flowers. The story-teller plucks many of the flowers; then he tries to pluck the thistle.

But this proved a very difficult task. Not only did the stalk prick on every side – even through the handkerchief I wrapped round my hand – but it was so tough that I had to struggle with it for nearly five minutes, breaking the fibres one by one; and when I had at last plucked it, the stalk was all frayed and the flower itself no longer seemed so fresh and beautiful. Moreover, owing to its coarseness and stiffness, it did not seem in place among the delicate blossoms of my nosegay.

This imagery has the deceptive simplicity of Tolstoy at his best. By contrast, the sort of image which appears in his social-religious art is an insult to the intelligence – the obnoxious parable of the pump-handle in A Confession, for instance, the simplicity of which deceives

[1] Simmons, Leo Tolstoy.

nobody except Tolstoy. 'If he moves the handle he will understand that it works a pump, that the pump draws water and that the water irrigates the garden beds.' Tolstoy's demand for answers to unanswerable questions has resulted in a conception of God as mechanic ('His soul needed cleansing as a watch does' – *Resurrection*), but the artist in him is in constant revolt. The ignoble struggle with the Tartar thistle suggests what Tolstoy has been doing to his later art. He has wished to force life to submit to his improvements, instead of regarding it with respect, especially the thorns, and has seen the latter as a personal challenge to himself. One must accept the necessary distance between oneself and others as well as rejoice in the measure of nearness, the avenues of communication which exist.

In *Hadji Murad* Tolstoy allows free play to his responsiveness to living situations. He forgets for the last time the rules he commands everyone to observe in order to bring about the kingdom of heaven.

CHEKHOV: THE STORIES

9. The Party: A Prelude

The Party, though not a particularly early work, is Chekhov's first considerable artistic success. It is an account of the tensions which build up during the course of one day in an apparently happy household. At the end, the lady of the house loses the child she is bearing. The subject of the story is the tragedy people generate for themselves, which they cannot prevent but for which they suffer the burden of responsibility.

The Party is full of echoes from Anna Karenina – like other stories written at this time when Chekhov is beginning to discover himself as a writer. It awakens memories of the painful quarrels between men and women in Anna Karenina, and of the baffled hatred for life of Anna at the end. Both Tolstoy and Chekhov set themselves as artists to acquire and impart understanding. Their aim is to see clearly.

When the story opens a house party has been going on for many hours. It is hot, thundery weather; the hostess, whose husband's name-day it is, escapes briefly into the garden. She is filled with nervous irritation, worn out by the strain of entertaining many people. The quiet she has been used to in the last months is shattered. She recaptures it in the garden but is almost at once the involuntary witness of a conversation between her husband and a young girl, one of the guests. Largely because of her exhaustion, the scene mortifies her. She expresses her feelings childishly, in a manner reminiscent of Tolstoy's characters.

She could understand that her husband was worried, dissatisfied with himself and ashamed, and when people are ashamed they hold aloof, above all from those nearest to them, and are unreserved with strangers; she could understand, also, that she had nothing to fear from Lubotchka, or from those women who were now drinking coffee indoors. But everything in general was terrible, incomprehensible . . .

'He has no right to do it!' she muttered, trying to formulate her jealousy and her vexation with her husband. 'He has no right at all. I will tell him so plainly!'[1]

But she does not, for she cannot put her disquiet into words.

[1] All the quotations from Chekhov's stories will be from Constance Garnett's translation.

Her rage builds up over the day. Soon she finds herself hating her husband for his self-confident bearing, which she despises because she knows that it is affected to deceive others. Only at the end – at the moment of disaster – will she remember that she is in love. They both are, but their own inner lives are more vivid to them than one another's. They are clumsy with each other. The wife's anger cannot be put into words for it is largely the product of her physical condition; and this is something she inevitably will not recognise. What is her rage about? That is the worst of it, and makes it dangerous. The lack of clarity in her emotions is unacceptable to her, an irritant which drives her to near hysteria, for her attempts to analyse her feelings merely add confusion. Her feelings have no ready outlet largely because she is a highly intelligent, educated woman. Chekhov leaves us in no doubt about this as he follows her through the tormenting day. Her education[1] makes her helpless because it hampers her in expressing her emotions freely.

Chekhov follows his heroine's sensations throughout her drama, never seeming to lose the almost physical connection he possesses with her. Within an incredibly short space he has captured a total experience lasting many hours. The story is like a sequence of short chapters in a Tolstoy novel.

The secret lies in the accurate timing of each stage of the heroine's inner drama. There are sharply defined stages in the course of the day, points of no return as her state deteriorates. The exertion of pouring out tea for a large boisterous group of guests on an improvised river-expedition almost results in her nerve breaking. The innocuous tea party turns into brutal hard labour, the guests into callous taskmasters.

Finally the day is over and she can relax, but the hoped-for relaxation when she goes to bed does not come. Her husband is to blame for this. He is in no mood to try to understand what his wife wants from him.

'We all have our personal life, every one of us, and we are bound to have our secrets.'

---

[1] 'For philosophy you must apply to my wife. She has been at university lectures and knows all your Schopenhauers and Proudhons by heart . . .' Olga Mihalovna felt bored again. She walked again along a little path by apple and pear trees, and looked again as though she was on some very important errand.

He is ashamed of some undignified mistake he has recently made. His need to save face and lick his wounds in private is sympathised with by his wife in theory, but she cannot accept it in fact. The awareness that an episode in his 'personal life' was his talk with the young girl earlier in the day destroys her ability to think herself into his masculine world. With devastating frankness, she informs him of the hatred she is feeling for him, and he leaves the room. It is a passage which is related to the domestic quarrel at the beginning of *Anna Karenina*, and also to the later ones between Anna and Vronsky. In each case the woman is acutely aware of the indignity which her dependent position involves her in.

For some minutes she remained silent, with her mouth open, trembling all over and looking at the door by which her husband had gone out, and trying to understand what it meant . . . Olga Mihalovna remembered her cousin, a lively young officer, who often used to tell her, laughing, that when 'his spouse nagged at him' at night, he usually picked up his pillow and went whistling to spend the night in his study, leaving his wife in a foolish and ridiculous position.

At this moment of humiliation, which is not perceived by the man responsible because it is outside his own experience, she takes the one course which seems open to her. She uses her ultimate weapon — a carefully aimed insult which instantly destroys for ever the trust that there is between them. She realises this immediately. The disaster which she has feared all day has at last occurred as if by some sinister magic, and results in the loss of the child she is bearing. In fact her instinctive nervousness about the security of the child has led her to seek out and in the end bring about what has most terrified her.

There has been a touch of satire in her attitude towards herself right up to the climactic moment, yet this has prevented nothing.

'You hate me because I am richer than you! You will never forgive me for that and will always be lying to me!' ('Feminine logic!' flashed through her mind . . .)

The husband perceives the cause of the outburst and the extent of his own responsibility for it, yet this does not mitigate the shock he receives. He understands that she does not mean what she says, and yet he will never be able to convince himself of this. They both understand exactly what has happened, yet after all the suffering, all the mutual forgiveness and demonstrations of affection the story ends as follows:

'Olya,' he said, wringing his hands, big tears suddenly dropping from his eyes. 'Olya, I don't care about your property . . . Why didn't we take care of our child? Oh, it's no good talking!'

Chekhov does not believe in the efficacy of 'talking things through'.

The tragedy is not final. Nothing is in Chekhov. The marriage is likely to continue and even to be a reasonably successful one, for the couple are clearly well-matched, knowledgeable about one another, and generous. Chekhov perceives that human freedom is limited because the means of communication between people are constantly breaking down in unexpected ways. This is the perception which dominates Chekhov's art. It has evidently been the preoccupation determining the way he has interpreted Tolstoy's *Anna Karenina*. It has been a fruitful interpretation.

Chekhov's conception of art is an extension in one direction of Tolstoy's – an aid to communication – but Chekhov will become increasingly less sanguine than Tolstoy. Communication seems less and less easy to him. Eventually, as a writer of plays, he will disappear behind the backdrop, leaving his characters to be interpreted by others. In *The Party* we are in a world that looks very like Tolstoy's world still. But this only adds to our uneasiness when we realise that it is not Tolstoy's world at all. It is the same world only a generation later, yet the difference is crucial for Chekhov belongs to our time. His perception is already our perception.

10. Chekhov and the Later Tolstoy
Studies in Death

The Death of Ivan Ilych was written in 1886, *A Dreary Story* in 1889. The eclipse of Tolstoy as a major artist and the achievement of major status by Chekhov are marked by these two stories, each of them about death.

The Death of Ivan Ilych comes after the crisis in Tolstoy's life, when the terrible question facing him wherever he turned, 'Is there any meaning in my life that the inevitable death awaiting me does not destroy?'[1] had almost driven him to suicide. The personal crisis had started while Tolstoy was finishing *Anna Karenina*. Levin's return to a life of simple religious faith, to the consciousness of being in the hands of a guiding divinity, is an early product of it. But, as Tolstoy shows, Levin is well-equipped by circumstance and personality to see life so clearly. He has the last word in the novel, and Tolstoy wishes that this could be the last word.

'. . . my whole life, independently of anything that may happen to me, is every moment of it no longer meaningless as it was before, but has an unquestionable meaning of goodness with which I have the power to invest it.'

Levin is privileged to be able to see his life like this. He is fortunate to be the one intellectual in his neighbourhood. By remaining upon his estate, he will always receive his less sanguine Moscow half-brother upon his own home ground from now on.

As a whole, *Anna Karenina* demonstrated that there is no such thing as a last word about anything. Levin's final words rang true because they had a convincing context. One certainly cannot imagine that the sordid end of the suburban Ivan Ilych could be lighted with the same kind of Christian illumination which a Levin might look forward to. It is too late in the day to try to convince people that they may sprout wings on their deathbeds, and this is what Tolstoy suddenly does. He is no longer grasping the world to him, but

[1] *A Confession.*

rather a shrunken replica of it which he can domineer over. He will write *The Kreutzer Sonata* to show what threatens those who do not conform to his decrees on how men and women must live together. He will sneer at Shakespeare for creating people who are impossibilities in the Tolstoy universe.

Tolstoy's persistent questions about the meaning of life and the purpose of art are the more disturbing because the answers he foists on one with an air of triumph are unacceptable. They were questions which he made it impossible to evade. They were the statement on Russia's behalf of that enormous late nineteenth-century collapse of confidence, the apparently irreparable loss of the old beliefs, the inexorable advance of a new world to grow accustomed to – that of the approaching twentieth century. A Russian writer who took himself as seriously as Chekhov did, could not but tackle the great question so bluntly stated by Tolstoy – 'What is life for?' – and work out his attitude to it, and try to make a new start in art at the point where Tolstoy had so frighteningly broken down. Chekhov's nightmare throughout his life was Tolstoy's. Perhaps art was a useless activity, perhaps it was meaningless and worthless, merely telling people what they knew already or else did not need to know anyway. The great obstacles Tolstoy was placing in the path of contemporary Russian artists had somehow to be surmounted. This is why Chekhov had to write his story about the way a contemporary might really experience death. *A Dreary Story* is Chekhov's answer to the Tolstoy contemporary with himself. Whether or not it was more specifically his answer to *The Death of Ivan Ilych* does not really matter, though it seems likely. When Chekhov wrote *A Dreary Story* Tolstoy had marked out his new course with such things as *A Confession, A Union of the Four Gospels, What I Believe, What then Must We Do?* – very little creative work as yet, other than *The Death of Ivan Ilych*. Certainly *A Dreary Story* challenges comparison with *The Death of Ivan Ilych*, and when Chekhov's story appeared reviewers referred to Tolstoy's story as a matter of course.

In *The Death of Ivan Ilych* Tolstoy's customary power has turned into something that feels very like bullying. Tolstoy has secretly lost his pride in himself, his faith in his own strength. His desire to fill us with the fear of death is a desire to find companionship in his own fear.

The Death of Ivan Ilych was the first substantial work of art after the completion of *Anna Karenina* ten years before, and the critics said of Tolstoy: 'At last his train has come out of its tunnel.' The intensely observing eye is still at work, but the scope of its vision is narrowed. Tolstoy is now suspicious, disapproving; he wishes to remove what disturbs him.

At the beginning of the story, Ivan Ilych's 'friends' enter the house in which his dead body lies.

... near the cloak-stand was a coffin-lid covered with cloth of gold, ornamented with gold cord and tassels, that had been polished up with metal powder.

That last phrase strikes a note one is not prepared for if one goes on to the story after reading *Anna Karenina*, but which one will hear continuously from now on. In the past, Tolstoy selected details in order to widen one's vision. Here he selects his details in order to narrow it down. At first it seems that, as before, Tolstoy wishes us to look at life through fresh eyes, to take a second look at obvious facts. But the result is unexpected: a growing sense of constraint, of being on a conducted tour – a sense that we are being pushed in a pre-selected direction, that our freedom of movement is being obstructed.

There is the amusing episode at the beginning when a visitor to the house of the deceased Ivan Ilych condoles with the widow whilst struggling with a collapsible and squeaky pouffe on which he has unluckily sat down. One wonders why the interjections of the pouffe during the conversation fail to produce the intended Dickensian effect. Dickens's satirical set pieces where he rings the changes on a single image are great dissipations of anger into laughter. Here the anger is not transformed in this way. Rather, it is nurtured and fostered by means of the repetitions. They have a nagging quality. Tolstoy chills one's sympathetic laughter.

... the struggle with the pouffe had cooled Peter Ivanovich's emotions and he sat there with a sullen look on his face.

Tolstoy is on the hunt for misdemeanours. Having decided to espouse a theological system of sin and repentance, he takes a poor view of human nature. One will be interested in Ivan Ilych only as 'the average man' confronted with death – not as a various and individual personality. Tolstoy represents as normal Ivan Ilych's coldness towards those nearest him, the selfishness which motivates

even his last-minute utterance of the routine passwords to Heaven –
his 'forgiveness' of others.

Tolstoy's Faustian desire to search out the secrets of the universe
has resulted in anticlimax. He has decided that the miseries of
human life are caused by sin against divine commands. His
ambition has led to an equally Faustian diminution in his own
stature. Tolstoy now pries and snoops, searching for the sins which
account for the terrors of human existence and for its final terror.
A visitor to the house of mourning bumps into Ivan Ilych's son –
'His tear-stained eyes had in them the look that is seen in the eyes of
boys of thirteen or fourteen who are not pure-minded . . . he
scowled morosely and shamefacedly.' Tolstoy's determination to
find a logical explanation for the horrors of death has led him to
commit unexpected acts of meanness.

Yet *The Death of Ivan Ilych* maintains its hold on the reader to the
end, in spite of the many annoyances on the way. And the reason is
simply the success with which Ivan Ilych's mortal illness is described. Physical fear rules Ivan Ilych in his last months – a fear
which Tolstoy is not ashamed to show that he shares. He puts the
whole of himself into his work with total lack of inhibition. This
unconcern with decorum, ignorance even of the need to conceal
himself behind his personae, accounts for the rare boldness, the
brave assurance of his great art – and also the gross and palpable
absurdities in his later writing. Artists put themselves into their art,
but most cultivate the quality of 'detachment'. Tolstoy exposes
himself at all points. He has an aristocratic unawareness of that need
for privacy which is so important to most people, artists included.
He gives the reader free access to his life, lavish hospitality. His
personal generosity is paradoxically at variance with the undeviating
rigidity of the opinions he later adopts, and which overset his
reason. It is the quality of shared living which redeems *The Death of
Ivan Ilych* from failure, indeed it redeems everything by Tolstoy from
failure – all his later work, even *The Kreutzer Sonata* (Chekhov talked
of its defects 'scattering like feathers before the wind' as one reads
it).

In *The Death of Ivan Ilych* Tolstoy is really imagining his own death.
The story is a great outcry of pain and despair – this is what makes
it so spellbinding.

The slow progress of Ivan Ilych's illness from a ridiculously slight
beginning, a knock he got while fixing up a curtain rod, elicits little

sympathy in his family for a long time. The explanation is simple. Ivan Ilych's marriage and career were mistaken. Ivan Ilych's illness makes him progressively more irritable towards his wife, and 'the more she pitied herself the more she hated her husband'. But soon he is finding that his rows with his wife have become welcome to him, a means of escape from his plight.

. . . then he did not think about It. It was invisible.

But then, when he was moving something . . . his wife would say: 'Let the servants do it. You will hurt yourself again.' And suddenly It would flash through the screen and he would see it. It was just a flash, and he hoped it would disappear, but he would involuntarily pay attention to his side. 'It sits there as before, gnawing just the same!' And he could no longer forget It, but could distinctly see it looking at him from behind the flowers. 'What is it all for?' . . .

He would go to this study, lie down, and again be alone with It: face to face with It. And nothing could be done with It except to look at it and shudder.

It is seldom that Ivan Ilych can bring himself to call 'It' by its right name. The terrible withdrawal of the dying man, his rather disgusting obsession with his entrails, alienates all around him. But surely this must be only part of the whole story. It is all we are told, though. Tolstoy imposes a strict censorship on all information about the family irrelevant to the dénouement he has prepared for us – the revelation of the errors of his ways to the dying man – the errors of a life which, as Tolstoy asserts at the outset, was 'most ordinary and therefore most terrible'.

There is little to alleviate the agony of dying alone, hemmed in by falsehood, his own and that of others.

'Why must I die, and die in agony? . . .'

The answer comes:

'Maybe I did not live as I ought to have done?'

Chekhov, writing about the later phase in Tolstoy's art, can still talk about the 'sincerity' of it, the 'sincerity of a man afraid of death and refusing to admit it and clutching at texts and Holy Scripture'.[1] He is talking about *Resurrection* here, but it is this 'sincerity' which redeems *The Death of Ivan Ilych* too. Only artificiality can totally neutralise a work of art – the artist depicting something he does not share in.

---

[1] Letter to Maxim Gorky, February 1900.

There is nothing artificial in *The Death of Ivan Ilych*. Tolstoy is desperately sincere throughout, but there is a great emptiness somewhere in the story. It leaves the reader with a sense of sadness, of loss.

It is customary to decry Tolstoy for his pigheadedness in hampering his creative gift in order to conduct his religious crusade. But it is important to try to establish exactly what it was that he was throwing away. We enter into Ivan Ilych's suffering – the hollowness of his life which makes his death so terrible – but we become aware that Tolstoy possesses answers, explanations which carry their own weight for him, ideas which have not been arrived at in the course of writing, but are there already, and then the element of collaboration is missing, of shared exploration. Tolstoy's work is no longer in the making as he writes. He has his solutions ready. The most eagerly awaited parts arrive prefabricated. Some of the excitement of the making is missing for the artist (and this loss is passed on to the reader), some of the mystery of discovering the unsuspected within a work which his own hands have made, of the construction as it grows demanding fresh forms which the artist must evolve out of what is already there, the work all the time teetering precariously on the edge of non-completion, of never being found. Now Tolstoy has stopped looking and in so doing has annihilated much potential creation. The losses are incalculable.

The following represents the spirit in which Tolstoy once wrote:

'The chapter describing how Vronsky accepted his part after the interview had long since been written. I began to correct it, and quite unexpectedly for me, but beyond any doubt whatever, Vronsky prepared to shoot himself. Then it appeared to me that this was organically indispensable for what followed.'[1]

The element of unexpectedness for the artist himself communicates itself to the reader and matters to him almost more than anything – the illusion of the artist and the reader being simultaneously aware of the growth of the work in the same way.

The greatest art is never predictable. It is always new. The moment Tolstoy's work became predictable he ceased to belong to the first rank of writers. One should never be able to foretell what is to happen any distance before it does. On the other hand, one should be convinced that each incident as it occurs is what must happen.

[1] Quoted in E. J. Simmons, *Introduction to Russian Realism* (Indiana, 1967), p. 172.

Chekhov's *A Dreary Story* reveals the unsatisfactoriness of *The Death of Ivan Ilych* perfectly. Chekhov writes on a similar subject in order to discover where it will lead him, and discovers a great deal that Tolstoy has neglected to find in the same region, Tolstoy having decided that everything has been found there already. The exploration which Chekhov undertook supplied him with experiences and discoveries vital to his subsequent development.

Chekhov's work from the moment he seriously took up writing is filled with echoes from Tolstoy. One does not need such things as Gorky's reminiscences of Tolstoy and Chekhov,[1] or the many references to Tolstoy in Chekhov's stories and letters, to become aware of these echoes. The sudden transformation of the apparently serene giant of Russian art into a bastion of traditional beliefs which seemed to be still tenable for him as a member of the older generation and of Russia's oldest ruling class, but were untenable for Chekhov, deeply shocked Chekhov.

' . . how much that is personal there is in it! The day before yesterday I read his 'Afterword'. Strike me dead! but it is stupider and stuffier than 'Letters to a Governor's Wife', which I despise. The devil take the philosophy of the great ones of this world! All the great sages are as despotic as generals, and as ignorant and as indelicate as generals, because they feel secure.[2]

Later, Chekhov will be able to look at Tolstoy's contemporary work more calmly, seeing him as 'a man afraid of death and refusing to admit it and clutching at texts and Holy Scripture'. By then Chekhov has his own achievement solidly there.

In *A Dreary Story* Chekhov writes about the last months in the life of a successful and intelligent man, months of failure and deep despair, disturbing because they seem unavoidable. Each aspect of Nikolay Stepanovitch's case is followed through patiently and laboriously. Chekhov has chosen to depict the onset of death as it is most likely to occur. He is not deliberately setting out to work on our fears, for he does not know in advance how the work will develop. It is an absorbing exploration. This is how Chekhov wrote about the story near the outset:

[1] 'For Chekhov his [Tolstoy's] love is paternal – in this love is the feeling of the pride of a creator.' Maxim Gorky, *Reminiscences of Tolstoy, Chekhov and Andreyev*, trans. S. S. Koteliansky and Leonard Woolf (New York, 1959), p. 4.
[2] Letter to Souvorin, September 1891.

My goal is to kill two birds with one stone: to paint life in its true aspects, and to show how far this life falls short of the ideal life. I don't know what this ideal life is, as it is unknown to all of us. We all know what a dishonest deed is, but who has looked upon the face of honour?[1]

The hero Chekhov has chosen is, for all his doubts and contradictions, a very impressive man, more intelligent and sensitive than his self-criticism allows him to accept. A science professor with an international reputation, he is a symbol of success. 'My name is closely associated with the conception of a highly distinguished man of great gifts and unquestionable usefulness.' Now he is conscious of approaching death and knows that none of his splendid, specialised knowledge, his originality within his chosen field is of use to him any longer.

The first person Nikolay Stepanovitch sees every morning is his wife. There is an amazingly convincing portrayal of the strained relationship between the old couple. His wife has become terrified of life, scared by money problems and by having to keep up their social position. The old man tells himself that he is not worried, but soon it is clear that he is as anxious as his wife. He thinks that his children ought to make some gesture towards alleviating his poverty. He despises his secret grievance against them as unworthy of the ideals he wishes to live up to. He fears his weakness, the weakness of old age, for the approach of death seems to be magnifying faults which must have existed in him all along, and this is what makes it intolerable – the discovery of his own ugliness when there is nothing left for him but to contemplate it helplessly. This is the nightmarish 'It' which he faces. It is worse than what the comparatively limited Ivan Ilych is up against.

Nikolay Stepanovitch's social and professional life is crumbling. His wide circle of eminent friends – critics, writers and artists among them – has faded away, and he is left with academic associates who bore him. He is a man with a vital intelligence which is being corroded through lack of stimulus as well as from physical causes. This is indeed a tragedy of old age. Nikolay Stepanovitch is now the associate of failures, and this intensifies his own conviction of failure. He finds that he is unequipped to deal with the situation he is in. With touching modesty he remarks: 'Unfortunately, I am not a philosopher and not a theologian' (– the kind of deceptive naïveté of

[1] Letter to A. N. Pleshcheyev, April 1889.

phrase with which Tolstoy also renders people's private thoughts).

Finally, worst of all, there is the responsibility Nikolay Stepanovitch feels for the person he loves most – his ward, Katya. This
trouble outweighs all the others. He sees his relationship with her
as a series of failures spanning many years of his life. He did not
discourage Katya's longing to go on the stage; now he feels that the
disasters which have befallen her were his fault. This is too painful
a subject to mention even to himself, and yet we so much live the
life of the old man that we know exactly what is going on within
him.

Chekhov said harshly:

'... one of my hero's chief characteristics is that he cares far too little
about the inner life of those who surround him ... Were he a different
sort of man, Liza [his daughter who marries a sponger] and Katya might
not have come to grief.'[1]

This is one of the many possible ways of looking at him. The old
man has been too tolerant, too acquiescent. He has taken life too
calmly. In some contexts his very virtues have been faults. The value
of every quality depends on the context in which it operates.

The old scientist is engaged in writing up the last notes on that
apparently abortive experiment, his life, carefully selecting what
seem to him the salient facts in his existence. We see more in them
than he does, for no man ever succeeds in seeing himself objectively.
Nikolay Stepanovitch, who suffers from a deep sense of failure, is
biased against himself. His most generous feelings are therefore
played down in the telling. And this self-discipline gradually
becomes more absorbing to contemplate than even the agonies of
Ivan Ilych. The courage of the man earns progressively more of one's
respect.

A large proportion of the story is about art and its importance to a
full, human life. The old man cannot find the means to express what
he feels. He finds himself dumb just when he most wishes to speak.
This is at the root of his feelings of helplessness at the end of his life.

Katya lives near by, having lost an illegitimate child, her life
ruined. Irritation at his home life builds up in the old man. He
regularly leaves the house to visit Katya. Another regular visitor, a
young colleague of his, arrives there too. Mihail Fyodorovitch, a
witty raconteur, reduces them to bitter and painful mirth. It is

[1] Letter to A. N. Pleshcheyev, September 1889.

plain that Mihail is in love with Katya; his witty conversation is a kind of love-call. In the lulls between satirical laughter, the thinking it overlays can be seen to have been banal. Katya says: 'I have seen in my day many of your students and young scientific men and many actors ... It's all the same mediocrity, puffed up with self-conceit.' By contrast, the old man's inner thoughts are charitable and sensible – if pompously expressed.

All these failings have a casual, transitory character, and are completely dependent on conditions of life; in some ten years they will have disappeared or given place to other fresh defects, which are all inevitable and will in their turn alarm the faint-hearted.

This might once have been the habitual Olympian detachment of a man who was himself successful and in the midst of creative work, but it does not ring true any more. He goes away in disgust with himself, having joined later in expressing very different thoughts from those he has lived with until recently. Hatred is poisoning him. It is the malice, the disgust of failure. Katya and he incite one another in it. It is clearly they who encourage Mihail Fyodorovitch to give effective expression to it for them. Nikolay Stepanovitch can do nothing to restrain the pettiness that seems to have taken possession of him.

The one person who still genuinely seems to expect to get help from him is Katya. 'What am I to do?' she cries. He thinks: 'It is easy to say "work", or "give your possessions to the poor", or "know yourself", and because it is so easy to say that, I don't know what to answer.' In practice, love does not necessarily unite – it can make a gulf in understanding seem wider.

As Nikolay Stepanovitch's death comes nearer, Katya begins to call on him for help more and more importunately. Abruptly she blurts out the reason for her despair. She has no talent. She has been too proud to admit it all this time. The practice of art is seen as the most dangerous as well as the most rewarding of all activities. Paradoxically, the old man has been fortunate in his life.

His present misery reaches its climax one night when his suppressed fear of death suddenly takes over and he wakes up in terror. The description is as gripping as the climactic moment when Ivan Ilych first became fully aware of what was happening to him. Chekhov seems to be deliberately vying with Tolstoy here in rendering the experience.

I hid my head under the pillow, closed my eyes, and waited and waited . . .
My spine was cold; it seemed to be drawn inwards, and I felt as though
death were coming upon me stealthily from behind.

In both writers there is the same amazingly intimate awareness of the
physical life of those they present.

There are uncanny repercussions among those who live close to
the dying man, those who have the deepest connection with him.
They come as a revelation of what he really means in the lives of
others. Nikolay Stepanovitch is in no condition to perceive this.
To him, these events represent a series of crushing failures. But we
can see more than he does, although it is he who tells the story. This
is typical of Chekhov, the reason for his success as a dramatist.

Nikolay Stepanovitch's wife runs in to say that there is something
the matter with his daughter. He drags himself to her room.

'My kind papa! . . .' she sobbed — 'my dear good papa . . . my good
papa . . . my darling, my pet, I don't know what is the matter with me . . .
I am miserable!'
She hugged me, kissed me, and babbled fond words I used to hear from
her when she was a child.
'Calm yourself, my child, God be with you,' I said. 'There is no need to
cry. I am miserable, too.'
I tried to tuck her in; my wife gave her water, and we awkwardly
stumbled by her bedside; my shoulder jostled against her shoulder, and
meanwhile I was thinking how we used to give our children their bath
together.
'Help her! help her!' my wife implored me. 'Do something!'
What could I do? I could do nothing.

Tolstoy is obviously the influence behind this. Just as obviously, it is
not the Tolstoy of The Death of Ivan Ilych. It is the Tolstoy who could
re-create domestic situations expressive of life-long intimacy, and
register them by means of perhaps only one detail, just enough to
elicit the reader's co-operation in constructing the rest.

A touch of dismal absurdity is added to the scene when dogs start
howling outside. It is indeed a night of high drama, as Nikolay
Stepanovitch has wryly intimated when introducing his account of
it — about the nearest most people come to high drama in real life.

Shortly afterwards we find Nikolay Stepanovitch sitting in a hotel
room, having taken a train to Harkov on family business. This rail
journey has transported him out of life, and the end is to be very
soon. One is reminded of an earlier description of Katya. 'Her

expression . . . is cold, apathetic, and absent-minded, like that of passengers who have had to wait too long for a train.' Nikolay Stepanovitch sits on a hotel bed, listening to a clock in the corridor. He ponders helplessly:

In my passion for science, in my desire to live, in this sitting on a strange bed, and in this striving to know myself – in all the thoughts, feelings, and ideas I form about everything, there is no common bond to connect it all into one whole. Every feeling and every thought exists apart in me; . . . all my criticisms of science, the theatre, literature, my pupils . . .

His thoughts are undirected even at the end. It would be absurd to expect a blinding light of revelation such as Ivan Ilych experienced when, as Tolstoy chose to put it, 'what had happened to him was like the sensation one sometimes experiences in a railway carriage when one thinks one is going backwards while one is really going forwards and suddenly becomes aware of the real direction'. Chekhov's characters in *A Dreary Story* are aware that they are travelling nowhere. They are sitting on the platform, waiting, their expectations sinking lower and lower. In Tolstoy and in Chekhov, trains are favourite symbols. They mock those who have no destination. The opportunities they offer are illusory.

Suddenly Katya is there, having pursued Nikolay Stepanovitch in the desperate hope that he may at last be able to help her, illumined as he must be now that he has reached the end. It is a ruthless and a superstitious action arising from her desperate mood.

This is death, the death of a man who does not know why he has lived and who is horrified at the discovery that he is not able to think, that every thought he formulates comes out a platitude, quite meaningless. In reply to Katya, who has broken down in hysterical tears, all he can finally say in his confusion is 'let us have lunch'. She leaves, and does not look back.

The old man cannot understand himself. His professional life is at an end, and the habitual means of self-expression are gone.

The story is in the first rank of Chekhov's stories. It is filled with the fresh perceptions of a young man picking his way through bewildering difficulties, finding out what he can do. Chekhov is at a crucial stage in his development – about where Tolstoy was at the beginning of *War and Peace*. At this stage, in both, there is the same excitement of the search, the same lack of real despair, in spite of depression. It is depression but at the same time buoyant with hope, with the certainty that what they are now doing is an important step in a progression towards some discovery. Chekhov is casting about, trying to find his direction as an artist, and by the end of the story he has succeeded.

Nikolay Stepanovitch is much more interesting than Ivan Ilych, more honest at the end, in other words less of a failure than he thinks. The whole of Ivan Ilych's self-pitying reminiscences of his childhood, which prelude his 'resurrection', are not worth that one memory touched off when Nikolay Stepanovitch and his wife jostle each other at the bedside of their daughter. The old man means more to us. That is his final triumph. He earns our esteem for his honesty with himself, his recognition of his own banality, his own dullness. Paradoxically, he becomes increasingly alive, increasingly aware, the more certain he becomes that he understands nothing. At the end he refuses to bestow upon Katya the impressive 'last words' which she imagines will illuminate her life. He knows in advance that this would ultimately add to her disillusionment, her helplessness. The success of the story lies in the amazing closeness that is achieved to the old man – the Tolstoyan illusion of entering into his life.

Tolstoy's train never came out of its tunnel. The major contrast between the two stories is that The Death of Ivan Ilych really is a work of despair. There is the real smell of death in it, the real terror, and there is little beyond the terror. Tolstoy's progress as an artist has been halted. He has lost his faith in himself, in the value of his own achievements.

F

11. Chekhov's 'Ideas'

Chekhov's realism involves the perception that one can make no judgements about life which are not liable to be cancelled out by fresh evidence. All Chekhov's works are illustrations of this. He often selects two contradictory points of view from which his material can be interpreted – employing Tolstoy's favourite method. Sometimes these contradictions occur in the mind of the main character, or else the narrator, who is often a young doctor or district official. Sometimes they are roughly divided out between two or more characters whose opinions constitute a dialogue. This dialogue often leads to hostilities; can even turn into a duel. It does so literally in the story of that name.

The Duel is about the hatred of two young men for each other, a scientist and a bewildered ex-student of the Petersburg University Arts Faculty. The dilemma is between the demand for effective, instant remedies for humanity's vast malaise, and an inarticulate lack of confidence in such remedies. The fundamental opposition between Tolstoy's Prince Andrew and Pierre Bezukhov continues in Chekhov's stories. The two attitudes clash, and often cancel each other out. Both kinds of men wish for a world that they cannot have, and have in any case no conception of what the world they desire would be like.

In Chekhov there are no permanent solutions such as Pierre and Levin arrive at. Chekhov characters are never rewarded with peace of mind, however fleeting. They achieve no respite. They do not discover God. They either become increasingly listless and despondent, or else they decide to be active and to work hard. When the latter happens they become admirable people, the sort of people who are an inspiration to others. But their dissatisfaction with themselves never allows them peace. Peace is suspect to Chekhov. It is synonymous with ceasing to be aware and, therefore, alive. He advocates perpetual warfare with delusion and apathy. He detests the later Tolstoy for the false confidence he exudes. There is nothing to be confident about, and the first duty of the artist, in Chekhov's view, is to make this plain. He must force people to see the world as it really is, so that they will re-think their lives and the worth of their activities.

Chekhov has no permanent solutions. He makes this plain in all his work. It is his purpose to challenge his audience to find their own immediate solutions. Like Tolstoy, he exhorts people to change their approach to living, and like Tolstoy at his greatest he does not tell them how to do so. Tolstoy, when he dealt with the torments and struggles of Levin and Pierre, was showing by implication how difficult it was for intelligent men even in the most privileged circumstances to achieve peace of mind. For Chekhov such privileged circumstances in any case are about to fade irrevocably into the past. One should, however, remember that this is recognised by Tolstoy too – to a certain extent. There is a faint nostalgia in the portrayal of Tolstoy's heroes, a regret for a fast disappearing innocence which has produced beauty in the past. Chekhov in his last work will ponder the precise value of this innocence.[1] The Cherry Orchard is the next generation's postscript to Tolstoy's masterpieces. The examples of Levin and Pierre cannot be generally followed.

Chekhov refuses to accept anything at its face value. This is an attitude he shares with the Tolstoy of War and Peace and Anna Karenina – the eternal restlessness of these books. Chekhov does not avoid inconsistency and paradox any more than Tolstoy did. He sees that nothing stands for long, and that the theories and presuppositions one brings to experience are never adequate to it. He sees that the most urgent of man's desires is the desire to find meaning in his existence. He also sees all the obstacles to the satisfaction of this desire. Man is enslaved by his material needs. The pursuit of physical comfort leads to mental discomfort. Man's instinct to satisfy the flesh is as fundamental as his instinct to satisfy his spirit, but it is a great deal easier to follow. Man occupies his time satisfying fresh material needs which he acquires in order to deaden the increasing dissatisfaction he feels. Chekhov is aware of mental slaveries of all kinds, the mind-forged manacles which man places on himself and others. He understands them in much the same way as the Tolstoy contemporary with himself does. But he admits that he does not know how men ought to live. He only understands the ways in which men torment themselves.

[1] The Tolstoy contemporary with Chekhov was pondering it too, but in a very different spirit.

Man's dissatisfaction leads to his tormenting himself and others in infinitely various ways, both subtle and crude. It is only the crudest activities, the enslavement of the weaker by the stronger, for which there are obvious, universally applicable remedies. Chekhov assumes that they will eventually be applied. He believes in 'progress' to this extent, though even here he admits to feeling a good deal more helpless than Tolstoy does as a member of the class accustomed to exercising social power. Chekhov proposes only the simplest and most obvious remedies.

... all, without exception, strong and weak, rich and poor, should take part equally in the struggle for existence, each one on his own account ... there was no better means for equalising things in that way than manual labour, in the form of universal service, compulsory for all.

Yet, when the speaker (in the story My Life) attempts to practise this in his own life, he fails miserably. Chekhov realises that a new social order is all but impossible to achieve in the short run. Apart from this, he recommends nothing. What he does do over and over again in his best work is to depict people who come to see the world around them in a new way – if only for a brief instant. The discovery that the world is different from what one has supposed, the ability to develop, constitutes life. The inability to understand things in more than one way constitutes death. Chekhov's subject is this. The overtly didactic stories scattered throughout his career, stories such as Lights, The Duel, An Artist's Story, A Doctor's Visit, are about this. Most of them are conversation pieces.

Lights was written in 1888, a year in which Chekhov was becoming absorbed with the question of where his art was taking him, and with the choice between his two careers of doctor and artist. The immense fertility of the previous two years, in which he had written an average of fifty short stories a year, disappeared. Chekhov had regarded his writing as a lucrative hobby and had found the exercise of his talent for inference and interpretation an absorbing activity. Gradually this ceased to be enough. Chekhov grew dissatisfied, even ashamed of easy writing. He became more and more concerned about the function of his art. What had all his sketches added up to? He began to ponder the vast questions which lie in wait behind the distractions of day-to-day living. He altered his focus and looked beyond the surface phenomena he had occupied himself with.

In Lights, this has begun. All Chekhov's work from now on is in a sense about art, about the expression man finds or fails to find for his spiritual aspirations and discoveries. Chekhov has begun to know in part what his art is for. He never knows in full. He is tormented by this, but it is the struggle to find out which produces his art. His work is always inconclusive in part, as Tolstoy's great art often is. Chekhov's art never satisfies, but it is never remote. One is not discontented with Chekhov for withholding answers, but, rather, with oneself for being as incapable of finding them as the characters Chekhov so mercilessly exposes for their emotional weakness, their self-deception and their mental sloth.

In *Lights* a railway-line is being built across an empty landscape. An engineer and his assistant supervise the work; the latter is a student and the former a good-natured and sentimental family man. A doctor spends an evening with them. A doctor is often the observing presence in Chekhov. Human illness is frequently spiritual in origin rather than physical. The doctor's calling therefore involves him in mysteries which he is unequipped to deal with. He is trapped into being a counsellor although he needs counsel himself. The figure of the doctor, the physician who cannot heal himself, is often used by Chekhov to represent all men who suffer from eternal discontent, from an awareness of human inadequacy.

Railways, those symbols of technological progress, are used with increasing effect by Chekhov. His attitude to progress as to everything else is mingled with reservations. But one attitude he never indulges in is the self-satisfied 'pessimism' of the young student in *Lights*.

Now we are making a railway, are standing here philosophising, but two thousand years will pass – and of this embankment and of all those men, asleep after their hard work, not one grain of dust will remain.

The thought is a platitude because of the person who utters it. The engineer will express thoughts very like this later, but we will listen to him. Ideas in the abstract do not exist for Chekhov. He perceives only people, their faces, their voices and intonations, the reasons for their speaking as they do rather than the logical correctness of the words they utter. The engineer's musings on the improvements railways facilitate have preceded the student's speech – 'good men will build a factory, a school, a hospital, and things will begin to move!' The student has decided to cap this, and indeed the argument of the young man sounds more profound. But his calm contempt for the older man is not quite in harmony with the tenor of his words. The older man is distressed at the young man's attitude.

On the face of it, the argument which has developed between these two men may not seem worth pursuing. This is the first of Chekhov's 'dreary' stories. Clumsy gropings and philosophisings about life by two rather dull people are not likely to add to one's intellectual equipment. The engineer starts a long, meandering narrative which forms the bulk of the story. He is not good at what is normally called self-expression.

Apparently he had no distaste for abstract subjects, was fond of them, indeed, but had neither skill nor practice in the handling of them.

He tells the story of an affair he had in his youth – when he returned to his provincial town and seduced a married woman. His attitude to her was self-centred. He was proud of the powers of discernment he had acquired in the city.

I was embarrassed, but not touched. Kisotchka's tears, her trembling, and the blank expression of her face suggested to me a trivial French or Little Russian melodrama, in which every ounce of cheap shallow feeling is washed down with pints of tears. I didn't understand her, and knew I did not understand her . . . When people cry, they don't like their tears to be seen. And I lighted match after match and went on striking till the box was empty.

He looks at her face as at some unfathomable mystery which he refuses to accept. It is only when he is on board the train on which he flees from her that his agony begins.

My conscience tormented me . . . The most incongruous ideas crowded one after another in disorder, getting more and more tangled, thwarting each other, and I, the thinker . . . could make out nothing and could not find my bearings in this mass of essential and non-essential ideas . . . For the first time in my life I was really thinking eagerly and intensely, and that seemed to me so monstrous that I said to myself: 'I am going off my head.' . . . my whole intellectual and moral wealth consisted of specialist knowledge, fragments, useless memories, other people's ideas – and nothing else; and my mental processes were as lacking in complexity, as useless and as rudimentary as a Yakut's.

One does not need to be an intellectual to learn from experience. Words are symbols for things which have to have been experienced before one knows what the words refer to. No man can hope to convey his awareness of guilt, or sorrow, or love to a man who has not experienced them. Yet the inexperienced man can use these words and construct arguments out of them which sound identical with those used by the man who knows what they mean. The engineer's attempt to convey his knowledge to the student is doomed to failure. The younger man does not see what the engineer is arguing about and despises him for his inability to make himself understood.

In any case, every man's experience is unique and therefore communicable only in part, even to the most imaginative observer. Every man is a new beginning, and no generalisation can cover his case completely. The truth for every man lies in his own experience. The thinker who reduces mankind to a set of generalised human types merely misleads.

In The Duel Laevsky, the arts faculty student, disgusts Von Koren, the young scientist, by his habit of finding parallels in literature for his failings, justifying his weaknesses and sins out of novels. Laevsky glibly pretends to despise himself for the habit too.

'I'm bound to look for an explanation and justification of my absurd existence in somebody else's theories, in literary types – in the idea that we, upper-class Russians, are degenerating, for instance, and so on. Last night, for example, I comforted myself by thinking all the time: "Ah, how true Tolstoy is, how mercilessly true!" And that did me good.'

There is self-congratulation in his deprecation of the habit. Laevsky is cut off from reality by his easy application of formulae which superficially appear to fit his situation. But Von Koren's explanation for Laevsky's irritating and squalid behaviour is also a crude application of theories, just as egocentric and unimaginative.

. . . we ought to look after the destruction of the rotten and worthless . . . otherwise, when the Laevskys multiply, civilisation will perish and mankind will degenerate utterly.

The theories of both are shown up in their infantile absurdity when real things begin to happen to them. To his horror, Laevsky suffers a nervous collapse at a time when he is plotting to desert his mistress whom he thinks he no longer loves. A little later he discovers the girl making love to the local police chief. This results in his love for her being brought to consciousness. Next, he is fingering a bullet mark on his neck after a duel with Von Koren, who has worked himself up to murderous fury, disgusted at the abject weakness of Laevsky. To Von Koren's amazement, Laevsky now marries his mistress and sets about earning his living. A few weeks later a slightly chastened Von Koren remarks with comic inadequacy: 'If I could have foreseen this change, then I might have become his best friend.' There is no science of human nature. Each case must be examined on its own terms. The artist who presents and the critic who envisages types in art, rather than unique individuals, simplify dangerously. Laevsky, the literary man, did more damage to himself and those around him than even Von Koren.

The theme of The Duel haunted Chekhov, embodying as it did the only answer he could find to the question 'What is Art?' It was an answer he could only express through example and illustration, as Tolstoy once did in his story Schoolboys and Art. The theme is taken up once again in An Artist's Story. This was written in 1896, the year of The Seagull (Chekhov's play about art). The story tells of a confrontation between an artist, who can no longer bring himself to work at his art, and a capable young woman who organises hospitals and schools and knows exactly what her life is for. The artist is in love with her younger sister, and his behaviour is influenced by this; he tries to undermine the authority of the older girl. In the end she removes her sister from his demoralising influence.

The artist feels himself completely helpless in the modern world — or says he does. He has given up. The forces of materialism have proved too much for him. It is impossible to say on which side Chekhov is in this story. The fact that the artist tells the story is no clue. It simply awakens our suspicion that the tale he tells has been loaded by him in his own favour. We are the observers of a clash of personality. It is this clash which is the story. Neither character has our sympathy, and it is their personalities which have determined their arguments. Their obvious self-obsession nullifies what looks at first like profound thinking. An argument is impressive only if the person who uses it is. The artist who poses as a spiritual dreamer is no better than the angular committee-woman he dislikes.

Scientific men, writers, artists, are hard at work; thanks to them, the conveniences of life are multiplied from day to day. Our physical demands increase, yet truth is still a long way off, and man still remains the most rapacious and dirty animal ... In such conditions an artist's work has no meaning, and the more talented he is, the stranger and the more unintelligible is his position ... it is evident that he is working for the amusement of a rapacious and unclean animal, and is supporting the existing order. And I don't care to work and I won't work.

This painter of landscapes has perhaps even less charity or real interest in his fellow man than his adversary.

The people who interest Chekhov most are those who suffer dumbly and are scarcely conscious of the depth of their suffering. He sees them as constituting the vast majority of the human race. Art exists to show people the truth about themselves and one another, and never has this been more necessary. Many Chekhov stories (*A Nightmare, The Schoolmistress, A Doctor's Visit*) diagnose the circumstances which deny the majority of people an opportunity to understand themselves. The majority of people are forced to lead empty lives. Those with an opportunity to think are a privileged minority. The reflections of the poor deacon, a minor character in *The Duel*, haunt the memory.

'Why, how few even outwardly decent people there were in the world! It was true that Laevsky was flighty, dissipated, queer, but he did not steal, did not spit loudly on the floor; he did not abuse his wife and say, "You'll eat till you burst, but you don't want to work"; he would not beat a child with reins, or give his servants stinking meat to eat – surely this was reason enough to be indulgent to him? Besides, he was the chief sufferer from his failings, like a sick man from his sores. Instead of being led by boredom and some sort of misunderstanding to look for degeneracy, extinction, heredity, and other such incomprehensible things in each other, would they not do better to stoop a little lower and turn their hatred and anger where whole streets resounded with moanings from coarse ignorance, greed, scolding, impurity, swearing, the shrieks of women.'

The sufferings of those who are articulate are often nothing to the sufferings of the dumb. Words can be used to provide a screen from reality. The privileged few often misuse their privilege to think; they deceive themselves with their own words. Chekhov is aware of the value of the opportunity to think, and of the responsibilities it entails – especially his personal responsibility to try to understand others, not man in the mass but every individual he comes into human contact with. Chekhov's thousands of character studies bear witness to the seriousness with which he took his responsibility. Only through learning to perceive others can one understand oneself.

12. Chekhov as Social Realist –
Peasants and In the Ravine

Peasants and *In the Ravine* are the best-known of Chekhov's many portrayals of the social horrors of his time. *Peasants* caused the same stir as Tolstoy's *Resurrection* was to do and, like it, braved the ill-will of the authorities. Poverty in the country is more difficult to portray than that in towns, for the horror and filth of peasant villages appear to be offset by the beauties of nature.

Like a practical physician, Chekhov examines sights which most people instinctively avert their eyes from. He also penetrates the minds of people who exist habitually on a borderline between life and death. He can see the world through their eyes and think with their thoughts. He understands something of the hierarchies among them, and has studied those who profit from their helplessness. *In the Ravine* is about the latter. It is a more disturbing story than *Peasants*. *Peasants* is about the humanity of those scarcely recognisable as human beings; *In the Ravine* is about the wickedness of those who at a first glance look more gentle than their victims.

Peasants was written in 1897, shortly after Chekhov wrote *The Seagull*, a witness to the extraordinary range of his art. In his story, Chekhov shows that peasants are not a separate order of beings whose elementary life is natural to them.

Tolstoy disliked *Peasants*, though he was struck by *In the Ravine* which is about petty merchants. He called *Peasants* 'a sin against the common people'[1] and stated that Chekhov did not 'know his peasant'. Tolstoy knew that there were bad peasants, as one can see from Nekhludoff's experiences with peasants in *Resurrection*, but Tolstoy was convinced that in general the peasant was closer to God than any other sort of man. It is easy to put oneself imaginatively in the position of Chekhov's peasants, whereas Tolstoy's remain in large measure incomprehensible. Their thoughts are often unexpected and reveal unfamiliar insights, which have been acquired through a total experience of life alien to one's own. They are like outcrops suggesting a rich deposit of folk wisdom below. But

[1] R. Hingley, *Chekhov* (London, 1950).

Chekhov does not trust folk wisdom very far. He observes that it is a luxury the peasants do not seem to have much time to develop. The sort of 'wisdom' Chekhov sees is that touched on by Tolstoy when Nekhludoff interviews an old hag about his illegitimate child. She tells of a 'wise woman' who made money by carrying unwanted babies to the Moscow orphanage.

'Eh, what food? Only just a pretence of food ... She said she just managed to get it to Moscow and there it died. She brought a certificate – all in order. She was such a wise woman.'

Chekhov feels qualified to show such a figure more from inside than Tolstoy usually risks doing. Chekhov sees both peasant vice and peasant wisdom as determined by degrees of poverty.

Tolstoy stresses the difference between peasants and other men, whereas Chekhov insists that the concerns of the peasant are no different from those of anyone else. His joys and sorrows are the same. The folk ritual of his life, the dressing up and the communal singing, which Chekhov shows us in *Peasants*, are more picturesque from afar than near at hand.

Chekhov with his quiet, matter-of-fact gaze seems to see everything, to leave no gaps. And yet Tolstoy's Karataev, the peasant figure used in *War and Peace*, is not quite so easy to dispose of as he seems to be when seen through Chekhovian eyes. He lives in the memory. Inevitably there are things which Tolstoy the landowner sees, or feels, which Chekhov does not. Tolstoy is still in touch with an older world. There is the vital difference in generations between him and Chekhov. In the story *Peasants* one notices that the inhabitants of the dilapidated hut Chekhov shows us are not entirely rural types. The village they inhabit sends young men to serve as waiters in Moscow. Granny, the frightening old crone who rules the family, has been in service at a great house near by. The family's labours on the land are scarcely mentioned.

It is true that Tolstoy, when he deals with peasants, cannot restrain himself from coming to bold conclusions on the evidence he possesses, whereas Chekhov is careful only to draw such conclusions as his evidence forces on him. Tolstoy in his later work produces Tolstoy peasants. Yet it remains true also that Tolstoy never entirely forgets the disturbing remoteness from his own way of looking at things which he once recognised and respected in his portrayal of the peasant Karataev. Chekhov and Tolstoy complement each other, speak for different worlds. The faintly urbanised Chekhov peasant, like all Chekhov's creations, is recognisably modern. The past out of which he comes is not felt by him, nor is it recognised by Chekhov, to whom the past seldom means much. Chekhov is busy with the present. He is the least nostalgic of writers. He is more interested in the practical things which may be achieved in the future.

Peasants, like all Chekhov's stories, leaves an impression of being much larger than it actually is, and the details seem thrown together almost carelessly. Tolstoy compared Chekhov's method to that of Impressionist painting – 'The illusion of truth in Chekhov', he said, 'is complete, his pieces produce the impression of a stereoscope. It seems as though he is flinging words around in any fashion, but like an Impressionist artist he achieves wonderful results with the strokes of his brush.'[1] Tolstoy himself has the same apparently effortless and casual way of assembling his impressions. The Impressionists also had predecessors whose similarity to them was not at first noticed. It is easier to see such things in retrospect.

Olga, the young Moscow wife, looks across the valley from the dilapidated village which is to be her home.

'It's lovely here in your parts!' . . .
Two little girls, down below, who were dragging up a pail of water, looked round at the church to listen to the bell.

The best must be made of the only life available to Olga's sick husband who has brought his family home. Soon the worst is known. A night has been spent in the hut. 'One had only to look round at the village to remember vividly all that had happened the day before, and the illusion of happiness which seemed to surround them vanished instantly.'

The struggle to remain alive has made the oldest people in the village almost unrecognisable as human beings. Granny, the frightening ruler of the household, is the worst. Her one remaining passion seems to be anger. It is necessary, for it both keeps her alive and is the fuel on which everything runs. Almost immediately, she beats her little Moscow grand-daughter, training her into the life of fear and subservience.

The deepest emotion in peasant lives seems to be fear. Pointing to the church, Sasha, whose mother has told her about religion, says

[1] Quoted in E. J. Simmons, *Chekhov* (London, 1963), p. 496.

to a little cousin: 'At night God walks about the church, and with
him the Holy Mother of God and Saint Nikolay, thud, thud, thud!...
And the watchman is terrified, terrified.' When a small fire breaks
out in the village the peasants are paralysed with fear and can do
nothing. This fear works in unexpected ways, for the majority of
them do not appear to fear death. It rather seems to be a fear of fresh
evil befalling them in life.

One night, the old people engage in reminiscences. The hideous,
mechanical Granny turns out to be the best story-teller. She recalls
her youth spent as a servant.

She described her mistress, a kind, God-fearing woman, whose husband
was a profligate and a rake, and all of whose daughters made unlucky
marriages: one married a drunkard, another married a workman, the
other eloped secretly (Granny herself, at that time, a young girl, helped
in the elopement), and they had all three as well as their mother died
early from grief. And remembering all this, Granny positively began to
shed tears.

Granny cannot die of grief – her energies are devoted to preventing
herself from dying of starvation. Her lot is worse than those lives
which provide her with an object for weeping. Her tears suggest that
there are many ways in which she might have been different.

The peasants are for reasons beyond their understanding poorer
than before. They have ceased to exercise their imaginations because
their entire energies are concentrated on facts. Whether the sense of
mystery will ever return cannot be known. The peasants hard-
headed enough to grow richer in the grim struggle for existence do
not allow themselves to be side-tracked by religion. For the poorest,
the yearly August procession of an icon, 'the Holy Mother, the giver
of life', through the village stirs up hope. The material appearance of
this icon in their midst awakens the hope that somewhere their
plight might be an object of concern. 'Defender! Mother! Defender!'
they shout for help. This is the only manifestation in them of a
larger view of human life.

When her husband dies, killed by a quack doctor, Olga leaves with
her daughter to become a servant in Moscow again. Since she is
leaving she can look at village life with detachment. '...to live
with them was terrible; but yet, they were human beings, they
suffered and wept like human beings, and there was nothing in
their lives for which one could not find excuse.'

Peasants ends with mother and daughter begging their way back to Moscow, the mother having taught her daughter how to do it. ' "Good Christian folk," Sasha began chanting, "give, for Christ's sake, with God's blessing, the Heavenly Kingdom . . ." ' This is the last sentence. Chekhov usually knows when the last word has been said. The story effects more than all the documentation and the exhortation for a religious awakening and a return to peasant piety, peasant simplicity of *Resurrection* (which started to come out the year after *Peasants* was published). Chekhov's story alters one's view of the people he tells us about. The humanity one shares with them is acknowledged not only by the mind but by the feelings. This is the purpose of all Chekhov's writings. Chekhov stated to all those who, like Tolstoy, saw no 'purpose' in many of his works – 'I am not a liberal, not a conservative, not a believer in gradual progress, not a monk, not an indifferentist . . . My holy of holies is the human body, health, intelligence, talent, inspiration, love, and the most absolute freedom.'[1]

Chekhov's art is intended to extend the reader's knowledge of human life, enable him to understand people who appear to be different from himself and thereby understand himself better. Chekhov seeks to liberate men by demolishing the barriers of ignorance which separate man from man.

The conditions described in *Peasants* beget evil. Unscrupulous storekeepers and factory owners, who use the peasants as a source of cheap labour and pollute their land and drinking-water with industrial refuse, render the hideousness of rural life more hideous still. *In the Ravine* is the natural companion to *Peasants*. The half-industrialised village lying concealed at the bottom of an unhealthy valley has less character than the one shown in *Peasants*. The process which Tolstoy unrealistically intends to arrest has gone further here than in the other village. Yet the more tender human instincts still manage to make their appearance. They are as impossible to eradicate completely as wickedness is.

The spruce Tsybukin spreads death and ruin among his destitute customers. His sons are sickly, but their father's position demands that they should have vigorous and beautiful wives. One of them, who is deaf, marries Aksinya, a girl whose activity amazes the old father. She darts about with a smile on her face from morning till

[1] Letter to A. N. Pleshcheyev, October 1889.

night, a demon of avarice. Her mind is impossible to penetrate, or, rather, for a long time it is difficult to accept that it contains so little. Chekhov cannot help us there.

The story tells of the marriage of Anisim, the elder son of Tsybukin, a little small-town fop. The household needs another woman. She should be hardworking but docile, so as not to get in the way of the other women. Lipa, a terrified little creature, her spirit crushed by poverty, is acquired. The household is an organisation for making money. It is a friendly household. This is what makes it so sinister – the quiet friendliness of its members towards one another. Their situation, surrounded by hostility and fear, engenders a sort of practical comradeship among them. Lipa does not fit in. The others are kind to her, but she fears them. She does not know why.

Soon the news comes that Anisim has been arrested for forgery. The family ambition of the old man becomes centred on Lipa's baby son. A piece of land owned by the family has been transformed by Aksinya into a lucrative brickworks. She is amassing great quantities of money, and regards the land as her own. Tsybukin makes a will, leaving it to his grandson. Aksinya, demented at this obstacle to her ruling passion, throws a cauldron of boiling water over the baby. As suddenly, she is herself again. The obstacle has been removed.

Lipa returns from the hospital that evening, the dead baby in her arms. She rests by a pond.

A woman brought a horse down to drink and the horse did not drink. 'What more do you want?' said the woman to it softly. 'What do you want?'

A boy in a red shirt, sitting at the water's edge, was washing his father's boots. And not another soul was in sight either in the village or on the hill.

'It's not drinking,' said Lipa, looking at the horse.

Then the woman with the horse and the boy with the boots walked away, and there was no one left at all.

Lipa watches the activities of the first people she has seen on the road. She is still attached to life and drawn along by it. The great mystery is why life should go on. She meets an old peasant whose life has been a hell, but he tells her that he wishes to go on living – 'I would be glad to live another twenty years; so there has been more of the good. And great is our Mother Russia!'

The old man yawned and made the sign of the Cross over his mouth.

'Never mind,' he repeated. 'Yours is not the worst of sorrows. Life is long, there will be good and bad to come, there will be everything. Great is Mother Russia . . .'

His wisdom is more for his own comfort than hers. He yawns because he feels tired, not sufficiently moved at the sorrow of Lipa with her dead child to prevent himself. Hers 'is not the worst of sorrows' because his own are worse to him. Lipa is journeying back to a house which will reject her because she is of no further use. The journey illustrates an eternal truth about the human situation; sufferings must always be borne alone.

The old 'Tolstoyan' peasant says 'Great is Mother Russia'. Perhaps for him her boundaries are the boundaries of the world, or perhaps he is just absent-mindedly mumbling out a habitual formula. It is typical of Chekhov that there is no means of telling. The old man seems to be expressing wonder at the endless possibilities that there are in life, but perhaps the wonder is not in him but in the peasant formula he is using. Man has the animal instinct to live and to remain alive.

'We can't know everything, how and wherefore,' said the old man. 'It is ordained for the bird to have not four wings but two because it is able to fly with two; and so it is ordained for man not to know everything but only a half or a quarter. As much as he needs to know so as to live, so much he knows.'

Life is held on to most tenaciously by those to whom it offers least.

Both stories are attempts to show how it is that men create a hell around them. Chekhov can see no further, and he admits this. Granny and her rages can be explained. Aksinya cannot. There is nothing to soften the cold realities Chekhov sees In the Ravine – the mystery of human evil in particular, the almost unalleviated harshness of the human situation in general. The two stories show Chekhov in a grim mood, and he is often grim.

13. Chekhov as Novelist – *Three Years*

What his art is for, and why he, Chekhov, should be an artist are Chekhov's constant preoccupation. When Chekhov attempts to visualise the artist, Tolstoy, the greatest of novelists, has a way of occurring in his thoughts ('of authors my favourite is Tolstoy').[1] Many of Chekhov's conceptions of art arise from his reading of Tolstoy as well as from his own creative experience. In a letter to Gorky he quotes Tolstoy –

He said: 'You can invent anything you like, but you can't invent psychology and in Gorky one comes across just psychological inventions; he describes what he has never felt.'[2]

In the same letter Chekhov refers to a situation in his personal life.

From Petersburg I get painful letters, as it were, from the damned, and it's painful to me as I don't know what to answer, how to behave. Life when it's not a psychological invention is a difficult business . . .

For Chekhov there is no separation between the intelligence he brings to bear in art and in life. He is inexorable in the demands he makes both on himself and on fellow artists for complete frankness with themselves as to their motives for writing. What Chekhov seeks for in art is the pang of recognition that a situation has been stated correctly. Tolstoy's tribute to Chekhov is worth quoting here – 'Just as one may find in Pushkin's verses an echo of one's own personal experiences, so this is true of Chekhov's tales.'

In a letter written in 1888, when Chekhov feels he has reached an impasse produced by his early mastery of magazine sketches, he worries his way through to a thought which is to become more and more distinctly the main theme in his thinking about art.

You are right in demanding that an artist should take an intelligent attitude to his work, but you confuse two things: *solving a problem* and *stating a problem correctly*. It is only the second that is obligatory for the

---

[1] A letter in which he outlines his biography to V. A. Tikhonov, February 1892.
[2] Letter to Maxim Gorky, April 1899.

artist. In 'Anna Karenina' and 'Evgeni Onegin' not a single problem is solved, but they satisfy you completely because all the problems in these works are correctly stated. It is the business of the judge to put the right questions, but the answers must be given by the jury according to their own lights.[1]

Chekhov has just completed The Party, and the experience of writing it is probably behind this.

The question which constantly recurs in one's mind, and in Chekhov's too, is why he does not write a novel. There is a deeper reason inhibiting his attempts than his apprenticeship in the short story and a consequent inability 'to master the technique'. The clue is contained in the quotation above, which reveals the way Chekhov read Tolstoy — 'solving a problem and stating a problem correctly. It is only the second that is obligatory for the artist.' If Chekhov had become convinced that the first was also obligatory he would have ceased to write. He is honest with himself. The majestic unrolling of War and Peace and Anna Karenina is impossible for him. He lacks the kind of vision which can detect a pattern in the kaleidoscopic fragments of experience, can shape great masses. Tolstoy perceives his characters' lives as unities. He follows what he sees as the sure contours of life. This is the monolithic quality of Tolstoy's art. The novels appear to have the calm and grandeur of great sculpture. The peace which his work generates may be illusory or temporary, the safeness of it did not help him personally, but it is there as far as it ever can be in novels.

The arrogance of Tolstoy is immense. Having annexed past and present, he then attempts to annex the future. When a friend accused him in later life of being in the power of 'Lucifer, the incarnation of pride', Tolstoy replied, 'of course I'm proud to be the only one who has put his hand on the truth'.[2] Even in the early Tolstoy there is an impression of autocracy, hard to define, a freedom from personal constraint, an air of easy self-confidence which Chekhov can never hope to emulate however much he may wish to. The air of deliberation and inner certainty in Tolstoy is illusory — the calm, decisive gravity, the majestic control. By contrast Chekhov's is a thin, tentative voice which sometimes drifts uncertainly into a pensive silence.

[1] Letter to Souvorin, October 1888.
[2] Quoted in Simmons, Leo Tolstoy.

The voice wavers yet does not fear to expose its uncertainty before an audience. Chekhov fundamentally respects the intelligence of his audience. He takes his equality with it for granted, in a different way from Tolstoy. He does not flatter it by lofty assumptions as to its necessary fellow-feeling with himself, as Tolstoy does. Chekhov refers to a 'sort of hypnotism' in Tolstoy – a forceful companionable reasonableness. Chekhov himself has refused to be hypnotised by Tolstoy. He is democratic and therefore his world is small. It is our world, and it is necessary for us to understand it. But the world we wish for also is Tolstoy's. Chekhov knew this, painfully. The novel for him was Tolstoy's kind of novel, which Chekhov's honesty with himself, his conscience, did not allow him to emulate. Although he could not foresee it, Chekhov is nevertheless a novelist in twentieth-century terms. His longer works can be called novels. Certainly Three Years is a novel by modern measurements.

Three Years is a novel about small urban people. There are no small people in Tolstoy or, if there are, Tolstoy looks imperiously past them and does not pause to attend to them sympathetically. Tolstoy's close attention to servants and subordinates in his later work is felt as oppressive. In Chekhov, everybody is small. Man has lost stature. Chekhov is reconciled to littleness, to impermanence, to the fragility of individual endeavour. These are facts which the later Tolstoy will not accept, and his stubbornness sometimes looks to us like madness – sometimes is madness. If Tolstoy teaches pride, then Chekhov teaches humility. Chekhov produces art in a period of drought.

There is no consciousness of human dignity in Chekhov. He has no personal sense of the past – of history – apart from the recent past. Chekhov is directly aware only of the immediate past and the immediate future. This is his predicament. He cannot be a historian or a prophet, for he can be sure of nothing. He cannot be sure what is to become of the Laptev family in Three Years or the family in The Cherry Orchard or Three Sisters for they either have no past or are shorn away from their past. For Tolstoy his ancestral past can be said to be part of his own experience. He can project himself back with ease; he can feel himself to have occupied a portion of the past as well as the present. Chekhov can only reveal the immediate successes and failures of his characters. He can only state findings in the particular case. The scientist in him does not allow him to base grand conclusions on insufficient evidence. Chekhov reflects the predicament of a country which has lost touch with its past. The sight of the old Tolstoy leading his followers back into the past moves him to laughter.

The past can only be felt to be part of the present by a society which is possessed of certainty about the present, which understands itself – a society in which everyone shares certain common assumptions. No artist can create these where they do not exist, and no man can tolerate those of the past when they cease to satisfy him. Tolstoy grows afraid of the passage of time. Time has become the destroyer for him – death. Tolstoy wishes people to remain as they have been, the country to remain separate from the town, the peasant to remain a peasant. For Chekhov, time flows, time is a creator. Time seldom brings what one hopes for, but seldom does it bring what one fears. Change is always unexpected – 'comes out of the unknown' in Lawrence's phrase. Generations change even physically and become total strangers to one another. This can be exhilarating and fascinating, not tragic. Men are the creatures of circumstance. For Tolstoy this is a nightmare, the nightmare of Prince Andrew in *War and Peace* – not so for Chekhov.

The difference between Tolstoy and Chekhov comes out most strongly in their attitude to education. Both work to establish schools and libraries. Tolstoy's purpose is to refine upon the peasant quality in peasants, to build upon old foundations. Chekhov wishes to bring out the individuality in everybody. He wishes simply to supply the materials of education and then see what happens – not to direct. Chekhov's is a new and raw society, feeding itself haphazardly with 'culture'. Laptev, the first intellectual in his Moscow merchant family, contemplates his position with surprise at the end of *Three Years*. The present is hardly what he has looked forward to three years ago, but it is sufficiently unexpected for the future to remain hopeful. Chekhov is the optimist, not Tolstoy any more. He welcomes the change which is coming over Russia. The tragi-comedy of half-educated men is the typical Chekhov comedy. It is very modern. Chekhov is certain that in the long run it will produce new life, a new vision of life. Taken together, the experience of Tolstoy and Chekhov is a reflection of two Russian generations. In these two generations developments take place which in Europe have spanned centuries.

Three Years traces the shifting pattern of human relationships which

develops round a man, even a timid and reticent man such as
Laptev, who lives a drab and uneventful life. *Three Years* is a 'slice of
life' – embarked on apparently at random, and dropped after the
three years are up. The hero of the story may be dreary and easily
dispirited, but he becomes interesting because of the author's deep
sympathy with him. He is alive because the man who writes about
him is vitally alive and aware of the life of others.

Chekhov is concerned as much as Tolstoy with the brotherhood of
man. The sort of closeness he wishes to engender between his
creations and the reader is shown by the way he himself reacts to art.
'What a glorious thing "Fathers and Children" is! It is positively
terrifying. Bazarov's illness is so powerfully done that I felt ill and
had a sensation as though I had caught the infection from him.'[1]
Laptev, the central character in *Three Years*, is brought close enough for
this to happen.

Laptev is a coward, and through Chekhov's analysis of his
cowardice the reader is brought to recognise his own cowardice.
Perhaps nowhere does the contrast between Chekhov and Tolstoy
come out so clearly. Laptev is a perfect foil to Tolstoy's heroes –
Levin, for instance, who is practically his antithesis except in his
restlessness, the residue of dissatisfaction in him after every achievement. Tolstoy admires courage. He is shocked by cowardice, and,
if he pities it, this is only because it seems terrible to him. Chekhov,
on the other hand, does not waste pity on it because for him the
coward is not a rare phenomenon, an error in nature. For him, the
majority of men are weaklings born and bred. He is less inspiriting
than Tolstoy who, with the half-conscious flattery of an extraordinary
man, assumes that he holds more in common with others than is
really the case. Chekhov has no illusions about his fellow men.

Laptev is acknowledged by his circle as a good man. He is
generous with money and is acutely sensitive to the attitude of
others towards himself, which makes him afraid of hurting them.
He has a reputation for kindness, but he is too defensive for real
generosity. His outlook is unenchanted. He is convinced that life
will never hold any joy for him. He ponders on his own shortcomings and on the shortcomings of those around him. He is
fastidious, a perfectionist who is convinced that perfection is
nowhere to be found. He is a man who travels through life with

[1] Letter to Souvorin, February 1893.

nowhere to go, unable to escape the twilight existence he despises himself for leading. The metropolis breeds many men like him, and an awareness of this is not the least of his troubles.

The opening of the story finds Laptev out of his normal setting, staying in a dreary provincial town to be near his sister who is dying of cancer. Connected with this break in the order of his life is the fact that he is passionately in love for the first time in his life. The girl is indifferent. His emotion is intensified by the fear that this may be the only chance of happiness life will afford him. There are excellent reasons for his pessimism. Laptev is intelligent and understands his case very well. The waste of his life is not his fault. Men's lives are wasted constantly, and in Chekhov's world the awareness of this arises in each generation, bringing fresh distress with it. Chekhov, in examining the lives of people like Laptev, looks for causes, but unlike Pierre in *War and Peace* he never finds it possible to ask the question 'what for?' Chekhov's Moscow is not the Holy City of a Hundred Churches which stood against Tolstoy's Napoleon.

Laptev knows that his sister is dying. It is the one item of information he can use to make himself interesting to strangers. It is inevitable that he should capitalise on it. He fails in his conversation with Yulia, the girl he is in love with, for he has already worn this and other subjects threadbare. That evening, all Laptev's thoughts have been centring around an ugly umbrella Yulia has left behind after a visit to Nina's bedside. Laptev, alone in his room, 'opened it over him, and he felt as though there were the fragrance of happiness about him'. The umbrella evidently fails to insulate him from his real life for he writes a letter to Moscow under its shadow; he writes of a 'certain person' whom he has been living with in Moscow.

The following day Laptev proposes marriage to Yulia. She treats him with shocked surprise, but later she feels she has just thrown away the only chance life is likely to offer. She can get no advice out of her father who 'for some reason fancied, that if he were left alone in that great house, he would have an apoplectic stroke'.

Laptev is a man of the city, and Yulia has a feeling that life might not be such a confused business with him. That she accepts him the following day does nothing for Laptev's self-esteem. There is obviously no love – there is even physical repulsion. Laptev is suspicious of sordid consultations between father and daughter.

He takes refuge in thoughts of the provincial vulgarity of her origins. 'The very name Yulia had a vulgar sound.' His status as a man who lives in the capital is all he has to hang on to.

In the train carrying them to Moscow Laptev's mind is filled with thoughts of the life he is about to resume under such strangely new conditions. Train-journeys in Chekhov, as in Tolstoy, give the illusion of freedom, although all routes are circular. The first person Laptev meets is his brother. As happens to Levin in *Anna Karenina*, Laptev's brother always disconcerts him by his likeness to himself, makes him conscious of weaknesses in his personality from which he may never escape. The brothers share the same past, the traditional self-righteous bullying in their gruesome old father's house of business. They have grown up in an atmosphere of fear. The fact that Laptev knows the reasons for his indecisiveness does not help to eradicate it. His father in his blind strength remains more powerful than he. Laptev's brother now seems to be as completely shattered in spirit as one of his father's clerks. Laptev has developed more of a personality because he was taken up by friends who helped him to develop away from his origins.

Soon we become aware that Laptev's marriage involves a third person – a woman he has been trying to avoid ever since his return to Moscow. He has discarded her love in a last-minute pursuit of something more. He is perpetually hungry because his appetite is weak and fastidious. He is critical out of an impotence to enjoy; he is impressionable through weakness, not strength.

The meeting with the woman he has deserted occurs abruptly. She suddenly appears before him during an interval at a concert, and fleetingly the relationship between the two is again present. There are numerous signs that they understand one another completely. They are both of the city, both victims of many wrongs, both a little eccentric as a result. They are talkative, ineffective, very conscious of the life around them. The great difference between them is that she is a fighter. She has a fearless spirit and the generosity which goes with strength.

It is not Chekhov's purpose merely to examine Laptev as a victim of city life. All that is good in Laptev, all that his wife later admires and respects, comes from Moscow too. Much has been developed as a result of his relationship with Polina Nikolaevna. Chekhov describes her wittily. She is untidy and awkward in her movements. Seen hurrying down the street she reminds one of a young monk.

Laptev sees her through such eyes now that circumstances are different, but she still dominates him.

The audience got up from their seats and went out very slowly, and Laptev could not go away without telling his wife. He had to stand at the door and wait.

'I'm dying for some tea,' Polina Nikolaevna said plaintively. 'My very soul is parched.'

Years of intimacy lie behind her assurance that he will follow her. Later, in her room, he is forced to remember all the bitterness of her life. She probes and tests his feelings mercilessly, trying to understand what their relation now is to each other. It is clear that their feelings towards each other are as strong as they ever were. Yet Laptev's feeling for his wife is something he has never had for Polina. She understands this and torments him with accusations which she knows to be half-truths, but which he cannot reply to adequately for fear of hurting her further. Her long nose turns an unpleasant waxy colour as she faints – and this only adds to his sadness. In two or three pages we have been convinced that the right and the necessary is also the impossible. Laptev is constantly oppressed by guilt at not having done what it was impossible for him to do. It is this universal human predicament which fascinates both Chekhov and Tolstoy.

Meanwhile, Yulia is finding her marriage impossible and is overwhelmed by guilt at finding it so. She lacks the training Polina has in expressing her feelings. To Laptev 'the conventional definiteness of her views and convictions seemed . . . a barrier, behind which the real truth could not be seen'. Communication is denied them at the moment, and their ignorance of one another leads to despair and enmity. It seems that there can be no escape from this situation, but it is characteristic of Chekhov that a few pages later it will have vanished with a chameleon change. Chekhov's knots never tighten. Like a game of cat's-cradle, they endlessly change position. Chekhov simply chooses the moment to withdraw his attention.

Laptev's circle of friends talk of art. They criticise theatre performances, and go on to talk about Laptev's brother 'and of it's being the fashion nowadays to adopt some pose or other. Fyodor, for instance, tried to appear like a plain merchant, though he had ceased to be one' – a great simplification of poor Fyodor's condition, as it turns out later. They clumsily try to create rules of conduct and behaviour for themselves, with nothing but their own limited experience to go on, and conscious of the crushing odds against them. The Laptev circle has outgrown the past, or at least this is the explanation it flatters itself with. Certainly it is irretrievably out of sympathy with the past.

Laptev owes much to Yartsev, who has hitherto been frequently mentioned in conversation. Now it is time for Chekhov to introduce him. Laptev's circle has been created around Yartsev. It seems to draw strength parasitically from the optimist and talker who teaches science at progressive schools and is interested in everything. Yartsev is enthusiastic about his pupils, especially the girls, and maintains that a remarkable generation is growing up. Many of his intimate friendships began at the university, where he met the Laptev brothers. Laptev first met Polina at his flat, and it was Yartsev who advised him at the age of twenty-two to leave his father's house.

Laptev's wife begins to find the people she lives among congenial. She is developing rapidly and ought to be happy. Ironically, the man who has introduced her to this new existence makes it impossible for her to partake of it fully. Yulia, like everyone else, relies on Yartsev to keep up her spirits. Laptev is tormented by jealousy. He subjects her to an emotional assault which is like a parody of Polina's efforts against himself. The desperate outburst of self-pity overwhelms Yulia with remorse. She now accepts part of the responsibility for their having married – a burden Laptev finds it impossible to shoulder alone, for he is a man without much pride in himself.

He suddenly kissed her foot and passionately hugged it. 'If only a spark of love,' he muttered. 'Come, lie to me; tell me a lie! Don't say it's a mistake!...'

But she went on crying, and he felt that she was only enduring his caresses as an inevitable consequence of her mistake. And the foot he had kissed she drew under her like a bird. He felt sorry for her.

He feels sorry for her because he knows from his own experience with Polina what she is going through. But this has not prevented him from acting as he is doing. Laptev has scored a victory, a change in Yulia's feelings towards him. He has thrown charity and consideration for others to the winds in blind self-assertion. He fights for what he needs. Yulia's reply, during the fight, to his insult that she married him for money has been 'I was afraid of spoiling your life and mine. And now I am suffering for my mistake. I'm suffering unbearably.' The reasons have shifted in her memory, significantly. They would perhaps have been her reasons now. The next day Yulia determines to visit her father at home. This registers that for her a definite stage has been reached in her life.

The episode of Yulia's return home is a carefully rounded Chekhov short story in itself. For the first time since her marriage we see her without Laptev. By the standards of the place she is going to, she has turned into a woman of the world. She has acquired a personality, and a warm, expansive one. For her the past is dead, and she is indeed lucky that she is free of it. Her choice was for Moscow, and she was right. A new certainty that she has done right for herself gives her a sense of self-sufficiency after her return.

Chekhov often withdraws himself unobtrusively, leaving it to us to explain things in our own way. Chekhov's characters usually do not know their own minds, and the author carefully arranges his information so that we can infer more about them than they can perceive themselves. Yet on occasion his own knowledge breaks down. There are certain mysterious transitions of feeling which elude explanation but certainly exist as Chekhov shows them. He is working from a knowledge of situations which develop in the way he shows them. Chekhov's first duty is to tell others exactly what he sees, and to make sure the reader is satisfied that no vital information has been left out.

Yulia, on returning to Moscow, continues to change. She makes the discovery that Laptev is not so cultivated as she had thought. She draws his attention to a picture which attracts her at an exhibition. Laptev's remarks once gave her the impression that all pictures were alike. She now tries to pass on to him what she has discovered for herself. Laptev's reaction depresses her.

Chekhov has not forgotten that the main preoccupation in his story must be Laptev. Laptev is being outstripped by his wife, who is suddenly freer, chafing at the fact that he is not sharing her discoveries.

A year passes, and Yulia has a baby. The men around her talk about love one evening at the summer villa where she is staying. Yartsev is inspired to romantic fervour by the awareness that Yulia is not in love with her husband. Yulia has asked him to write a historical play, since he is so good at history. On the way back to Moscow he dreams of Moscow's past glories. Alone in a cab which conveys him through the empty streets, he imagines scenes of high tragedy and wild slaughter out of the stirring past. But soon Yartsev is unwillingly face to face with real suffering and, a while later, with real tragedy. On entering his room he finds Polina asleep on the sofa. A few days later the news comes that Yulia and the baby have caught diphtheria. The baby dies.

Now, in her suffering, Yulia is completely exposed to Laptev's view, completely understood, or seems to be. Laptev contemplates her sadly as he has once contemplated Polina. It is also the way he has contemplated the pictures Yulia showed him. He looks, and it appears to him that he sees everything, yet he sees nothing. Yulia has seen the real pictures whereas he has not, and perhaps Yartsev has seen the real Moscow. Laptev has been drawn to both people, but he has not found what they seem to find in life.

Now that Polina is again strange to him, Laptev's feelings for her return, and recede from Yulia. A detached onlooker might call it heartless, but nobody has discovered the secret of controlling the feelings. Laptev clings to Polina and Yartsev with tenacious dependence. He wears out Yartsev with his perpetual questioning of life and prevents him from writing, until Polina has to tell him to stay away. He has been testing his pessimism against Yartsev's optimism, but has achieved nothing except endless definitions of his own condition.

'I am always in a gloomy mood or else indifferent . . . I consciously do good, and feel nothing but uneasiness or complete indifference. I explain all that, Gavrilitch, by my being a slave, the grandson of a serf . . .'

To which Yartsev retorts, 'That only proves once again how rich and varied Russian life is. Ah, how rich it is!' Laptev and his problems are beginning to bore those around him. Besides, he seems to be sapping even Yartsev's confidence a little.

Yartsev calls on Laptev to tell him that he is going to marry Polina. He seems almost apologetic for being satisfied with less than could satisfy Laptev – almost as though he sees Laptev's fastidiousness and discontent as a mark of superiority. Laptev feels let down – his relationship with Yartsev and Polina is now irrevocably different.

People change constantly, and life is full of new beginnings. It is brought home to Laptev that his relationship with his wife is entirely different too. He now faces the fact that, since the death of their child, he no longer loves her.

Laptev's brother one day shows him an article he has written. It turns out to be a vapid plea for the conventions to be respected, and for religion to be observed. Laptev tears the argument to shreds in a paroxysm of fury. It strikes him as an act of treachery to himself and to their past together. Fyodor seems to be acquiescing in what has been done to him. Living in his father's house, he has been at the mercy of people who have made him weaker than themselves. For the last three years he has been without the support of his fractionally stronger brother. Now this brother turns on him with hatred and contempt, tries to crush him as a reminder of his own deformity. He destroys the remnants of self-confidence in his brother, who has a nervous breakdown. This scares Yulia. She now sees that Laptev has destroyed her morale too.

'. . . why have I left off saying my prayers? What has become of my faith? Oh, why did you talk of religion before me? . . .' He put compresses on her forehead, chafed her hands, gave her tea to drink, while she huddled up to him in terror . . .

Laptev has been unable to do anything original with his life. He questions all conventions, all accepted beliefs, yet he cannot live differently from other people. He has always been attracted to free agents like Yartsev and Polina who seem to be in charge of their own fates, but he himself has feared taking risks. Even his marriage seems to him in retrospect to have been a conventional move in disguise. His wife, far from having helped him in his irresolute bid for freedom, is now determined that he should face what she sees as his responsibilities. She cannot bear the guilty, soured, inactive life she has been sharing with him, and she now forces him to look at the old sights of his youth again. She tries to re-establish Laptev in his father's business. Yulia has an eye on the family house, for she needs a sense of continuity with the past. She visits the old man. Now, after three years, Laptev's terrible old father reappears, the personification of a barbarous past when people were less squeamish about inflicting suffering on others, seeing their actions as the will of God.

The old man is now almost completely blind, an autocrat filled with rancour against those who have disobeyed him – significantly, Laptev is not one of that number. Yulia has not been a victim of the old man's active years; all she is aware of is the present state of his affairs, and in these she sees possibilities. Laptev's duties as the new head of the family are clear. He does what is necessary with a bad grace, though. 'I feel as though our life is already over, and that a grey half-life is beginning for us.'

This life will be dismal in appearance – simply the life of a Moscow businessman who has inherited his father's business. It has always been in store for Laptev. Like his brother, he is no rebel. He has been incapable of devising any alternative activity for himself. He has little imagination and no talent. There is only one place for him, it seems.

After going over the accounts and discovering the exact extent of his possessions, Laptev wanders out into the yard at the back. The yard awakens memories of the past and seems unchanged. An old cherry tree is in flower as he remembers it from his childhood. It is terrible to him that he should be back in a place he thought he had escaped from for ever. A dog lies in the yard, keeping him company. The dog will never run away. His case appears the same as Laptev's – training will always prove stronger than instinct. Laptev overhears a young man in the next garden talking to a girl – the mating ceremony of the average man. Laptev recalls all that has happened to him in the last three years and sees it as part of a predictable process, without individuality. He will 'begin to grow dull and old, die in the end, as the average man usually does die, in a decrepit, soured old-age, making everyone about him miserable and depressed'. But the 'average man' is a figment of his private and lonely imagination. The cherry tree and the black dog, which seem sinister and inert to him, are really unique and beautiful things, creatures of infinite variety like himself. The wife who has led him into the very life he wished to avoid leading, has her beauty too, but Yulia no longer fascinates him as a strange and alien creature.

The next day he visits Yulia who is staying in the country. He remembers the many changes which have occurred in his relations with her and the others there, even in the amazingly short space of three years. He knows that he himself has been developing with every change in his relations with others. It seems that there is hope in the very unexpectedness of everything – in the very fact of change.

When his wife meets him she is holding her old parasol – the one Laptev once held over himself, thinking of her. She hopes he will again look on her as he did then. 'You are precious to me, Kostya . . . I am so happy . . .' All Laptev can think of at the moment is his dinner. He is still angry over her satisfaction at having turned into the wife of the dull businessman he has become in his imagination. Ironically, it is his unceasing desire for more out of life which makes him attractive to her – the fact that he will never be satisfied.

Laptev has been forced by circumstances into the tacit admission that he is a practical man by nature, an owner of property and director of labour, not a dreamer. He has wished to be a dreamer and thinker, but is too hard-headed and cold by nature. He has become visibly more resolute and stronger. He has not got what he has wished for, but he never really knew what he wanted.

Yartsev looks at Yulia with longing. He sees something in her which Laptev does not see at the moment because she is associated in his mind with the prison-house of his childhood memories. Yulia sees something in Laptev, however. It is through her that we become aware of the new strength in him. In fact it suddenly seems to be Yartsev and Yulia who are the weaker ones – an unforeseen reversal.

Laptev could not help watching them while he thought that he had perhaps another thirteen, another thirty years of life before him . . . And what would he have to live through in that time? What is in store for us in the future?

And he thought: 'Let us live, and we shall see.'

What the future brings is seldom what we hope for, but it is seldom what we fear either. Laptev's life is sad and restless, but it is not ugly or mean. It has been refined and clarified by the help of others who have received very little gratitude from him. The thought that things last for ever has been the nightmare that has dogged him. Now it is lifted, and he breathes more freely. His fear has been of stagnation. In fact he has developed more than he realises, and this is a sign that he and those about him will go on developing in unexpected ways. There is unhappiness in his household, perhaps more than there was in the old Laptev's day. It is impossible to say. But Laptev is no longer a pessimist.

Three Years has been the story of a man whose overriding fear is that he is a prefabricated nonentity, 'the average man', and his discovery that such a being is an impossibility. To a limited but significant degree, he has acquired the sense of freedom which Chekhov always seeks to impart.

CHEKHOV: THE PLAYS

14. Chekhov's Apprenticeship as a Playwright
(Uncle Vanya and The Seagull)

Chekhov had a major share in the innovations at the end of the nineteenth century which determined the theatre of today. Many of his basic ideas were preceded by those of Ibsen and Strindberg. Ibsen wished his audience to feel that it was directly watching life itself. He avoided soliloquies and set debates between pairs of characters, and eliminated surprise entrances. In 1887 the Théâtre Libre was started in Paris, inspired by the work of Ibsen and others; André Antoine, its founder, trained actors for the new generation of playwrights he foresaw. 'The actor will no longer "speak his lines" in the classic manner; he will say them naturally, which is just as difficult to learn.'[1] Antoine was ridiculed for his willingness to turn his back on the audience if natural behaviour on the stage should require it.

The most brilliant exponent of these new ideas was Strindberg. (His Scandinavian Experimental Theatre was started in 1888.) In his opinion a new type of drama had not yet been achieved, certainly not by Ibsen. Here is an example of Strindberg's acting instructions for The Father:

A deceived husband is a comic figure in the eyes of the world, and especially to a theatre audience. He must show that he is aware of this, and that he too would laugh if only the man in question were someone other than himself. This is what is modern in my tragedy, and alas for me and the clown who acts it if he goes to town and plays an 1887 version of the Pirate King! No screams, no preachings! Subtle, calm, resigned! – the way a normally healthy spirit accepts his fate today.[2]

In the Preface to Miss Julie he says that the philosophy of 'character' has strangled free creativity in the drama.

Originally it meant the dominant feature in a person's psyche, and was

---

[1] Quoted in Strindberg, The Plays, introd. and trans. Michael Meyer (London, 1964).
[2] Letter to Axel Lundegård, October 1887. In Meyer, Strindberg.

synonymous with temperament. Then it became the middle-class euphemism for an automaton; so that an individual who had stopped developing, or had moulded himself to a fixed role in life – in other words stopped growing – came to be called a 'character' . . . And these summary judgements that authors pronounce upon people . . . 'He is stupid, he is brutal, he is jealous, he is mean,' etc. – ought to be challenged by naturalists, who know how richly complex a human soul is and who are aware that 'vice' has a reverse image not dissimilar to virtue . . .

. . . This multiplicity of motives is, I like to think, typical of our times. And if others have done this before me, then I congratulate myself in not being alone in my belief in these 'paradoxes' (the word always used to describe new discoveries).

An awareness of the personality as it really is will of itself produce realistic dialogue. Strindberg's thinking, for all its incidental eccentricities, is profounder than Ibsen's.

Strindberg dreamt of a time when the dramatist would no longer be 'a lay preacher [he still saw Ibsen as that] hawking contemporary ideas in a popular form, popular enough for the middle classes . . . to be able to grasp without too much effort what the minority is arguing about'.[1] An audience should be given much harder work to do. Strindberg indicates the technique his conception of dramatic character demands:

. . . I have somewhat broken with tradition by not making my characters catechists who sit asking stupid questions in order to evoke some witty retort. I have . . . allowed their minds to work irregularly, as people's do in real life, when, in conversation, no subject is fully exhausted, but one mind discovers in another a cog which it has a chance to engage. Consequently, the dialogue, too, wanders, providing itself in the opening scenes with matter which is later taken up, worked upon, repeated, expanded and added to, like the theme in a musical composition.[2]

This technique was arrived at independently by Chekhov who was the new voice in Russian literature. The route he took was less precipitate. The results were the product of trial and error, of laborious common sense in place of the startling brilliance one associates with Strindberg. Nevertheless Chekhov in his much calmer manner can be as disturbing a playwright as Strindberg.

Chekhov's dramatic art was affected by the general movement

[1] Preface to Miss Julie, in Meyer, Strindberg.
[2] Ibid.

towards realism on the stage, but there is no need to search through
the work of specific dramatists for his sources. In particular it is
absurd to point to Turgenev as his precursor. The play often alluded
to is *A Month in the Country*, written as early as 1850. In it, motives are
sometimes concealed behind fragmentary, naturalistic conversation.
At a cursory glance this might look like Chekhov, but Turgenev's
dialogue with its delicate innuendoes is the product of his own
chivalrous idea of the relations between men and women. The
suggestiveness is simply a roundabout way of expressing devotion,
jealousy, slighted love and the like. The sugary nobility of Turgenev's
characters has nothing to do with Chekhov. This means that any
resemblance between the techniques Chekhov and Turgenev employ
in the furtherance of their very different ends is bound to be
accidental.

Chekhov was drawn to the drama from the beginning. One of his
first works is the ungainly play, Platonov, written at the age of
twenty-one. It is intended as a large-scale portrayal of contemporary
Russian life. At its centre is the contemporary intellectual, a man
bewildered and helpless in the face of the hateful lethargy which
smothers his country, a man who does not know where to begin to
set things right.

This unwieldy piece should have been a novel. The reason why it
was written as a play can be gathered from the description of
Platonov by one of the characters, a representative of the older
generation.

He's the hero of our best modern novel, one that hasn't yet been written . . .
Vagueness seems to me typical of modern society, and your Russian
novelist senses it. He's baffled and bewildered, he has nothing to hold on
to, he doesn't understand.[1]

At this early stage Chekhov has decided that he is unequipped to be
a novelist, at least not a major one like Tolstoy. He does not know
enough. He can show Platonov talking, and reproduce a few people's
reactions to him. Thereafter, all he can do is hope that a work of art
will emerge if he puts enough down. It does not, but Chekhov has
learnt something of the advantages of the dramatic form.

Many years later, after rigorous training as a writer ('I must study,
study everything from the beginning, for I, as a littérateur, am a mass

[1] *The Oxford Chekhov*, ed. and trans. Ronald Hingley (London, 1964), III.

of ignorance')[1] Chekhov restates his doubts about his qualifications
as a writer. The novelist Trigorin in The Seagull unburdens himself to a
young fellow writer.

'... I dislike myself as a writer. But the worst of it is that I live in a sort of
haze, and I often don't understand what I'm writing ... As an author, I feel
I'm in duty bound to write about the people, their sufferings, their future –
and about science, the rights of man, and so on, and so forth ... I see
science and society forging ahead, while I drop further and further behind,
like a peasant who's just missed his train, and in the end I feel that all I
can do is to paint landscapes, and that everything else I write is a sham –
false to the very core.'[2]

This is Chekhov's fear as a writer too – not to understand what he is
writing, to allow his pen to drift. The definiteness of the dramatic
form attracted him more and more.

Henry James, who was equally concerned that the life around him
should not evade his grasp, a life which was beginning to elude easy
definitions, was also aware of the dramatic method as a means to
fix it.

'Exhibition' may mean in a story twenty different ways, fifty excursions,
alternatives, excrescences, and the novel, as largely practised in English,
is the perfect paradise of the loose end. The play consents to the logic
of but one way, mathematically right.[3]

In his early years, when writing magazine sketches, Chekhov had
instinctively limited himself to dialogue and scene-setting. On
occasion, between the years 1885 and 1895, he was able to bring in
money by turning five of these early sketches into one-act plays. He
merely added to the existing dialogue. More of his stories have been
adapted by others since (as has happened with James too). 'Going
behind' and 'telling about the figures'[4] started to happen during the
years 1888 to 1889, when Chekhov felt that he really knew enough
about the life around him to speak about it with authority. By that
time, he had served a long apprenticeship in the story form, but his
apprenticeship in the drama was only beginning.

[1] Letter to A. S. Souvorin, December 1889.
[2] Plays by Anton Chekhov, trans. and introd. Elisaveta Fen (Harmondsworth,
1959). All subsequent quotations from Chekhov's plays will be taken
from this translation, unless otherwise stated.
[3] Preface to The Awkward Age.
[4] Ibid.

When Chekhov began deliberately writing four-act plays in 1888 and 1889 they were far less accomplished than the long short-stories he was then writing, and this gap between the quality of his plays and his stories continued up to the turn of the century. Chekhov's awareness of the advantages of the dramatic method was of value to his narrative work in the first place. Till nearly the end of his life it seemed likely that he would continue to be a story writer who had conducted a fruitful flirtation with the drama. But as a result of Chekhov's last-minute achievement in Three Sisters and The Cherry Orchard, the stories and the plays came to complement one another in a unique way. Together, they project the total vision of a major artist.

After the lukewarm reception of Ivanov, Chekhov's second attempt at a play, the mastery of the stage became an urgent preoccupation with him. He could not rest until he had achieved it. One reason was the total transformation that came over his written work upon the stage, to which the production of Ivanov had awakened him. 'Nikolay, Shekhtel, and Levitan – all of them painters – assure me that on the stage it is so original that it is quite strange to look at. In reading one does not notice this.'[1] Chekhov's creation had taken on a movement and vigour which he himself had not realised it possessed. His contemporary subject matter was often such that even a Tolstoy could not have presented it on the written page with more vigour than Chekhov had succeeded in doing. Yet the movements and voices of actors and actresses had shown beyond doubt that Chekhov's modern people were as alive as those of Tolstoy. In the future there would be the gallant Russian army and an admiring provincial society in Three Sisters. There would be the native gaiety of Madame Ranyevskaia ('nothing but death could subdue a woman like that')[2] in The Cherry Orchard. On the surface, and it is a surface only the drama can show, Chekhov's world would be vividly, surprisingly alive.

In Ivanov Chekhov is feeling his way, but he has not yet discovered how much material a play is able to carry. There is not enough for the characters to talk about – there is only Ivanov. In The Wood Demon, written the following year, there is, on the other hand, too much. Chekhov has overcompensated by creating three sets of characters.

[1] Letter to Alexandr Chekhov, December 1887.
[2] Letter to O. L. Knipper, October 1903. Quoted in D. Magarshack, Chekhov the Dramatist (London, 1952), p. 272.

Chekhov goes on tinkering with both plays, learning from mistakes in his original forecasting of effects on the stage. The result of many delicate rearrangements of material is Uncle Vanya, emerging over the early nineties, though probably given its finishing touches just after The Seagull. Uncle Vanya is essentially a dialogue between two main characters, and is the result of extracting all the successful sequences out of The Wood Demon and putting them back together again in a tighter and, as it turns out, totally different pattern. It is a fascinating object-lesson in the relationship between conversations and the contexts in which they occur. Identical dialogues have completely different meanings in each play. As a result of the exercise, Chekhov finds out a great deal about the medium, discovers that it is even more difficult than he has imagined.

Uncle Vanya is interesting as an exercise, but it is a little hard and mechanical. The Seagull, on the other hand, is over-ambitious. It is the last of Chekhov's experiments with the drama, a qualified success.

Each play so far, except Uncle Vanya, contains one act at least which fails to come off, and Chekhov's play-writing efforts have wrung curses from him about the wastage of story material which their necessary tightness of construction involves. 'Oh, why did I write plays and not short novels? I've lost good plots, lost them irretrievably.'[1]

Ivanov and The Wood Demon were written or being worked up at about the same time as A Dreary Story was written. The disparity between Chekhov's achievement in the two forms at this period is immense.

Chekhov at first ascribed the heaviness of Ivanov to poor acting, which may have been partly true. But the fact remained that it was over-written. Chekhov had to discover how to keep his talk as natural as it was in his stories, and yet convey very much more through it than was necessary in a story. Chekhov would always rely heavily on unobtrusive stage directions, telegraphic and suggestive, the result of his training in the other medium, but there was much else that he had to learn to do without. Narrative techniques had developed far ahead of the drama, and Chekhov found that he had undertaken the task of re-establishing connections between the two forms, so that each in their different way should be capable of

[1] Letter to Souvorin, December 1896. In Magarshack, Chekhov the Dramatist, p. 204.

absorbing the same material. Chekhov's lifelong interest in the theatre made him aware that the drama, in Russia at least, was not in touch with contemporary life.

There are already some inspired moments in Ivanov. They come when the characters say exactly what they would say in real life, but usually they say too much and therefore leave an impression of prolonged nagging and moaning. Ivanov feels stifled at his failure to change any of the people around him. He seeks to undermine their self-confidence, and often displays a quiet and chilling malice in his remarks to them. Such moments tell one all one needs to know. They provide Chekhov with the clues he uses later. But in Ivanov Chekhov is not awake to the fact that talk in a play is a much more sensitive instrument than talk in a story because the attention of the audience is concentrated upon it.

Chekhov tries to tone down the heavy portentousness of his hero by making him aware of it himself. Ivanov mocks himself to the girl he leans on for support.

. . . my whining inspires you with a sort of reverent awe, you seem to think that you've got hold of a second Hamlet in me . . .

I've acted Hamlet and you've acted a high-minded young woman – but we can't go on like that . . .

The self-mockery of Ivanov as a tinpot Hamlet comes in during the revisions of the play which continued into 1889. Ivanov is certainly not Hamlet. The play Hamlet may fractionally include Ivanov's situation, but it covers much else. Hamlet discovers himself in a universe quite different from the one he had assumed himself to be in. It has changed its aspect as in an optical trick where an apparently solid object hollows out while one is looking at it, and remains obstinately present as something else. It is a revelation on a different scale from Ivanov's awareness that he cannot change the society he lives in, that he is the product of a mediocre age and is probably a mediocrity himself. Throughout his life Chekhov makes many references to Hamlet in his letters. The play is part of his awareness of the world, and is present least in the work where it is mentioned most.

In Ivanov Chekhov is still giving his audiences a great deal that they are accustomed to. The elements in it which probably had the most success are precisely the ones which gradually fade out in the plays which follow. Fragments of Ivanov answer to a convention of stage behaviour which strikes one as odd precisely because of the pervasive influence Chekhov has had on the way plays are now written. There are vestiges of stage farce. There is a long hortatory speech in which a young girl stands up and tells a roomful of people to pull themselves together. She is allowed to have her say, which does not usually happen to youthful idealists in Chekhov.

Also, it was tempting to take the usual way of insuring against failure, eliciting the responses which any audience can be made to produce. The easiest one is sympathy with the stage victim of mis-understanding, the person who makes his case perfectly clear to the audience yet seems unable to get the same response from those insensitive fools who are his companions on the stage. The audience sits frustrated, in a state of painful excitement.

IVANOV (*suffocating*). Stop, for God's sake! I can't answer for myself like this! I feel absolutely suffocated with rage, and I ... I might say something insulting to you ...

Although the effects are calculated with greater nicety, the fact remains that this will still be the fuel on which Uncle Vanya is fired. One does not have to make people any more obtuse on the stage than they are in life.[1] Chekhov takes a long time to find out how quick an audience can be in its responses.

Ivanov is immediately followed by The Wood Demon, which is intended as a portrait of a narrow provincial society and the tensions generated within it. The whole is given a modicum of coherence by the figure of Kruschov, an idealist nicknamed the Wood Demon. He campaigns to preserve the fertility of the countryside by replacing trees that get used up for firewood. The main action concerns the Voinitsky household. A professor has come to the country to spend his retirement with Voinitsky, his brother-in-law. Voinitsky is poisoned with resentment at having wasted his time and talents in the country while the professor has been a successful figure in the city, living off the proceeds of the estate. The professor is extremely irritating, but he is a more prepossessing figure than he will become in Uncle Vanya —

... I starved and worried because I was living at someone else's expense. Then I went to Heidelberg to the university, but I saw nothing of Heidel-

---

[1] Strindberg's characters are not at all obtuse.

berg. I went to Paris, but I saw nothing of Paris . . . And when I became professor I served scholarship with faith and truth. I always have and still am. So, haven't I, I ask you, the right to be pampered and cared for . . .[1]

It is understandable when he turns vicious under Voinitsky's taunts ('a writing-machine') and suggests that the estate which binds their lives together should be sold.

The Wood Demon is shapeless, a dreary succession of squabbles with now and then a short-lived reconciliation. Chekhov realised about half-way through that the whole thing was failing to cohere. Experience was teaching him the necessity for what James called 'ferocious, really quite heroic compression . . . where the "cross references" of the action are as thick as the green leaves of a garden, but none the less, as they have scenically to be, counted and disposed'.[2] Chekhov eventually tried to force the action to some conclusion by making Voinitsky commit suicide.

Voinitsky's death comes like a thunderbolt out of an empty sky and achieves little impact on an audience other than surprise. The ambitious scale of the play has brought Chekhov face to face with fresh difficulties, and has caused him even more disappointment than Ivanov did. Chekhov the narrative artist can link up his material in a variety of ways. But he has so far only found the crudest means to turn his plays into unities — through moralising commentaries and through administering shocks which shake the characters together and give them something obviously in common.

Putting a slice of life on the stage has been found to be all too easy, and not what Chekhov wants after all. On the other hand, the means of giving a play the appearance of a slice of life has not been fully discovered. Chekhov still seems to be hoping that a work of art will emerge if he goes on writing long enough. It is seldom that anything really original comes easily. The Chekhovian drama has a slow and painful birth.

All the scenes in the later Chekhov plays will be scenes which register changes in a situation, changes which steal up almost unnoticed but which are irrevocable and will inevitably have their consequences. Critical moments occur in people's lives and often pass unnoticed by those around them. There is the impression of

---

[1] Six Plays of Chekhov, trans. and introd. Robert W. Corrigan (New York, 1962).
[2] Preface to The Awkward Age.

life being lived at its normal pace, but everything in fact happens very fast; before our eyes, people are being altered through living together. Such sequences did occur in The Wood Demon, if we were alert to them, and these are the ones Chekhov extracts and reworks in Uncle Vanya. There is the identical ending of the first act in both plays, for instance, in which Voinitsky reveals his desire for Yeliena.

YELIENA. (Speaking of her husband) . . . at lunch today you argued with Alexandre again. How petty it all is!
VOINITSKY. But if I detest him?
YELIENA. There is nothing you can detest Alexandre for – he's just like anyone else. He's no worse than you are.
VOINITSKY. If only you could see your face, your movements! . . . You give the impression that life is too much of an effort for you . . . Oh, such an effort!
YELIENA. Oh, yes, such an effort and such a bore! Everyone blames my husband, everyone looks at me with compassion: an unfortunate woman – . . . oh, how well I understand it! . . .

. . . Don't look at me like that, I don't like it!

Short sketches like this in The Wood Demon are suggestive, but need a different context to bring out their possibilities. Voinitsky and Yeliena in Uncle Vanya are slightly different people. Voinitsky is warmer; it is his good qualities which have made him an easy prey to selfish relatives, particularly the professor. Yeliena, on the other hand, is far more complicated than she was, good-natured still, but selfish by upbringing and environment. Both are real people, and therefore the scene becomes a real scene. The behaviour of Voinitsky shocks one by its unexpectedness. With desperate clumsiness he attempts to seize the life which has passed him by. There is the irony, again true to life, that the person he chooses should be a woman such as Yeliena, the sort of 'sophisticated' woman whom men like Voinitsky can know nothing about.

In Uncle Vanya Voinitsky goes through agonies of humiliation over Yeliena. This is why, when the professor attempts to seize the family property, Voinitsky runs berserk and takes shots at him with a revolver. When this occurs one sees immediately that this is what must happen. Chekhov has worked off the failure of The Wood Demon. He was a man who could not submit to an artistic failure.

Six of the characters in The Wood Demon are left out of Uncle Vanya as an irrelevant nuisance, but one of the characters who remains is

the 'Wood Demon' himself. He now answers to the name of Astrov.
Astrov is bitterly aware that he is regarded as a crank. He occasionally
drinks to bolster his confidence. It is clear that his day-dreams are an
escape from the terrible sights he sees in the course of his routine
labours as a country doctor. Yet Astrov remains obstinately the
Wood Demon, though heavily disguised, and through him Chekhov
tries to maintain a commentary which his slender material –
stripped-down episodes out of the previous play – will not sustain.

Tolstoy, for one, did not read the two main characters in the way
Chekhov intended:

. . . he keeps the spectator's attention fixed on the fate of the unhappy
Uncle Vanya and his friend Dr. Astrov, but he is sorry for them only
because they are unhappy, without attempting to prove whether or not
they deserve pity. He makes them say that once upon a time they were the
best people in the district, but he does not show us in what way they were
good. I can't help feeling that they have always been worthless creatures
and that their sufferings cannot therefore be worthy of our attention.[1]

This is fair comment. The play provokes little or no thought because
the situation shown really reflects little in life beyond itself. In fact
the play only becomes interesting if one sees it as a technical
exercise deliberately planned and carefully executed.

The most significant of the technical advances Chekhov has made
in the play is the creation of a successful last act for the first time.
In the previous plays he bundled his characters out unceremoniously,
afflicting an early version of Ivanov with a heart attack, shooting him
in a later version, and getting several indefinite characters in *The
Wood Demon* to marry one another.

In *Uncle Vanya*, Chekhov's arrangements have been so successful
that the audience dreads the explosion of hysteria just before it
occurs. The aftermath in Act Four is a copybook result of good
planning. The audience is able to speculate about it with some hope
of accuracy, and its predictions are borne out in essentials, the
surprises simply coming in small details which we immediately feel
we ought to have foreseen.

The characters successfully embody the theory Chekhov was
developing as he went along – that much of the drama of a person
resides inside him. One is able to perceive enough about the

---

[1] From an interview published in the journal *Slovo*, quoted in Magarshack,
Chekhov the Dramatist, p. 16.

characters to be able to construe their reactions to what is going on in front of them even when they are saying little themselves.

Uncle Vanya is a great stride forward technically, but the subject is limited. By contrast, *The Seagull* is less accomplished, but this is because Chekhov feels ready to do much more. In fact he takes an enormous stride forward. It is a work of art which embodies speculation about the eternal mystery 'what is art'? Like Keats's *Ode to a Nightingale* and *Ode on a Grecian Urn*, it is intended to enchant us and 'tease us out of thought'. There is the living Nina and there are the works of art which Trigorin and his rival, Konstantin Trepliov, create out of her. There is the riddle posed by the relations of the two actresses, Arkadina (the mother of Konstantin) and Nina, to their art. There is the even more elusive problem of the precise relation between the arts of actor and writer.

Chekhov tries to deal with too many themes all at once, so that nothing can be examined in any detail. The play, therefore, remains a puzzling sketch in the last analysis. Time passes rapidly, personalities harden, artists develop their skills, and a sparse, suggestive dialogue must carry it all.

Chekhov's main purpose with *The Seagull* is to educate audiences into a new attitude to the drama. He feels qualified to do this now. He wishes to point the connection between what occurs on the stage and the lives being lived by those who watch. He hopes that the discussions started on the stage will be continued among the audience. In a neglected medium Chekhov is re-stating the relationship between art and life.[1] One of the leading characters, Trigorin, is a novelist and short-story writer. The materials he turns into his kind of art (himself included) are re-illuminated on the stage.

On the stage, as the play opens, is a poverty-stricken, dull schoolmaster in the company of an intelligent but desperately lonely girl he is in love with.

MEDVIEDENKO. Why do you always wear black?
MASHA. I am in mourning for my life. I'm unhappy.
MEDVIEDENKO. But why? (*Meditatively.*) I can't understand it. You're in good health. Your father isn't rich, but he's comfortably off. My life is much harder than yours. I only get twenty-three roubles a month, and from that my superannuation is deducted. Yet I don't wear mourning.

---

[1] A seagull came to be chosen as the symbol of the Moscow Art Theatre.

These are the raw materials of life. Behind these people, a stage is being erected on which Nina for the first time in her life is going to act, Trepliov's first play. The situation of Masha and Medviedenko is potential material for art, but Trepliov does not realise it. He flaunts his talent before the two women in his life, Nina and his mother. He bitterly denounces his mother for her selfishness, revealing what is in large part his motive for writing. 'You mustn't praise anybody but her . . . you must acclaim her and go into raptures over her wonderful acting in The Lady with the Camellias, or The Fumes of Love.'

After Trepliov's outburst against Arkadina, it is difficult to take his criticisms of the modern theatre at their face value.

. . . when I watch these great and talented people . . . when I hear them trying to squeeze a moral out of the tritest words and emptiest scenes – some petty little moral that's easy to understand and suitable for use in the home; when I'm presented with a thousand variations of the same old thing, the same thing again and again – well, I just have to escape. I run away . . . We need new art forms. New forms are wanted . . .

Trepliov is intelligent and the objects of his iconoclastic urge are the right ones, but everything is against his achieving anything. His talent has been discouraged, his self-confidence undermined. The direction he takes has been chosen arbitrarily.

Trepliov mentions Trigorin, his mother's lover –

It's all very clever and charming, but . . . if you've been reading Tolstoy, or Zola, you don't feel like reading Trigorin afterwards.

Of course he is jealous. One is left pondering the factors which go to produce artistic failure or success. They are seemingly as accidental as life itself. But since one is not quite sure what Trigorin writes, there is not enough evidence to weigh up. Chekhov is putting his audience in an impossible position. One is constantly being invited to make judgements on insufficient evidence.

The fragment of a play which the terribly nervous Trepliov allows his audience to see is pretentious and vapid. He has chosen a huge subject in order to evade a detailed examination of experience, which he is not equipped for. Nina and he are at an age when it is impossible to predict how they may develop. Dorn, the local doctor, is the best judge of them simply because he has no vested interest in art. Trigorin is silent and non-committal. Arkadina's damaging interjections during the performance are a display of cowardice at any threat to her own kind of drama. The first act of *The Seagull* has been a close-packed commentary on the apparently impossible conditions in which works of art get produced.

The act ends with Dorn trying to talk seriously to Trepliov about his play, but all Trepliov can think of is the disappearance of Nina. She has talked to Trigorin and shown her admiration for him. She is now ignoring Trepliov. She does not know enough to discount the obvious contempt for Trepliov's play which her elders show. She has not liked it much herself in any case. She has told him beforehand, 'there's hardly any action in your play, there are only speeches. And then I do think there ought to be love in a play.' The act ends as it began with a reminder of all that Trepliov has not included in his play about the 'common soul of the world'. Masha approaches Dorn.

MASHA. . . . You must help me. Help me, or I'll do something stupid, something that'll make a mockery of my life and mess it up . . . I can't go on like this . . .
DORN. But what is it? How am I to help you?
MASHA. I'm so unhappy. Nobody, nobody knows how unhappy I am! . . . I love Konstantin.

Masha will reappear as the central character in *Three Sisters*. She represents the everyday tragedy which Chekhov feels that plays ought to include.

In the second act Trepliov makes a histrionic entrance, carrying a seagull he has shot. He lays it at Nina's feet – 'Soon I shall kill myself in the same way.' Nina finds his grand gesture strident and slightly ridiculous. Killing the bird appears cruel because it has effected nothing. Trepliov wishes to communicate his sorrow. He fails. Trigorin uses the same seagull to great poetic effect in his subsequent talk to Nina. One asks whether the seagull has died in vain. The question which follows is whether anything justifies suffering and sacrifice, whether Nina, like the seagull, should have been left alone. People have their lives taken from them in order that a few ephemeral objects or performances may be produced. Perhaps these are not worth the suffering their creation entails. Dorn is the most admirable person in the play. People in the play turn to him for help, not to the artists, who are self-absorbed and cut off from he others. Dorn helps those around him, and Trigorin does the reverse but is of importance to others whom he will never see – his public.

Trigorin approaches. He notes down in a pocketbook a few details he has observed about Masha. He is pleased to meet Nina –

I've forgotten what it feels like to be eighteen or nineteen, indeed I can't imagine it at all clearly. That's why the girls in my novels and stories are usually so artificial.

He notices Nina's envy of his success as an artist, and wishes for her sympathy. His personal life is empty.

...I feel as though I'm devouring my own life, that for the sake of the honey I give to all and sundry I'm despoiling my best flowers of their pollen, that I'm plucking the flowers themselves and trampling on their roots.

All the time, he is toying with the situation he is in as a possible subject for his art.

The worst distress Trigorin suffers is a constant dissatisfaction with his work, which allows him no peace. 'I feel that . . . everything . . . I write is a sham – false to the very core.' Nina, who has not yet achieved anything, cannot understand this. She cannot see beyond the triumph of a first achievement to the penalties it will involve, personal and artistic, the dissatisfaction, the fear that one has reached a point beyond which one is for ever unequipped to go. Trigorin can foresee the sort of thing that is likely to happen to her, but he does not give her any advice.[1] He sees that life can never be arranged for another person, that the advantages and disadvantages of anybody's course of action can never be weighed in advance.

The subject of a story comes to him when he notices the seagull –

...a young girl, like you, has lived beside a lake from childhood. She loves the lake as a seagull does, and she's happy and free as a seagull. But a man chances to come along, sees her, and having nothing better to do, destroys her, just like this seagull here.

Evidence of the truth of this story, in which Nina is cast as the heroine, is that it occurs. Trigorin will be the man. Perhaps he foresees it, but he knows that if it is not he it will be someone else.

Art operates in a region of probabilities. Trigorin is very observant

---

[1] At the beginning of Act Three Nina will ask him whether she should go on the stage. 'One can't give advice about that' is the reply.

— it is his job, but as a result he is cold to the stuff of his art. Perhaps this is the penalty of accuracy. It is so in Trigorin's case. He is only moved by the objects he makes.

In Act Three Trigorin has decided to fall in love with Nina, and he begins to act out the story he stated as a theme suitable for his art. He tries to get Arkadina to release him. She overwhelms him with endearments, frightened of losing an influential lover at her age. His surrender is rapid. Trigorin has not been entirely serious in his histrionic description of his love for Nina.

Young love, enchanting, poetical — love that carries you off into a world of dreams — it's the only thing that can bring happiness on this earth!

This is in fact as far as the play goes. There is a sudden, startling drop in quality from now on. Chekhov has posed his situations. He now has to resolve them. What will become of Trepliov, Trigorin and Nina? All are on the brink of making some discovery about themselves, of bringing out in themselves what is potentially there, if anything. Chekhov has run out of space, and the rest is huddled and unconvincing. Trigorin and Trepliov, in their separate ways, pay the penalty of their personal ineffectuality. Trepliov's ruined self-esteem incapacitates him from deciding what to do with his art. Trigorin cannot get deeply involved with life, so that both he and his art remain doomed to sterile cleverness. Nina, by contrast, is forced to throw the whole of her gift for living into her art. She lives a full life in her art, and finds that this makes up to her for everything. It is a little vague and plangent, giving one a misty sense of edification if one is not alert.

Two years elapse in the play between Act Three and Act Four. Chekhov is rushing the end. He himself was dubious about the play the moment he finished it — 'I began it forte and ended it pianissimo.'[1]

At the beginning of Act Four Trepliov is starting to make his way as a writer. His private life is melancholy as ever. He has followed Nina's tragic life from a distance — the loss of her child, her desertion by Trigorin. He has watched her first failures on the professional stage. Trigorin is visiting the house.

TRIGORIN. I think I'll go back to Moscow tomorrow. I've got to, really. I'm in a hurry to finish a novel, and besides, I've promised to give them something for an anthology. In short, it's just the same as ever.

[1] Letter to Souvorin, November 1895.

He says this happily to the struggling young writer. Arkadina admits to not having read a word by her son. The heartlessness of these celebrities increases the poignancy of the situation of Trepliov and of Nina who, it turns out, is lurking in the cold outside. Trigorin's character seems to have suffered a lightning change immediately after the period dealt with in Act Three, for Nina will inform Trepliov that during her life with Trigorin 'he didn't believe in the theatre, he was always laughing at my dreams'. The previous Trigorin took such things a little more seriously.

The characters in the fourth act all 'represent' things. Their opinions no longer shade into one another. They stand there pollarded, hard to recognise, acting out a sad little lesson. 'I think,' says Nina,

I now know, Kostia, that what matters in our work – whether you act on the stage or write stories – what really matters is not fame, or glamour, not the things I used to dream about – but knowing how to endure things. How to bear one's cross and have faith. I have faith now and I'm not suffering quite so much, and when I think of my vocation I'm not afraid of life.

Chekhov is putting up a smoke-screen to cover up the fact that his play has fizzled out. The last act is an exhibition of mournfulness, filling audiences, flattered at being required to ponder about 'Art', with a nameless sadness and spiritual uplift.

Chekhov saw Nina as the key figure in the play. All the questions in the play involve her. She creates and at the same time is material for the creations of others. She is broken into service as an instrument to further the work of others, and yet has an independent life of her own, is both creator and created. Nina's personal life becomes ruined, unlike that of Arkadina who considers her roles simply as vehicles for self-display and has no respect for the art of others.

The play would exert greater fascination if Nina were capable of carrying the weight of significance which is placed on her. In fact there is no proof that she is a finer artist than the other three (Trigorin, Trepliov, Arkadina), and so one cannot decide finally on the merits of the others relative to hers. We do not see Nina's performance. We have to take it on trust, and Chekhov has not created a personality on the stage which is sufficiently fascinating to permit us to do this. He has not given her enough to do. She needs more space to develop in.

The Moscow Art Theatre built up The Seagull as the representative

Chekhov masterpiece. The shaky last act has done great damage to Chekhov's image. It is indeed 'wistful' and 'poignant' and all the things that Chekhov is to many people. There was always the danger that the theme, the relationship between art and life, was too delicate a matter for Chekhov's first attempt at a major work in a medium he had still not entirely mastered, and so it turned out. The first three acts are filled with insights; the play is a more important play than the relatively elementary *Uncle Vanya*, but only with his last two plays will Chekhov's apprenticeship be over.

Tolstoy said of *The Seagull* —

The play is chock full of all sorts of things, but no one really knows what they are for. And Europe shouts, 'Wonderful!' Chekhov is one of our most gifted writers, but *The Seagull* is a very bad play . . .

. . . In his short story *My Life*, Chekhov makes his hero read Ostrovsky and say, 'All this can happen in life,' but had he read *The Seagull*, he would never have said that.[1]

Part of this is not wholly fair to *The Seagull*. Much does ring disturbingly true as one watches the play. It is just that in our memory the falsity of the last act reflects discredit upon what preceded it. In the theatre the audience is in danger of assuming that the characters it sees in the last act were like this previously.

The sort of play Chekhov envisaged would do some things better than a story could. But there is a wider separation between the narrative and the drama than he at first estimated. He hoped that a realistic play would turn out to be more 'real' than a realistic narrative, a closer approximation to the way we experience people in daily life. Seeing a person before one's eyes on a stage ought to be an improvement on being told about him. In fact, if the writer is not careful, it is a quite unexpectedly separate kind of experience. At the time Chekhov wrote *Ivanov* he was already saying:

Let things that happen on the stage be as complex and yet just as simple as they are in life. For instance, people are having a meal at the table, just having a meal, but at the same time their happiness is being created or their lives are being smashed up.[2]

[1] Souvorin's Diary, February 1897. Quoted in Magarshack, *Chekhov the Dramatist*, p. 17.
[2] Fen, *Plays by Anton Chekhov*. Quoted in Introduction.

It turns out to be a fallacy that watching people having a meal on the stage will be like watching people having a meal at home. Such an illusion is extremely difficult to create. On a stage everything becomes larger than life, and all conversation carries far greater weight than it normally does. Chekhov, for one thing, did not intend his plays to be as sad as they turned out to be on the stage. He was frequently disappointed with performances of them.

The collaboration between actor and author is one of the many teasing problems set in *The Seagull*. Chekhov was fascinated by the infinite variety of effects which occur when a written text is brought to life on a stage. Several individualities react on one another and produce a totality which will vary with every performance. Chekhov instructed the actors of the Moscow Art Theatre: 'You must create a character which is entirely different from the character created by the author, and when these two characters – the author's and the actor's – merge into one, you will get a work of art.'[1] Chekhov's major problem, nevertheless, was to forestall dramatic interpretations which worked against his own intention – to prevent the atmosphere in the theatre from becoming overcharged, prevent talk from appearing like garrulity, a fit of weeping from looking like the prelude to a suicide attempt, and an intentionally weak joke from masquerading as an epigram. Chekhov gradually discovered that one way to prevent overstatement on the stage was to understate everything in the text.

The deftness of the stories is completely there only in *Three Sisters* and *The Cherry Orchard*. These plays will be on the same level of achievement as some of the best of Chekhov's stories, but they will not be stage duplicates of the stories. The one medium can do things the other cannot. One can see discoveries being made about this, information being built up as the early plays succeed one another. In the plays, the Chekhovian sense of physical closeness to individual characters cannot be present. Instead, the attention of the audience is concentrated on groups of people, several people in simultaneous action and the patterns and cross-currents which are set up among them. Nothing can be underlined by the author, and this is why there is much to argue about after each act – but there should not be too much, as there is in *The Seagull*.

It requires great skill in the dramatist to supply us with all the information we need. It must appear to be left to the audience,

[1] Magarshack, *Chekhov the Dramatist*, p. 152.

strangers observing from outside, to see things the participants miss, or no longer see because they are preoccupied with living their lives. This can be done in a narrative too, but it is usually done in a different way. In Chekhov's plays the onlookers are conceived as strangers; in the stories they tend to be conceived as intimates although it is accepted that even the closest intimates must remain strangers to some degree. One's opinions about characters in Chekhov's plays are more extreme, but must remain less accurate, more controversial. With Chekhov's stories one's opinions about the characters are never as clear-cut. One knows too much about them, or imagines one does. One knows less about the characters in Chekhov's plays, or perhaps one simply knows them in a different way. The plays complement the stories. Chekhov approaches life from many angles.

In solving his problems with the drama, Chekhov was inventing a new use of the stage. Nobody before had achieved quite that illusion of private life, the onlookers being apparently left completely to their own resources, to make their own sense of the glimpses the transparent fourth wall of the stage afforded them.

15. Three Sisters – 'laughter shining through tears'

Chekhov was the enemy of clichés and conventions, of everything that imposed a mechanical pattern on a man's life, making him dull, blundering and dangerous in his conduct. He saw the contemporary theatre as a bad influence, filled with impossible people, pernicious sentiments and lies.

> ... It is not the public that is to blame for our theatres being so wretched. The public is always and everywhere the same: intelligent and stupid, sympathetic and pitiless, according to mood. It has always been a flock which needs good shepherds and dogs, and it has always gone in the direction in which the shepherds and the dogs drove it.[1]

Chekhov wished to open people's eyes to the life around them. He wished to permit access to experiences which can rarely be transmitted in full in real life, while at the same time producing the illusion that his audience is sitting comfortably out of sight watching real people talking their everyday prose and exposing their everyday selves to one another. While attempting to create the impression of transmitting only the information about other people that is available in daily life, Chekhov tried somehow to make his characters as transparent as they can be made in a story. He gradually mastered this problem – the difficulty of coaxing sufficient information out of his characters, packing natural, freely flowing talk with self-revelations, while maintaining an illusion of the reticences normal in conversation even between people accustomed to living together.

Three Sisters is an object lesson in the way a tight circle of intimates can prevent one another from acting independently – a study in frustration. The characters sap one another's confidence and undermine one another's resolve. At first there is no practical obstacle to at least two of the sisters leaving the town they live in and going back to Moscow, yet we see this steadily becoming impossible. Despondency turns into despair. The paralysis of the will they cause in one another results in poisonous complications. Moscow is a symbol in

[1] Letter to Souvorin, November 1888.

this play, as it is elsewhere in Chekhov, of a world where life is full
of incident, full of satisfying activity.

The sisters are well equipped to analyse the shortcomings of the
life they lead, but cannot visualise any other. They are gentle beings
with educated tastes and refined feelings, and they have not been
trained to act and think boldly. Courage is a matter of training as
much as intelligence. Their house attracts people who are equally
incapable of dealing with their difficulties. They demoralise one
another so that all become good for nothing. Power will soon go to
an occupant of the house who is not so constrained in her activities.
Natasha, who becomes the wife of the head of the household, is
without imagination and therefore without mercy.

The three sisters reminisce about their father's death, which has
occurred exactly a year ago. The day is the anniversary of a death and
a life, for it is also the youngest girl's name-day. The past seems
recent because little has happened since. The two unmarried sisters,
Olga the eldest and Irena the youngest, are convinced that they will
soon leave for Moscow. Masha is married and knows that her
opportunities are lost. Young officers wander in from a nearby
room; Vershinin, their new commander, is mentioned. A few
remarks by the nicest of them, Toozenbach, sketch Vershinin's
character – he is all right, but he talks too much.

For the sisters it is no ordinary day, and this soon gives the
conversation a deeper note than, we already gather, it ordinarily
has. Irena and Toozenbach, young people full of energy, talk
heatedly about filling their time with work instead of doing nothing
all day. They are against the way society is constituted. They feel that
their fate will be different from that of the previous generation.
Masha can stand no more talk and makes a move to leave.

Masha is the female character one watches most in the play. In so
far as there is a central character, it will be Masha. She has said
nothing up to now, just irritated the others by whistling to herself
and reading a book. She has attracted attention to herself by not
speaking. Olga starts weeping; Masha turns on her and tells her to
stop snivelling. Chekhov gave careful instructions about acting the
part. 'You can look angry, that's all right, but not sad',[1] and 'make
them (the audience) feel you're cleverer than your sisters – or at
least that you think yourself cleverer'.[2] Masha is stronger than her

[1] Quoted in The Oxford Chekhov, III, 313.   [2] Ibid. p. 314.

sisters, yet the bonds which tie her to her present life are too strong
for her.

Vershinin, the colonel from Moscow, once a subordinate of their
father, calls to pay his respects. He enjoys holding forth to those
younger than himself on the glorious future of the human race as he
sees it. One feels Toozenbach was probably right in his summary of
him. Vershinin talks too much. Poor Toozenbach is never listened
to by anyone because he is really the most original thinker among
them. He is often interrupted by the venomous poseur Soliony who
projects himself as a misunderstood genius and whose precarious
self-confidence is bolstered up when he senses a kindred spirit in
Vershinin. He will always be at his most offensive to Toozenbach
when Vershinin is present. Toozenbach is the man most isolated in
this small society.

Chekhov does not believe there is such a thing as an objective
idea. He judges people, not the ideas they hold. It is not so much
the arguments but the way they are presented that he is interested in.
One has to study not the logic but the context, the speaker, and how
his words are received. Vershinin soothes the three sisters by telling
them that their mere presence in a provincial town is a civilising
influence. 'After you've gone, perhaps six more people like you will
turn up, then twelve and so on, until in the end most people will
have become like you.' This will be accomplished in 'two or three
hundred years'. Vershinin is an older man complimenting three
young women. The result of his little speech is that Masha, who
thinks she is 'cleverer' than the others, decides to stay to lunch.
Chekhov does not intend any of the talk in *Three Sisters* to be on a
profound intellectual level. He intends the reverse. These people
have become dull and repetitive. Vershinin is a shining light only
when compared with Masha's husband Koolyghin, a foolish
schoolmaster.

Andrey Prozorov – the head of the household – has revealed his
incompetence by falling in love with a stupid girl called Natasha.
There is an instinctive enmity between her and the others. At the
beginning of the next act, Natasha has become mistress of the household, and she already holds absolute power in it. Andrey has
abandoned the hope that he will ever get a job in Moscow. He feels
dishonoured; those he regards as his inferiors see that he is a failure.

It is carnival week. Everybody waits for a carnival party to begin.
Masha and Vershinin have the sort of conversation that has evidently

become habitual between them. She complains of her life. He is preoccupied with his latest family row, and although he feels the obligation to exhibit an elevated mind he cannot bring himself to talk of anything else. Irena comes in with Toozenbach. Vershinin and Toozenbach have become adversaries in a sporadic arguing game. Toozenbach, who is in love with Irena, has no quarrel with life at the moment. 'Life will be just the same as ever not merely in a couple of hundred years' time, but in a million years.' Toozenbach cannot communicate his contentment to the others. Opinions are as shifting, as variable, as the rest of life. Vershinin and Toozenbach each speak with a different emphasis from that in Act One. Vershinin is getting worn down by the miseries of his home life. There is a defensive and even rather querulous note in his remark that he did not have the advantages of the Military Academy as Toozenbach did. Toozenbach, on the other hand, is relaxed and self-confident in the knowledge that he is expressing himself better than the other man. The thoughts in themselves are not important. Real people stand before one in all their variousness. The thoughts take their complexion from the shifting moods of the speakers.

The spirits of those in the room begin to improve, and the guests are starting to become a little less subdued, when Natasha says that her son is ill and needs quiet. The visitors simply have to bow to the fact that they are no longer welcome. Everyone is too polite to say much. Natasha has proved her strength. From now on she acts with greater and greater assurance, her malice always covered over with a coating of sentimentality.

As in all Chekhov's plays, the third act is the climax. Fire is devastating one of the nearby streets. The situation brings to a crisis the panic at being trapped which is present at the end of Act Two. Natasha appears and starts threatening Olga, attacking her with wheedling spite for not sacking an old family servant who is of no use in the house. Olga tries to explain herself to Natasha. 'It may be that we've been brought up in a peculiar way, but anyway I just can't bear it. When people are treated like that, it gets me down, I feel quite ill.'

Toozenbach mentions that he is organising a concert to aid the homeless. He wishes Masha to take part, but he is the only person who sees her brilliance as a musician. She has given up playing years ago. When her talent is mentioned her husband replies: 'You're right, Baron. I'm very fond of Masha.' Originality seems useless where nobody recognises its existence. There is only one's private conscience to accuse one of failure, and there is no reward for success. Toozenbach is the only one who has made a decision about his life. He has taken a job at the brick-works. There seems to be no way out into a world of free, gracious activity.

In Act Four the soldiers are about to leave. Toozenbach seems to have rescued Irena. She is to be a teacher and will live with him at the brick-works. But there is a rumour that Soliony has challenged Toozenbach to a duel.

Koolyghin is the only person in a happy mood, but this in itself makes the occasion more sombre. There is the risk that the period we have witnessed might turn out to have been a time of comparative happiness. Mediocrity will now go unchallenged.

Toozenbach and Irena hold the stage briefly. Irena is in an abstracted mood, taking no action to prevent Toozenbach from meeting Soliony. When he says that the one thing missing on her side is love, out comes the hackneyed reply: 'I've never loved anyone in my life. Oh, I've had such dreams about being in love!' One infers that Toozenbach cannot bring himself to mention the duel he is about to fight, but wishes that Irena would – as a sign that she really desires a future with him. She still hopes for something better.

Irena sits on a swing and waits for what is to be. Andrey comes out and talks of his misery.

'Why do we become so dull and commonplace and uninteresting almost before we've begun to live? Why do we get lazy, indifferent, useless, unhappy?... There's never been a scholar or an artist or a saint in this place, never a single man sufficiently outstanding to make you feel passionately that you wanted to emulate him.'

He talks, and as he talks the lives of Toozenbach and Irena hang in the balance. One achievement would outweigh everything because it would make hope easier. But hope is never easy, and Toozenbach's death will lend weight to Andrey's despair and to that of his sisters.

Vershinin appears, to say goodbye to Masha. His talk is as banal as ever, 'the time isn't far off when the light will spread everywhere'. Vershinin leaves. Masha's husband enters. Like Vershinin, he is gentle and clinging. He needs her support as Vershinin did.

'Never mind, let her cry, let her... My dear Masha, my dear, sweet Masha... You're my wife, and I'm happy in spite of everything... We'll start our life over again in the same old way –'

Masha breaks down briefly. 'A green oak grows by a curving shore, and round that oak hangs a golden chain.' The opening lines of a poem she has forgotten have been on her lips all through the play – their beauty is elusive, yet has an appropriateness always just beyond her grasp, haunting and tormenting her. A pistol shot is heard in the distance. The proximity to death keeps their nerves on the stretch while the little world which they have all been inhabiting is dismantled with disturbing rapidity. In retrospect, it seems to have been snug and secure. The inability to destroy it of their own volition, to break away and go to 'Moscow' can be understood. The prospect of beginning something new is terrifying, but now it must be faced. As the troops form up to leave, Masha's last words say everything that is needed.

. . . 'They're leaving us . . . one of them's gone for good . . . for ever! We're left alone . . . to start our lives all over again. We must go on living . . . we must go on living.'

An episode in their lives is over.

Three Sisters shows the hell people bring about through cowardice and mental weakness.

'You say that you have wept over my plays. Yes, and not only you alone. But I did not write them for this purpose, it is Alekseev [Stanislavsky] who has made such crybabies of them. I desired something other. I only wished to tell people honestly: "Look at yourselves, see how badly and boringly you live!" '[1]

Most of Three Sisters seems to take place in stuffy rooms after dark. It is perhaps Chekhov's blackest work of art. Natasha is one of his most sinister figures, yet it is evident that her relentless activity, her erosion of the lives and liberties of the Prozorovs is brought about by their weakness. She is created by the sweet young people she victimises.

Chekhov derides Natasha's victims. He hates passivity, for evil comes of it. He does not hold the hands of the three spinsters (one of them nominally married) and weep with them. Chekhov 'was sincerely convinced', writes Stanislavsky, 'that it was a gay comedy, almost a farce. I cannot remember that he ever defended any of his opinions with such feeling as he defended this one.'[2] If it is comedy,

[1] Quoted in Simmons, Chekhov, p. 581.
[2] Quoted in The Oxford Chekhov, III, 314.

it is comedy of a peculiarly savage kind. Chekhov sees why potential old maids have always been a standing joke. Those more fortunate than they must protect themselves from being infected by their demoralisation. There is a streak of ruthlessness in Chekhov. He shows what sitting about feeling one another's pulses leads to. Too much identification with others, too much sympathy can damage the person who indulges in it. Too much pity encourages self-pity in the recipient and, even worse, in the giver.

... *solving a problem and stating a problem correctly.* It is only the second that is obligatory for the artist.

This statement of Chekhov's can be finally understood only after experiencing Chekhov's major art. In isolation it could be quoted to epitomise the lazily wistful Chekhov created by a past generation of critics — 'laughter shining through tears' — 'the delicate, humorous, compassionate mind which observed, understood and forgave'.[1] But the statement quoted above issues from the man who wrote *Three Sisters*. A fixed, seemingly impracticable human entanglement presented with sufficient accuracy may jolt an audience into achieving new insights. These in turn may make the discovery of solutions possible — still immensely difficult, but at least possible. For Chekhov stating a problem correctly was a disciplined and responsible exercise.

Tolstoy spoke sternly, as to a member of the opposite persuasion from himself, when he said to Chekhov:

Shakespeare ... grabs the reader by the scruff of the neck and leads him to a definite objective, not permitting him to wander off the road. But where are you going with your heroines? From the divan where they lie to the closet and back.[2]

Tolstoy did not realise that the differences between his own practice of art and Chekhov's required finer distinctions than this. Chekhov had already seen what Tolstoy was rather unnecessarily informing him about:

... the writers who we say are for all time or are simply good, and who intoxicate us have one common and very important characteristic; they

[1] Desmond MacCarthy. Quoted in Magarshack, *Chekhov the Dramatist*, Chapter I.
[2] Simmons, *Leo Tolstoy*.

are going towards something and are summoning you towards it, too, and you feel not with your mind, but with your whole being, that they have some object, just like the ghost of Hamlet's father, who did not come and disturb the imagination for nothing.[1]

How are the Prozorovs ever to break their constipated routine? This is what Chekhov's play is about. He has set out to 'disturb the imagination' of his audience with this.

As one looks back upon the play one can see that it contains implicit solutions. These result from the accuracy with which the problems have been stated. Gentleness and liberality are all very well, but there are situations in which they cannot operate. There are cases where tolerance is not a virtue. There are cases in life where violence is necessary – one thinks of Pierre's furious reaction in *War and Peace* when Prince Vasily tried to get too close to him. It cleared the air.

As one looks back, one's attention centres on Toozenbach, the figure on whom Chekhov has led one to pin one's hopes, only to dash them unceremoniously with a pistol shot. One remembers Pierre's duel in *War and Peace*. Pierre deserved to win. Toozenbach has lacked energy. Soliony's victimisation of him has steadily intensified, in parallel with Natasha's victimisation of the Prozorovs. The presence of Toozenbach has brought only the faintest breath of fresh air. He has carried no authority, has lacked confidence in himself. His gentle refinement is not needed. He goes out like a lamb going to the slaughter, and one watches his exit with mixed feelings – as Irena does. Perhaps she is right. Perhaps her withdrawal from Toozenbach is really the most hopeful thing in the play. Difficult judgements such as these are easier to make when the artist has not solved anything on our behalf – when he is not standing in our light.

Chekhov is not Toozenbach. Perhaps it is Toozenbach who is the 'willy wet-leg' of D. H. Lawrence's imagination. Certainly the nickname is not otherwise appropriate.

[1] Letter to Souvorin, November 1892.

16. 'I shall call the play a comedy' – The Cherry Orchard

In contrast with *Three Sisters*, *The Cherry Orchard* is astonishingly light and fresh – astonishingly so, when one thinks of the labour it exacted from Chekhov shortly before his death. The subject is the immense changes a generation lives through. This, one would have thought, was a daunting project – but, to the bewilderment of his friends, Chekhov declared: 'The play is gay and frivolous.' He meant that it was entirely without solutions such as Tolstoy was demanding from works of art.

It is art as Tolstoy had once seen it himself.

'The aim of an artist is not to solve a problem irrefutably but to make people love life in all its countless inexhaustible manifestations. If I were to be told that I could write a novel whereby I might irrefutably establish what seemed to me the correct point of view on all social problems, I would not even devote two hours' work to such a novel.'[1]

Chekhov cannot judge the people in his play because he refuses to withdraw his sympathy from any of them.

Chekhov's typical artistic innovation is the inconsequentiality of the dialogue in his plays and stories alike. Conversation flows on endlessly. It has no beginning or end. Fragments of it are caught fortuitously when the curtain is raised or a door is opened into a room; when someone approaches on a railway platform or is overheard in a garden. People engaged in conversation seldom listen attentively to one another because they are attending to themselves. Often a casual onlooker sees more essential detail than those who have grown used to each other and no longer hear or see one another. Talk is seldom original, but the person who talks is always interesting. One thinks of Chekhov's personal remark about Tolstoy –

I know Tolstoy, I feel that I know him well, and that I understand every movement of his brows – and yet I love him.[2]

[1] From a letter written in 1865, when he was publishing the first books of *War and Peace*. Quoted in Christian, *Tolstoy's 'War and Peace'*.
[2] Letter to L. A. Avilov, March 1899.

This is the way Chekhov attended to people.

Chekhov wishes to convey the awkwardness of life itself, the stupidities of even the most intelligent in unguarded moments, which are frequently far more revealing than their most polished utterances. The latter are projections of an Olympian wisdom which cannot exist in the real conditions of life. Chekhov was always aware of the special problems in which the recognition of such facts involved the writer.

> ... don't be afraid to show yourself foolish; we must have freedom of thinking, and only he is an emancipated thinker who is not afraid to write foolish things. Don't round things out, don't polish – but be awkward and impudent.[1]

There are no examples in English nineteenth-century fiction of talk as accurately natural and therefore inconsequential as Chekhov's. His art of dialogue is indeed startlingly original. The source of it is not Ibsen or Strindberg, because it does not occur in the plays alone – it is already there in the earlier stories. The most obvious literary source is Tolstoy. Most authors project people as thinking in a 'consistent, streamlined, polished, ultra-logical way', writes Tolstoy's friend V. V. Stasov:

> But is this the way we think? Of course not. I have only met one example up to now – Count Leo Tolstoy. He is the only person who in his novels and dramas gives us real monologues with all their irregularity, fortuitousness, incompleteness and jerkiness.[2]

Tolstoy knew that conversation is usually a matter of monologues. (One thinks of those between Vronsky and Anna Karenina.) The auditor usually hears what is uttered in his own way. Genuine communication, when it occurs, is often achieved in unexpected and apparently accidental ways. Such apparently casual moments are the most important ones in real life.[3] Tolstoy illustrates this in his

---

[1] Letter to Aleksandr Chekhov, April 1889.

[2] Christian, Tolstoy's 'War and Peace'.

[3] It is not accidental that D. H. Lawrence (at the time he was writing his own plays) was once an admirer of Chekhov.

> Tchekhov is a new thing in the drama. (April 1912)

> I believe that, just as an audience was found in Russia for Tchekhov, so an audience might be found in England for some of my stuff... It's the producer that is lacking, not the audience. I am sure we are

short story *Schoolboys and Art*, a story which has the apparent fortuitousness, the haphazard quality of a Chekhov piece. The coming
together of husband and wife at the end of *Family Happiness* is another
example. So is the snatch of conversation Vronsky hears as Anna
approaches him on the railway platform one moment before their
first meeting.

'All the same I don't agree with you,' said the lady's voice.
'It's the Petersburg view, madame.'
'Not Petersburg, but simply feminine,' she responded.

The human being strives to reveal himself, and never does so
completely. Nevertheless we do catch glimpses of one another in a

---

sick of the rather bony, bloodless drama we get nowadays. (February
1913).   *The Letters of D. H. Lawrence* (London, 1932)

The Tolstoy/Chekhov kind of reality is an important ingredient in
Lawrence's work. For him also, talk is usually the tip of the iceberg.
Misunderstanding and apparent deafness to surface meanings overlay the
real dialogue, which is partly wordless.

He became aware of the woman looking at him . . .
He did not know what to do, and turned to his sister. But the wide
grey eyes, almost vacant yet so moving, held him beyond himself.
'Mother, I may have it, mayn't I!' came the child's proud, silvery
tones. 'Mother' – she seemed always to be calling her mother to
remember her – 'mother' – and she had nothing to continue now her
mother had replied 'Yes, my child.' But, with ready invention, the
child stumbled and ran on 'What are those people's names?'
Brangwen heard the abstract:
'I don't know, dear.'
He went on down the road as if he were not living inside himself,
but somewhere outside.
'Who *was* that person?' his sister Effie asked.
'I couldn't tell you,' he answered unknowing.
'She's *somebody* very funny,' said Effie, almost in condemnation.
'That child's like one bewitched.'
'Bewitched – how bewitched?' he repeated.
'You can see for yourself. The mother's plain, I must say – but
that child is like a changeling. She'd be about thirty-five.'
But he took no notice. His sister talked on.
'There's your woman for you,' she continued. 'You'd better marry
her.' But still he took no notice. Things were as they were.
                                              (*The Rainbow*, Chapter 1)

variety of ways, and these are the clues Tolstoy and Chekhov capture as they search for an answer to the question *What is Art?*

Communication is never a matter of words only, but of the living presence of the speaker, and here again it is the quiet, almost accidental movements that are important (not stylised gestures pre-ordained like the rules of conversation). Chekhov felt that he sometimes needed the drama, to convey these. That is one of the reasons he wrote plays. He once described the sort of stage behaviour which his plays were creating.

Suffering ought to be expressed as it is in life – that is, not by the arms and legs, but by the tone and expression; not by gesticulation, but by grace.'

The scene, as the curtain opens on Act One of *The Cherry Orchard*, is fresh and cool. In a country mansion, Lopahin, a businessman, sits waiting to greet the returning Liubov Andryeevna. Essentially the play will be a confrontation between these two people.

The room in which Lopahin waits was formerly the old nursery. He had once been in it long ago when he was a peasant boy. The memory means much to him, though it would not be impaired if the room ceased to exist. The room itself is insubstantial to him, remote from his daily life.

Suddenly there is a Tolstoyan rush of life into the room. There is a whirl of joyous action and yet, at the same time, something is felt to be missing. It is like one of Nikolay Rostov's homecomings in *War and Peace* – Chekhov's favourite novel –

. . . the first minute of meeting them had been so blissful that his happiness now seemed a little thing, and he kept expecting something more and more and more.

If one looks upon an ever present awareness of the limits to human happiness as a weakness, then it is a weakness Chekhov shares with Tolstoy.

Everyone's news comes out quickly. It is the early dawn. The last reserves of energy are being drawn on, and there is not enough concentration to bestow on others. Liubov Andryeevna is magnificent to watch in her spontaneity, like the Rostovs,[2] with the charm, the elegant carelessness, even slovenliness of an old aristocracy. She has

---

[1] Letter to Olga Knipper, January 1900.
[2] Aspects of her character remind one of Anna Karenina too.

the grace of one who has been born to a life of absolute security. Such people are without fear, and so they have not learnt the means of self-defence. Tolstoy finds the same weakness, the same associated beauty, in them. But he grows to hate this beauty, drags it through the mud in *Resurrection* (1900), that strange antithesis to *War and Peace*.

The spontaneity of Liubov Andryeevna and her young daughter Ania is in brilliant contrast to the behaviour of their dependents and admirers – those who live without illusions, comparatively speaking. It was the same with the rather puzzled fellowship which existed between Natasha Rostov and Sonya in *War and Peace*; but Varia and, more importantly, Lopahin fully understand the criticisms which can be levelled against themselves. They understand and yet have the painful consciousness that they cannot help it. Tolstoy was not so generous in his portrayal of Sonya. He has no real interest in dull people. Chekhov quietly gives his attention to every member of the household.

The conflict over the orchard begins early. Lopahin tells Liubov Andryeevna his good news rapidly. She can turn financial disaster into victory by leasing her land for summer villas – of course the house and orchard will have to go.

LOPAHIN. The only outstanding thing about this orchard is that it's very large . . .

Gayev, Liubov Andryeevna's brother, who lives in the house, finds Lopahin an objectionable bore. She herself is sweet to him partly because she is sweet to everybody.[1] Lopahin, a sensitive man, understands this and yet behaves with the warmth that is occasionally found in people who have lived through oppression.

Lopahin has no taste. He has his visions, though: generations of prosperous townsmen who will inhabit the land as well as the towns, men like himself. Gayev puts Lopahin in his place. He pompously tries to start a family discussion over a bookcase which he has discovered to be a hundred years old. Everything surrounding the brother and sister is substantial and alive for them. They cannot take the responsibility for destroying it. For Lopahin, the developer,

---

[1] 'She is intelligent, very kind and absent-minded. She's nice to everybody and always has a smile on her face.' Letter to O. L. Knipper, October 1903. (Quotations from letters relating to the play are from the Appendices of *The Oxford Chekhov*, vol. III.)

H

the same things are insubstantial as a dream. In his eyes it is easy to replace them by something more solid – his own dream.

GAYEV (*opens another window*). The orchard is all white. You haven't forgotten, Liuba? How straight this long avenue is – quite straight, just like a ribbon that's been stretched taut. It glitters on moonlit nights. Do you remember? You haven't forgotten?

LIUBOV ANDRYEEVNA. . . . If only this burden could be taken from me. If only I could forget my past!

The imagery is simple. The issues are clear, and therefore insoluble, for there is nothing to unravel by argument. The rigidity of the avenue cut across land decorated by an infertile orchard expresses much. Much has come of this complete certainty about what is of importance in life – Liubov Andryeevna, for example. Like Keats's 'Cold Pastoral', the orchard 'teases us out of thought' as to the value of its beauty, the admiration it deserves, the priorities it should be given.

Liubov Andryeevna is endlessly fascinating, endlessly puzzling. Over and over again, she behaves in a way that makes one wonder how to value her spontaneity, her inner certainty. It is really much more formidable than Lopahin's decisiveness. Sometimes it is difficult not to see it as the quintessence of selfishness. The student, Trofimov, enters before she has been warned of his presence in the house. He was once the tutor of her little son, who died here.

LIUBOV ANDRYEEVNA (*quietly weeping*). My little boy was lost . . . drowned . . . What for? What for, my friend? (*More quietly*) Ania's asleep there, and here I am, shouting and making a scene. Well, Pyetia? How is it you've lost your good looks? Why have you aged so?

This strikes a slight chill, which passes. As always in Chekhov, there are many instants like this, awkwardnesses which hasten by. They produce an uncanny illusion of real conversation participated in silently by the observer. Ania needs her sleep. Hurting Trofimov is the quietest way for Liuba Andryeevna to relieve her feelings. Charmingly transparent on her part, but troubling all the same. It is wonderful that such simple language can arouse such complicated responses.

By the second act, Lopahin has been driven to desperation.

LOPAHIN. . . . Do you consent to lease your land for villas, or don't you? You can answer in one word: yes or no? Just one word!

After more evasiveness, Liubov Andryeevna inconsequentially embarks on the story of her life – futility and misery, and all her own doing except for the death of her son. She has allowed others to devour her life. Recently she has lived in France, unwilling to return to her own country. Her French villa has been sold to pay debts. Her lover has deserted her and is now ill in Paris.

LIUBOV ANDRYEEVNA. . . . I felt an urge to come back to Russia, to my own country and my little girl.

We know that her daughter fetched her here. She lies to herself as she talks. The little speech concludes with a dramatic climax. She produces a telegram from Paris and tears it up impulsively. This is all really her answer to Lopahin – like Gayev's lecture about his bookcase. After a pause, Lopahin, defending his own way of life, mentions a comic play he has just seen.[1] Liubov Andryeevna cuts him short.

LIUBOV ANDRYEEVNA. I'm sure it wasn't at all amusing . . . Just think what a drab kind of life you lead, what a lot of nonsense you talk!

Clearly, whatever the outcome, this is not going to be a long stay in Russia for Liubov Andryeevna. Her present desire that the loss of her old house might be averted is likely to be stronger than any subsequent wish to visit it. The object of her patriotic nostalgias must not disappear. Her ancestral setting would be gone and, with it, her sense of identity. She associates her attractiveness with the beauty of her ancient home. Charlotta, the stateless governess who amuses them all by performing conjuring tricks, spoke the first lines in Act Two:

. . . who I am, what I exist for, nobody knows . . .

She haunts the play like a comic skeleton at a feast. She embodies Liubov Andryeevna's personal nightmare.

The defensive irritability present in the second act comes to a head when Trofimov also proceeds to attack poor Lopahin:

. . . so far as a wild beast is necessary because it devours everything in its path and so converts one kind of matter into another, you are necessary . . .

Trofimov hates the appearance of smugness in Lopahin's social

[1] 'Writing Act Two was difficult, very much so, but I think it's turned out all right. I shall call the play a comedy.' (Letter from Chekhov to V. I. Nemirovich-Danchenko, September 1903.)

manner with a nervous hatred. He does not wish to know the reason
for it. He is careful not to blur the clarity of his sociology. This
being so, Trofimov is not very convincing when he states his dreams
of a great new society –

... We ought to stop all this self-admiration. We ought to – just work.

His desire for admiration, for assurance, has slipped out. Lopahin is
ignored when he makes the irritating retort that he does work. Each
nervously defends himself.

The sound which comes from the sky at this moment – like a taut
string breaking – disturbs them. Whatever its source,[1] it brings to the
surface forebodings of dissolution, the awareness that the passing
moments do not return, that much has been missed.

In Act Three, Liubov Andryeevna holds a party. The estate is up for
auction on this day. She seizes what is left of her time here. The
gaiety of the occasion, graced almost wholly by local petty officials,
is a travesty of those wonderful parties held by Tolstoy's Rostovs.
There is the same abundant activity compressed into a short space of
time. Almost as much is there in the text of the play as on the stage.
Like Tolstoy, Chekhov does not evoke or suggest – he presents in a
clear light. The experience offered is oddly different from Tolstoy's
though. It is of another age, another century. It is already our world.

The party is held because Liubov Andryeevna is frightened of being
alone. Her irresponsibility irritates Trofimov.

TROFIMOV. . . . for once in your life you must look the truth straight in
the face.
LIUBOV ANDRYEEVNA. What truth? . . . You're able to solve all your
problems in a resolute way . . . you're not old enough yet to have suffered
on account of your problems.

The 'truth' for her is that she loves the cherry orchard. This is a kind
of truth which one may face or turn one's back on. In either case it
will remain unchanged and insoluble for the person it affects.

LIUBOV ANDRYEEVNA. . . . I can't conceive life without the cherry
orchard, and if it really has to be sold, then sell me with it . . . (Embraces
TROFIMOV, kisses him on the forehead.) You know, my son was drowned
here . . .

---

[1] Chekhov commented on the problems this presented to sound-effects
men – 'What a lot of fuss about nothing.' (Letter to O. L. Knipper,
March 1904.)

Even as Liubov Andryeevna seeks pity from the baffled Trofimov, the handkerchief she pulls out brings a telegram from Paris along with it. She explains that she cannot live without the man who has ruined her. Trofimov's shocked reaction sparks off a strident and abusive retaliation – 'you're a ridiculous crank, a freak . . . Not to have a mistress at your age!' She has an instant of hatred for his lack of experience, his inability to comprehend her position. She needs understanding, not advice. Advice is impossible, but Trofimov does not yet know this. It is not his fault. Both are acutely aware of their own weakness, and jealously defend it from each other.

At the end of this act, Varia runs to the door in pursuit of a servant who has been insolent. In her rage she raises a stick. At this instant Lopahin enters. He is now the owner of the orchard. All that separates him from those he has ousted is uppermost in his mind – everything that has invested Varia with the right to wield sticks. Kindly though he is, his triumph breaks out after an embarrassed moment or two. He has been drinking to give himself courage. He has bought

. . . the most beautiful place on God's earth! . . . just you see the trees come crashing down! We're going to build a whole lot of new villas, and our children and great-grandchildren are going to see a new living world growing up here.

His feelings on possessing the orchard are as complicated in their way as Liubov Andryeevna's. To make the land his, he must destroy the beauty which he feels he has no right to inherit. He must disguise what he has stolen. This is the foremost consideration at the present instant. Lopahin has acted honourably for a long time, but generosity has its limits. He loves the orchard too. Love accounts for much in this play – the illogicality of everything in it. Lopahin abruptly exclaims: '. . . if only we could alter this distorted unhappy life somehow!'

In the last act, the moment of departure has come. Trofimov addresses a lonely, boycotted Lopahin, criticising him for his big talk, and magnificently refuses a gift of money from him. Lopahin, the older man, remarks after a while:

We show off in front of one another, and in the meantime life is slipping by.

There is something exhilarating about the departure, even for the former inhabitants. Inevitably, though, this act is filled with the most poignant nostalgia and regrets. Heartbreaking memories come up. The last person to speak will be Feers, an ancient family servant forgotten in the now empty house:

My life's gone as if I'd never lived.

The house has eaten up his life – countless lives, presumably. But for the others this is not so. There have been plenty of hints that there is much still to come, still to speculate about, for each of them. The objects of even the deepest love or devotion must change with time. The subject of The Cherry Orchard, as of all Chekhov's plays, is the vital importance of change. Stagnation is evil. The spell of the old orchard which grips even Lopahin accounts for the deepest, the most obscure motives in his present haste to chop it down. The moment the sound of an axe is heard, Trofimov, of all people, accuses him of tactlessness. Lopahin has the experience to know that some knots are best cut. One must have the courage to abandon one's dead. Both Lopahin and Liubov Andryeevna, for their various reasons, must abandon their ties with the orchard. When the moment comes it is not so difficult after all, it is not a tragic moment at all. Rather, it is a moment of release.

Chekhov always deals with the waste there is in life. The Cherry Orchard is no exception. Waste in Chekhov comes about through living according to habit or theory, living exclusively in the past or in the future, forfeiting the present in a variety of ways, through conventionality, timidity or inflexible principles of all kinds. In Chekhov's world there are endless ways in which people find it impossible to deal with the knowledge that the passing moment will not return, that life is short.

Much in Tolstoy is an exploration of this theme too. How is the cry to be answered which Tolstoy puts into the mouth of Anna Karenina?

'What do I know, what do I want, what is there I care for?'

The starting point is similar in Chekhov and Tolstoy, the reaction is different. Tolstoy has confidence in the larger movements of time, in the larger continuities, in those links with the great human past, those conventions of right and wrong conduct, those certainties which Chekhov has reservations about. Tolstoy spreads his events out in an orderly sequence spanning many years, hoping to discover the direction in which they tend, and thereafter to decide on the correct conduct of life. Chekhov brings out the immense amount which is there to be experienced in every moment.

Chekhov's wish to fit the maximum amount of information into the smallest space was bound to lead him to explore the possibilities of the drama. He is interested in the fugitive moment – in ways and means to convey an experience at the same speed as we would experience it in life. Tolstoy captures the mobility, the swiftness of life too, but he is not satisfied. He tries for more; that remains his greatness.

Chekhov experienced life as unsystematic, illogical. He sometimes felt that his failure to produce anything more than tight fragments of life implied a lack of fertility on his part, an inability to form massive structures of interrelated events. The real reason was a sense of honour which prevented him from making connections when he had not found any. He could not, whereas Tolstoy could.

A Note on
TOLSTOY and D. H. LAWRENCE

D. H. Lawrence said that it was the duty of a writer to hate his recent predecessors. There was no predecessor he hated so devoutly as Tolstoy, who stated that all happy marriages are alike, and who believed that the rules of conduct have been laid down for all time and apply in all situations. This was sheer hidebound nonsense to Lawrence. Marriages cannot be alike any more than people are alike; and a rule of conduct such as Tolstoy found in the Sermon on the Mount is only applicable in a society which will never exist. In real life it is often deeply wrong to turn the other cheek. The maintenance of love often entails fighting the other person with all the weapons at one's command. Lawrence cannot bear Tolstoy the doctrinaire nineteenth-century sage. He hates his dogmatic generalisations. Yet the human situations treated in *Anna Karenina* have lived vividly in Lawrence's memory. In *The Rainbow* they are reflected more noticeably than any other of Lawrence's literary experiences, apart from the Bible. The two massive studies of marriage are, therefore, intimately related to one another.

The interpretations by Lawrence and by Tolstoy of what *Anna Karenina* is about are not irreconcilable. *Anna Karenina* is ample enough for innumerable interpretations. In any case Tolstoy's interpretation is not so rigid as it might appear to be. His apparently smug statement about perfect marriage can be seen, after reading *Anna Karenina*, to refer to a goal all men strive to attain but never reach. The same thing applies to the search for perfect religion, which is related to the theme of marriage in *Anna Karenina*. Levin comes back to the church as a result of his marriage. Church services move him. He begins to pray. Meanwhile his theological speculations are secretly smiled at by Kitty who understands her husband in her own way and contrasts him privately with Varenka, the calm, practical Christian. Levin's theoretic conclusions seem mathematically clear and are neatly tabulated, like Tolstoy's own, perhaps. But in the novel they really mean nothing to Levin, any more than the latest theories about the universe do. The spoken word never does mean anything to him.

Lying on his back, he gazed up now into the high, cloudless sky. 'Do I not know that that is infinite space, and that it is not a round arch? But, however I screw up my eyes and strain my sight, I cannot see it not round and not bounded, and in spite of my knowing about infinite space, I am incontestably right when I see a solid blue dome, and more right than when I strain my eyes to see beyond it.'

One recalls Tom Brangwen's semi-mystical experience as he gazes at the blue church window at the back of the altar during Anna Brangwen's marriage. Levin and Tom Brangwen have the same inability to grasp clearly formulated theories. Levin feels uncomfortable, a fumbling, bucolic farmer, when he is caught in the same room with good conversationalists. He cannot grasp the scientific treatises he attempts to improve himself with, either.

He took up his book again. 'Very good, electricity and heat are the same thing; but is it possible to substitute the one quantity for the other in the equation for the solution of any problem? No. Well, then, what of it? The connection between all the forces of nature is felt instinctively . . . It's particularly nice if Pava's daughter should be a red-spotted cow, and all the herd will take after her, and the other three, too! Splendid! To go out with my wife and visitors to meet the herd . . . My wife says: "Kostya and I looked after that calf like a child." "How can it interest you so much?" says a visitor. "Everything that interests him interests me." But who will she be?'

Levin's wife will not in fact be interested in what he does, but her presence will transform all his activities in a quite unimaginable way. He cannot foresee how, but he knows that a transformation of his life is necessary to him. For Levin, marriage is 'the chief affair of life'. He does not know at this stage whether it will be with Kitty. 'Whether with her or with another, still it would be.' Tom Brangwen's understanding of his destiny is described in the same terms.

He was nothing. But with her, he would be real. If she were now walking across the frosty grass near the sheep-shelter, through the fretful bleating of the ewes and lambs, she would bring him completeness and perfection. And if it should be so, that she should come to him! It should be so – it was ordained so.
    . . . the business of love was, at the bottom of his soul, the most serious and terrifying of all to him.

When marriage comes it gives Tom Brangwen a sureness in all his dealings. As Levin changes, to his own surprise, into a tower of strength in his daily life, so does Tom Brangwen. Levin notes the new firmness in himself with wonder. 'Besides knowing thoroughly what he had to do, Levin knew in just the same way *how* he had to do it all, and what was more important than the rest.' He is aware of stability somewhere in him, but he remains perpetually dissatisfied. Like Tom Brangwen, Levin still suffers from an awareness of incompleteness which never disappears. Tom gazing dumbly at the blue church window knows he will never penetrate beyond it. 'My God – and one still was so unestablished – . . . Always it was so unfinished and unformed!' In the last paragraph of *Anna Karenina*, Levin states his position to himself.

. . . there will be still the same wall between the holy of holies of my soul and other people, even my wife; I shall still go on scolding her for my own terror, and being remorseful for it; I shall still be as unable to understand with my reason why I pray, and I shall still go on praying; but my life now, my whole life apart from anything that can happen to me, every minute of it is no more meaningless, as it was before, but it has the positive meaning of goodness, which I have the power to put into it.

The last phrases may look like a descent into muddy sentimentality. What really happens is that Levin's emotion seems falsified by its clumsy translation into words. This is no different in kind from Tom Brangwen's speech about angels at the wedding dinner of his daughter, which is met with faint derision by the auditors, but with a half-understanding nevertheless.

Lawrence disliked Tolstoy's presentation of his successfully married pair. He stated that the interest he found in the book was in the Anna–Vronsky relationship, and yet the firm ground he establishes, and from which he goes on to contemplate the perilous Ursula–Skrebensky relationship is not very different from the Levin part of *Anna Karenina*. The difference is that Lawrence leaves Tom Brangwen behind, drowned by the industrial waters, and projects Ursula forward as continuing her voyage into an unknown future. Tolstoy destroys Anna Karenina with machinery, and allows Levin to continue his journey. This is the essential difference between the two novels. In *Anna Karenina* Levin's journey is not yet finally over while Anna has not been strong enough to stand against a world created by men. In *The Rainbow*, Ursula Brangwen is able to hold her own.

Lawrence refers to Vronsky's 'phallic splendour'[1] in the course of an

1 'The novel', *Phoenix II* (London, 1968), p. 417.

onslaught on Tolstoy's conception of religion and doing good. Lawrence counters Tolstoy's religious conclusions with his own. Meanwhile the two novels stand as evidence against their own authors, who often forget the utterances of their art. Lawrence states:

Tolstoi has a perverse pleasure in making the later Vronsky abject and pitiable: because Tolstoi so meanly envied the healthy passionate male in the young Vronsky. Tolstoi cut off his vain nose to spite his face.[1]

Lawrence is here interpreting Vronsky's character in the light of his own antagonism to Tolstoy's social morality, but he is going against his own real understanding of what happens in the novel. Tolstoy's 'pleasure' in making Vronsky abject and pitiful is not so different from Lawrence's 'pleasure' when he does the same thing to Skrebensky. Tolstoy has selected the right figure to break the rules of society and then fail to create a life apart from society. Tolstoy's contention is that Vronsky should have left Anna alone since he could not fight his way through the consequences. It is not that Tolstoy envied 'the healthy passionate male' in Vronsky; it is rather that he had reservations on that score. In *Anna Karenina* it does not really matter what Tolstoy's theoretical moral position was. Tolstoy was true to the situation he described. Lawrence acknowledges this fact about the great Tolstoy in the course of his attacks on him — inconsistently.

Of course, Tolstoi, being a great creative artist, was true to his characters. But being a man with a philosophy, he wasn't true to his *own character*.[2]

Tolstoy sides with Levin against Vronsky, but the novel sides with him for the right reasons. Another man might not have sinned in eloping with Anna. The novel makes that plain. Whatever Tolstoy's ideas on the matter were, they are not obtrusive in the novel.

Lawrence talks about the 'quick' and the 'dead' in novels. Dead characters are those which can immediately be seen to be put in for a didactic purpose, to illustrate a morality.

The novel contains no didactic absolute. All that is quick, and all that is said and done by the quick, is in some way godly. So that Vronsky's taking of Anna Karenina we must count godly, since it is quick. And that Prince in *Resurrection*, following the convict girl we must count dead . . . The

[1] ' "Cavalleria Rusticana", by Giovanni Verga', *Phoenix* (London, 1936), p. 246.
[2] 'The Novel', *Phoenix II*, p. 423.

really quick, Tolstoi loved to kill them off or muss them over. Like a true Bolshevist . . . Men clotting together into social masses in order to limit their individual liabilities: this is humanity . . . And this is Tolstoi, the philosopher with a very nauseating Christian-brotherhood idea of himself.[1]

Lawrence is determined to read *Anna Karenina* in the light of Tolstoy's didactic intentions rather than his artistic statements. According to such a reading Levin should emerge as duller and stupider than Vronsky, because Tolstoy sides with Levin and Kitty against the social outcasts Anna and Vronsky; but in fact Levin is not 'dead'. The quality of the two relationships is examined, the quality of the two men, Vronsky and Levin. The same test is applied to Vronsky as Lawrence applies to Skrebensky when he uses the Brangwen family for comparison.

One remembers how Vronsky's 'stillness and quietness', his 'simple and elegant exterior', his 'quiet, soft and composed' voice, impress others. Here is Ursula's first impression of Skrebensky: 'He seemed simply acquiescent in the fact of his own being, as if he were beyond any change or question. He was himself . . . So he seemed perfectly, even fatally established.' Ursula finds out what underlies the impressive façade. She learns to her chagrin that Skrebensky exists 'in her own desire only', that he is more real to her when he is not physically present. Ursula tells him, during a moment of hatred for him:

'It seems to me as if you weren't anybody – as if there weren't anybody there, where you are. Are you anybody, really? You seem like nothing to me.'

Skrebensky's rather furtive physical desire for her, thought of in terms of 'playing with fire' disappoints her. It is not enough. He on his part is deeply attracted by her, by her superiority to himself – her 'passionate knowledge of religion and living' – but he does not know what she wants of him. It is the same with Vronsky's excited 'playing with fire' over Anna and his simultaneous realisation that this attraction goes further and is bewildering, that it is also a response to something Kitty has recognised in Anna too – 'a higher world of interests, complex and poetic'. The situation is not covered by Vronsky's ideas of a dashing affair as laid down by his military code. Vronsky's 'proud, gay smile' at the opera, alluding to his newly broached intrigue with Anna, is a piece of dramatic irony.

[1] Ibid. p. 420.

So is Skrebensky's talk of 'women' to Ursula at the beginning of their acquaintance.

The Levin–Shtcherbatsky family dismiss Vronsky easily as a man 'turned out by machinery'. He is an instrument forged by the State to serve its impersonal aims. In the end, Vronsky offers his body to the State. He returns with horror to the world Anna has failed to cut him loose from. He is superior to Skrebensky, the young man of a much later generation, who returns with relief. Lawrence's figure is a sinister phenomenon as Vronsky is not. Vronsky destroys life for mistaken reasons. Skrebensky merely avoids it. But they both are young men who do not have a place in the world as a birthright, and have placed themselves in an institution which lends them an identity. Lawrence gives a detailed analysis of Skrebensky as a type. (Tolstoy never defines his characters at such length, his method being more to allow them to reveal themselves.)

His life lay in the established order of things. He had his five senses too. They were to be gratified. Apart from this, he represented the great established, extant Idea of life, and as this he was important and beyond question.

There is the world of recreation allowed Skrebensky as long as it remains separate from his essential function. Both Skrebensky and Vronsky are great horsemen[1] (champions respectively at steeple-chasing and polo) and attractive lovers.

Vronsky has given himself with utter conviction to his career. He is capable of smashing things which hinder his purposes, but this is partly because he is not opposed with conviction. Anna is not Ursula. She has her life with Karenin behind her, and her life with Vronsky is far better than that. Her association with Vronsky eventually leads her to despair, yet she has no understanding of what she still lacks. She accepts without question Vronsky's conclusion that the painter Mihailov's vision of her is merely a matter of 'technique'. Her accusations later that Vronsky does not 'love' her are incomprehensible to him partly because they are not understood by Anna herself; she does not understand what is wrong with their life together. Vronsky spends money lavishly on her, takes her on

---

[1] Contrasting with Vronsky's disastrous horse-ride is the memory of Levin's ride over his family estate, watching the sowing, 'swaying rhythmically' with his horse, the horse drawing 'each hoof with a sucking sound out of the half-thawed ground.'

journeys, and establishes her in a house reminiscent of 'the best hotels'. It is an interlude in the real business of life which he wants to return to, respectably married to her. Ursula Brangwen *does* know what is wrong when Skrebensky offers the same distractions to her, taking her on expensive car trips and living with her in hotels in London and Paris, finally introducing her into a rented villa occupied by well-bred people sharing an escapade. This is when Ursula escapes as Anna cannot.

In Tolstoy's novel there was the prophetic episode of the horse-race. Vronsky's horse is in his service, with its allotted place in the recreational side of his life, fully under his control and loved by him. But at a crucial moment the life of the horse, its individual rhythm, is forgotten by Vronsky as he perceives the obstacle in front in his own way. The dislocation in the rhythm of the ride breaks the horse's back when the critical moment is reached, and Vronsky continues to ride in the same way, unaware for a while of what has happened. The rhythm of Vronsky's life, affected by his vision of what lies ahead in his life with Anna, is also unchanged by an awareness of her and her kind of knowledge. It is a relationship which should not have been entered into, but Anna had no alternative, hence the tragedy. It is a tragedy of a kind which Ursula, the heroine of *The Rainbow*, is able to avoid. *The Rainbow* is open-ended in the case of Ursula; she is left free to pursue her life, to continue her independent exploration of possibilities.

In his theoretical writing Lawrence expresses contempt at what he chooses to see as cowardice in Vronsky and Anna.

They couldn't live in the pride of their sincere passion, and spit in Mother Grundy's eye. And that that cowardice, was the real 'sin'. The novel makes it obvious, and knocks all old Leo's teeth out. 'As an officer I am still useful. But as a man, I am a ruin,' says Vronsky – or words to that effect. Well what a skunk, collapsing as a man and a male, and remaining merely as a social instrument; an 'officer', God love us! – merely because people at the opera turn their backs on him! As if people's backs weren't preferable to their faces, anyhow![1]

This statement is a damaging half-truth running counter to Lawrence's understanding of the novel. It is careless journalism with a bias. Lawrence must accuse Tolstoy of distorting Vronsky to inculcate a despicable morality. But Vronsky's tragedy is not caused

---

[1] 'The Novel', *Pheonix III*, p. 417.

by social cowardice. It is caused by a sincere and total commitment to a particular conception of himself. The misquotation is illuminating – 'As an officer I am still useful. But as a man, I am a ruin.' This is rather what Skrebensky furtively admits to himself at the end of The Rainbow.

Lawrence also misplaces the remark he assigns to Vronsky. He puts it in the scene where Anna is disgraced at the opera. This is the moment of Anna's defeat – the moment when her back is broken. Anna tries to gain an entry for Vronsky into the world of public life, hoping that this will re-establish his 'love' for her, remove the obstacle which she sees before them. Vronsky's inability to understand the reason for her action destroys her ultimately – not social cowardice.

The statement which Lawrence misplaces actually comes as Vronsky stands on the railway platform by a troop train shortly after Anna's suicide.

'Yes, as a weapon I may be of some use. But as a man, I'm a wreck,' he jerked out – he could hardly speak for the throbbing ache in his strong teeth.

Vronsky has plainly not collapsed as a male. He is now no longer an officer but a dangerous weapon. Lawrence's Skrebensky retreated to India and complacency, an officer of the crown, not really even a soldier but an engineer in uniform.

When thinking of Vronsky's last appearance one remembers the peasant Levin appeals to in his distress over the war –

'What should we think? Alexander Nikolaevitch our Emperor has thought for us; he thinks for us indeed in all things. It's clearer for him to see.'

Vronsky, too, is partly an anachronism. He has given his service to a master. He is not going to fight for economic welfare disguised as Pan Slavism. Vronsky's loyalty to the State is different from the loyalty of Karenin as expressed in his activities on various government committees – and that of Levin's half-brother Sergey who, like his counterpart in The Rainbow, the younger Tom Brangwen, manager of industry, represents the 'superior foreign element' in the family. The latter people are the future in the midst of which D. H. Lawrence finds himself.

Vronsky retains a glamour oddly at variance with the true facts of his position. He is misplaced amid the machinery of modern life.

Anna recognises this in him but cannot free him. Ursula recognises the same in Skrebensky to a lesser degree, but she understands that help is useless. One of the most haunting descriptions of Skrebensky is when he is seen off by Ursula on his departure for the Boer war. Tom Brangwen the younger is there too.

The three made a noticeable group on the station; the girl in her fur cap and tippet and her olive green costume, pale, tense with youth, isolated, unyielding; the soldierly young man in a crush hat and heavy overcoat, his face rather pale and reserved above his purple scarf, his whole figure neutral . . . The train gathered speed, it grew smaller and smaller. Still it ran in a straight line . . .

Ursula chooses not to join Skrebensky on his journey through life.

Levin provides the major contrast with Vronsky. Levin has escaped the influences which have shaped his acquaintances, Vronsky among them. A misfit in a world he senses to be illusory (the life, for instance, of his brother-in-law seems to him 'a mere phantom'), Levin retires with feelings of 'shame and self-dissatisfaction' to his activities in the country. He is disturbed when his half-brother Sergey pursues him to his retreat. Sergey talks about the necessity of changing his activities, of educating the labourers into an efficient and intelligent labour force. Levin feels obscurely threatened. He is like Tom Brangwen up against schoolmasters at the beginning of The Rainbow.

He was more sensuously developed, more refined in instinct than they. For their mechanical stupidity he hated them, and suffered cruel contempt for them. But when it came to mental things, then he was at a disadvantage. He was at their mercy. He was a fool. He had not the power to controvert even the most stupid argument, so that he was forced to admit things he did not in the least believe. And having admitted them, he did not know whether he believed them or not; he rather thought he did.

It is the same reaction Levin constantly suffers, especially in town where he is always made uncomfortable by the games people play.[1] It is like the conversation Levin took part in with a Moscow professor about the definition of life and death, or the episode at the table-

---

[1] 'What was it all?' . . . 'What did everything mean?' These are the inner exclamations typical of Levin and of all Tolstoy's seekers. These words are assigned by Lawrence to Tom Brangwen in Chapter I of The Rainbow.

turning session where Vronsky was present, in which Levin hotly exclaimed that he did not understand how spiritual forces could be demonstrated in physical experiments.

Levin comes near to losing his temper with his half-brother, who never loses his. Levin's solution in the country is to forget himself in physical labour. It is hay-harvesting time, and he goes out to mow his fields. The physical rhythm quells his mind, and he has moments of unconsciousness, living in the swing of his body only. A little later during the harvest, Levin spends a night under the stars. He dreams of reverting to the life of the peasant, escaping back through the generations. This would be an escape from those who harass him, whose certainties he distrusts, but whose confidence he envies. There is likely to be a return to 'shame and self-dissatisfaction' once more, but Levin is saved from this when the carriage bearing Kitty passes him on the road.

With a face full of light and thought, full of a subtle, complex inner life, that was remote from Levin, she was gazing beyond him at the glow of the sunrise.

. . . He recalled with horror his dreams of marrying a peasant girl. There only, in the carriage that had crossed over to the other side of the road, and was rapidly disappearing, there only could he find the solution of the riddle of his life, which had weighed so agonisingly upon him of late . . .

He glanced at the sky, expecting to find there the cloud-shell he had been admiring and taking as the symbol of the ideas and feelings of that night. There was nothing in the sky in the least like a shell. There, in the remote heights above, a mysterious change had been accomplished. There was no trace of a shell, and there was stretched over fully half the sky an even cover of tiny and even tinier cloudlets. The sky had grown blue and bright; and with the same softness, but with the same remoteness, it met his questioning gaze.

'No,' he said to himself, 'however good that life of simplicity and toil may be, I cannot go back to it. I love *her*.'

It is a moment of awakening like Tom Brangwen's vision of Lydia on the road — 'With her he would be real.'

Like the symbol of the rainbow in the Lawrence novel, the shell-like cloud marks the end of one epoch in the man's life and the beginning of another in which everything is profoundly changed. Levin's experience of marriage can be summed up without any distortion in words taken from *The Rainbow*:

. . . his eyes opened on a new universe, and he wondered in thinking of his triviality before. A new, calm relationship showed to him in the things he saw, in the cattle he used, the young wheat as it eddied in the wind.

And each time he returned home, he went steadily, expectantly, like a man who goes to a profound, unknown satisfaction.

Both Tolstoy and Lawrence seek in their art to arrive at some definition of fulfilment in life. They both see life as a quest for spiritual illumination which must be made anew by each individual in his own way according to his generation and his circumstances. They both believe that any illumination which is attained can only be made perfect when a man and a woman have come together in their lives. These conceptions underlie their great art. Starting from them, they travelled along widely divergent paths. But Lawrence always understood Tolstoy very well. One can see this beneath his harshest criticisms. He said of him:

'Count Tolstoi had that last weakness of a great man: he wanted the absolute.'[1]

This might serve as both their epitaphs.

[1] 'The Novel', *Phoenix II*, p. 24.

A study of the literary relationship between two great Russian authors. When Chekhov began to write, Tolstoy was the acknowledged master. Each admired the other's work, and part of Mr Speirs' argument is that Tolstoy's example helped Chekhov to see what he wanted to do and how to do it.

The author feels that both have an unequalled insight into the life of modern man, the one speaking for a generation when the old order was just breaking up, and the other for one in which the new order was being established. In his middle period, Tolstoy in the vast structures of *War and Peace* and *Anna Karenina* devised literary forms adequate to his insights; and, as Chekhov put it, this enabled him 'to state the problem correctly'. That was the point, to reflect all the facets of a situation, to make the reader see it as if he were both involved and a privileged spectator.

Mr Speirs begins with a large section on Tolstoy, where the main chapters are given to detailed and very helpful examinations of the structure and intentions of *War and Peace* and *Anna Karenina*. The study of Chekhov which follows builds on these perceptions about theme and method, showing the links and contrasts between the two authors. The short stories, the short novel *Three Years* and the plays are considered, as a developing achievement culminating in *Three Sisters* and *The Cherry Orchard*. A final note shows how the achievement of Tolstoy and Chekhov opened ways for writers in other countries; in particular how D. H. Lawrence was able to develop their methods for his own purposes. Mr Speirs writes directly and freshly, with admiration and understanding. His book marks an advance in Russian literary studies.